OPEN SKY

Also by Eric Nisenson

Blue: The Murder of Jazz
Ascension: John Coltrane and His Quest
'Round About Midnight: A Portrait of Miles Davis

OPEN SKY

Sonny Rollins and His World of Improvisation

Eric Nisenson

St. Martin's Press
New York

Library of Congress Cataloging-in-Publication Data

Nisenson, Eric.
    Open sky : Sonny Rollins and his world of improvisation/Eric Nisenson.
      p.   cm.
    ISBN 0-312-25330-3
    1. Rollins, Sonny.   2. Jazz musicians—United States—Biography.   I. Title.
ML419.R64N572000
788.7'165'092—dc21
[B]

                                                                99-055285

First Edition: March 2000

10 9   8   7   6   5   4   3   2   1

To the memory of Robert Palmer, my friend and colleague

Contents

Acknowledgments   ix

Foreword   xi

Introduction   xiii

1 Sonny Rollins Is in the House!   1

2 School Days   16

3 Blue Room   33

4 "Oleo"   49

5 Work Time   67

6 Saxophone Colossus   88

7 A Night at the Village Vanguard   104

8 The Freedom Suite   124

9 The Bridge   141

10 Now's the Time   162

11 Playin' in the Yard   176

12 Silver City   196

Notes   215

Acknowledgments

Writing this book was one of the most joyful experiences of my life. One of the best things about it is that so many have been supportive and helpful in one way or another. It was touching to discover how important Sonny Rollins is to so many people, and I owe all of them a huge debt.

First of all, I must express my deepest gratitude, of course, to Sonny and Lucille Rollins. Your generosity with time, your saintlike patience, and your kindness and consideration will remain with me as long as Sonny's music illuminates my life. Simply the fact that we have become friends has made this project so worthwhile to me.

I also must thank my editor, Jim Fitzgerald, who has been such a bulwark for me for many years now. Thanks, Jim, for believing in me and believing in this project. I must also thank Terri Hinte, Sonny's publicist at Fantasy Records: thank you for your help in getting this project initially off the ground. It could never have happened without you.

I am also deeply grateful to Bill Kenz for his research—your help was invaluable. And then I must thank Kresten Jespersen for proofreading and spiritual solace. I also thank Alice Schell for so many reasons. And special thanks to Maureen Barnes, the bravest person I know. Not only did you do a great job typing many of the transcripts, but you have been continually supportive of me and have helped lift me up so many times when I was feeling down. Also thanks to Joan Ariessohn and her sister Melanie, who also did a great job with the transcripts and helped me laugh when I needed it. I also have to thank Michael Bader, James Hale, Enrico Merlin, and Michael McLaughlin. Great thanks, too, to Nick Catalano for moral support and some great discussions.

In addition, thanks to Lewis Porter, Gene Lees, and Bill Kirchner for all their help. And I am deeply grateful to Jim Hall, Jackie McLean, Orrin Keepnews, and Bob Cranshaw for their time and insights.

And I must thank my wonderful father, Jules Nisenson, and my brother Peter, who turned me on to this music in the first place. I am also grateful to John Falencki for being such a great doctor. Also, thanks to Sean Ducker for some reason or another. I can only hope that this book is worthy of the generosity and support I have received from all of these terrific people.

Foreword

When Eric Nisenson wrote to me some time ago seeking my cooperation for a book he intended to write about me, I reluctantly agreed, feeling that it would probably be written anyway, and that at least in this case something of my own remembrances would be represented.

During the course of the numerous interviews we did, we would quite often digress from the topic at hand to discuss current events, environmental issues, race relations, politics, and the like. Over the course of time, I found that we were in general agreement about what needs to be done and what should be done about many of these matters. So the process of discussing my life with someone I'd never met turned out to be not nearly as painful as I had feared.

Although I feel uncomfortable praising a book in which I am portrayed in such glowing terms, I do feel that Eric has done an excellent job in depicting my life and my evolution as a musician, and the book has many valuable insights (although I do not necessarily agree with all of his opinions). I have a special appreciation for his understanding of how social and cultural issues have shaped my life, both as a man and an artist.

—Sonny Rollins, September 1999

Introduction

Every jazz fan has a favorite story about Sonny Rollins. Here is mine: When I was living in northern California in the early 1970s, Sonny appeared for a week at the most important jazz club in San Francisco, the Keystone Korner. He had not been playing live for quite a while, and his return to performing was exhilarating news for most jazz listeners. Being a longtime Rollins fan, I attended his opening night with a friend. I had great expectations. Sonny was magnificent at the time, playing at his peak. His inventiveness bordered on the miraculous; he took lengthy solos that were like musical roller-coaster rides, constantly veering in unexpected directions, at some points dramatic and at others sardonically humorous, evoking obvious joy in both the audience and his band.

At the time I lived in a flat facing the San Francisco Panhandle. Living above me was a couple named Frenchy and Carol, who were also jazz lovers. Frenchy, however, had no use for Sonny Rollins. He had never seen Sonny play live; he had probably heard one of Sonny's lesser albums and jumped to his conclusion. His disparagement of Sonny may have been a result of the ludicrous comparisons some in the jazz world continually made between Sonny and his close friend John Coltrane. I insisted to Frenchy that if he caught Sonny playing at the Keystone, his opinion would be altered forever. So he reluctantly agreed to go with me to see Rollins perform that Saturday night.

As you may have already guessed, on that Saturday night Sonny was terrible. It was, by far, the worst I have ever heard him play, either in live performance or on record. He would start a tune, attempt a solo, and simply hit a stone wall. After a few bars he would shake his head in discouragement and sit on a stool facing the audience, his face mournful, as the rhythm section played on. I am certain that he was neither high or ill; it simply wasn't happening for him that night.

Well, you can imagine what Frenchy had to say. Of course, I was quite disappointed, as well as mortified. I was also fascinated. This incident made it utterly clear to me that Sonny improvised "without nets"—that he was completely dependent on the inspiration of the moment and dedicated to genuine spontaneity. Unlike many jazz musicians, he didn't rely on memorized solos or old licks when inspiration was absent. Sonny has told me that he believed Charlie Parker was right when he said, "You play what you have experienced that day." If the music wasn't happening that night, well, there was not much he could do about it. He was unable to fake it. Few musicians would ever reach the creative nadir of the performance I had dragged Frenchy to. And few have ever come near the heights of fervid creativity that Sonny had achieved during the earlier show.

After the second show, I realized that jazz improvisation is more than a musical technique; it is a holistic way of looking at the world. It was obvious to me that nobody ever understood this more profoundly than Sonny Rollins has. (Incidentally, Sonny's wife, Lucille, who has been listening to Sonny since 1957, told me that he no longer has nights as unproductive as that Saturday-night show.)

Let me warn the reader: like my previous books about Miles Davis and John Coltrane, this is neither an "as-told-to" autobiography, nor a formal, authorized biography, nor a definitive biography. This is according to Sonny's own wishes. He is planning to write an autobiography after he retires, and it should be a fascinating and important book. Although this book includes most of the facts of Sonny's life, it is instead about the evolution of a great jazzman's sensibility and musical conception, and how his life has meshed with his art. My primary focus is on Sonny's years of *development*. This does not mean that he has ceased to grow as both an artist and a man in the past quarter-century or so. But I have purposely limited the scope of this book. I'm hoping the more recent years will be more fully covered when Sonny writes his own book.

I have loved jazz for a very long time. Over all these years I have wondered and speculated about how a great jazz improviser goes about creating his music. I knew that nobody was a more "pure" inmproviser than Sonny Rollins, and I hoped he could answer many of my questions. Writing about him seemed like a wonderful idea, since Sonny has long been one of my favorite jazzmen and I knew that he was a thoughtful and articulate man.

I decided that I could write this book only if Sonny cooperated with me. This was a long shot, because Sonny has long been wary of the press. He is a private person who, except when he is performing, is rarely in public view. And I was certain that others must have asked him to cooperate with—or collaborate on—a book.

I decided to pursue the idea anyway. I called Rollins's publicist, Terri Hinte, who told me that he was getting ready for a three-week tour of Japan. But she agreed to give him a letter I had written describing the project I wished to do as well as a copy of my book *Ascension: John Coltrane and His Quest*. Around the time Sonny was due back from Japan I called Terri, who told me that Lucille Rollins had sent her an E-mail saying that Sonny did not want to do a book at this time and that if and when he did they had other writers in mind. Disappointed, but not terribly surprised, I reluctantly pushed this project out of my mind and turned to another one. The very day I spoke to my editor about it, I received a fairly long letter handwritten by Sonny Rollins. I was bowled over.

Rollins explained that he had read my book *'Round About Midnight: A Portrait of Miles Davis* a while back and "found it a "serious study respectfully done." He told me that he had never previously agreed to do a book because, in his own words, of "all the time it would take from my current activities—and the fact that I want to accomplish a little more to be written about!" But, he said, if I could work with him without interfering too much with his musical regimen or his private life, he would cooperate with me. He concluded the letter by saying "Again, there is an air of finality about biographies that I cringe from as I truly feel unfinished in my present contributions. My whole life is dedicated to the achievement of some important breakthroughs, and I would die disappointed if I couldn't reach them. I feel I have been blessed and I want to live up to my promise—not just for me, but for the music."

We did a seemingly endless (at least from Sonny's point of view) series of phone interviews. Sonny has been consistently forthcoming and helpful, always conscientious and generous with his time. He is a remarkable person. Virtually everyone I talked to who has known him said the same thing—that Sonny is a "special guy" (although Sonny thinks of himself as being just an "average Joe").

Sonny Rollins, as we shall see, has often struggled with the idea of being a performer. On more than one occasion, he dropped out of the jazz scene altogether. But he has always returned to the music. This book will, I hope, explain why.

Therefore, for the most illuminated souls who have ever lived in this world—their whole life was music. From the miniature music which we understand, they expanded themselves to the whole universe of music, and in that way they were able to inspire. The one who finds the key to the music of the whole working of life—it is he who becomes intuitive; it is he to whom revelations manifest, for then his language becomes music.
—Hazrat Inayat Khan

Music is an open sky.
—Sonny Rollins

OPEN SKY

Sonny Rollins Is in the House!

The rewards for an audience catching Sonny Rollins on a good night go beyond hearing the actual music itself. Being able to actually watch Rollins as he improvises is a fascinating spectacle; there is a powerful physicality in the way he produces sound through his tenor saxophone. The fierce determination that he devotes to producing his flow of sound brings to mind the image of Ahab trying to kill his quarry. The great slabs of sound Rollins produces are so viscerally compelling that they seem to have actual physical properties. We almost feel we can touch the notes.

As members of his audience, we can only guess at the mental, physical, and emotional processes and strategies through which Sonny creates his music. But on Rollins's best nights, we in the audience become so uplifted in Sonny's grip that we have no thoughts about how he achieves what he does. We are just so glad to be in this place, listening to him, right now, right here, in this moment. If you have never been fortunate enough to catch Sonny Rollins on one of his better nights, here is a sketch:

We hear Sonny before we see him. After his band settles in, he begins playing, still backstage; as he gets closer to the stage his sound grows in intensity. When he finally strolls onstage he continues to play—usually a favorite standard; perhaps "I'm Old-Fashioned"—without any acknowledgment of his audience. He begins his improvisation with only slight variations of the melody as he restlessly prowls around the stand, in step with the rhythm. At first, his improvising is tentative and probing, as if he is testing various directions for the best course to follow. When he takes off, the atmosphere becomes molten. He continues to pace the stage (he has a small microphone in the bell of his horn), almost as if trying to find the spot most conducive to his sound. Now we can hear his tenor saxophone in all its glory, that big burly tone; just the *sound* of Rollins's horn is so muscular that we are immediately enthralled. His tone, by turns gruff and cello-like, is so full that it seems to envelop the entire venue. Tonal variation is as important to Sonny's improvising as his melodic line or rhythmic conception.

Sonny himself is an imposing figure: tall, with an elegant beard, sharply yet tastefully dressed, charismatic, deadly serious. He walks with the physical confidence we usually associate with great athletes; and, like a great athlete, he seems in command of everything around him. Despite the fact that his hair is now gray, he walks with a youthful gait, steady and confident. When he plays, the veins in his head are pronounced; his powerful torso and arms are taut. But it is his eyes that draw us in; his eyes are sad and wise, ancient and compassionate.

Viewing Sonny as he plays, chorus after chorus, growing more and more impassioned and inventive, it becomes clear that every atom of his being is engaged into the production of his music. It is not just Sonny's breath that is being blown through his horn; it is his entire being. His physical, emotional, and spiritual self is blown through the reed, into the mouthpiece, around the curves of his horn, and past the keys. Finally, this essence of Sonny Rollins flows out of the gleaming golden bell of his saxophone, changed by the alchemy of his genius into the cosmic geometry of music.

The strength of his playing makes the band coalesce into a tight singular unit, both supporting and propelling him as he stretches out and soars. He is truly wailing now, arching back. The lights dance over his golden saxophone as he walks and rocks in time with the rhythm. After he has been playing this first solo for fifteen or twenty minutes, we become aware of his stamina; just as it seems that he must be running out of ideas, he soars even further afield. His phrasing is more often speechlike than legato, yet even that is never predictable. Sometimes he seems to be talking to us directly through his horn, telling us stories or sharing insights and ironies with us. We wonder how he can have the resources not only to play with such intensity for so long but also to continually create so many fresh ideas.

The longer he solos, the more complex his lines. He never seems to repeat himself. He returns back to the theme, repeats it another time or two, and then his improvising becomes even more intense. His harmonic conception often seems like a kind of musical Möbius strip: he seems to be zigging and zagging both inside and outside the chord changes, sometimes in a single phrase.

At times Sonny's playing is daringly chromatic, but then he will follow such a passage with sly quotes from other tunes, ranging from "Night and Day" to "Stars and Stripes Forever." But these quotes are not used in lieu of invention, nor do they reflect cleverness for its own sake (although Rollins has a musical sense of humor not unlike that of his great mentor, Thelonious Monk). Instead, Sonny fits these quotes snugly into the overall design of his solo, making perfect, and witty, sense in the context of the entire performance. His ability to create musical puns and self-referential paradoxes makes Sonny the jazz equivalent of Vladimir Nabokov.

We follow his solo breathlessly, feeling that Sonny is addressing us directly, speaking of great truths and ironies, reaching us on a level deeper than language itself, exhorting us to awareness of our lives right here in this moment. We notice that we are not the only ones astounded by Rollins's inventiveness; Sonny's sidemen break into small smiles and quiet laughter every time Sonny takes an unexpected course or creates one of his wonderful musical puns.

Perhaps Sonny's greatest musical sorcery is rhythmic. No one, including Charlie Parker, could create such rhythmic legerdemain. At certain points, Sonny seemingly stops the flow of time itself; at others, he seems to flatten rhythm, creating the illusion that time is floating over and against the flow of the rhythm section, almost giving rhythm an actual life of its own. Yet as magical and amazing as these aural illusions may seem,

Rollins's protean strength and determination stamp everything he plays with a muscular authority.

As Sonny's solo goes on for chorus after chorus, many of us are undoubtedly comparing him with John Coltrane, his friend and colleague who also played improvisations of great length. The two have often been compared, but their musical sensibilities are profoundly different. Coltrane's long, long, powerful solos seemed to provide emotional and spiritual catharsis. The incendiary intensity of his improvisations seared our souls and blew our minds. But Sonny's long solos celebrate the sheer joy of improvising and express the infinite possibilities of both music and life. Sonny does not seem to be ripping apart his soul, but rather to be inviting us to dance with our minds. Coltrane's playing always seemed like one brave man's plunge into the void; but it is difficult to imagine Sonny playing as he does *without* an audience. As audience, we are his partners in creation, as necessary for his musical calculus as his horn or breath.

Finally, Sonny's long, long solo reaches an end. He starts another tune and plays briefly, letting the other members of his group solo. They are all superb musicians, but following a lengthy, superb Rollins solo is a daunting task for even the greatest of jazzmen. The audience, overwhelmed, may find it hard to even focus on anything else. But at least the other solos give Sonny a chance to regain his strength. Earlier in his career he often played with just bass and drums, and sometimes with no other players at all. Now, well into his sixties, he no longer feels strong enough to play in such a demanding and exhausting context. Despite his age (quite an advanced age for a jazz musician) he continues to improvise on a level that few have equaled.

After a series of fours between Sonny and the drummer, he plays the theme and takes the tune out. Next is a ballad—say, "For All We Know." Sonny's ballad style reminds us of such classic tenormen as Coleman Hawkins, Don Byas, and Ben Webster. Like them, Rollins uses his big sound and his sense of drama to wonderful effect. Playing ballads is one of the great challenges for a jazz musician. Overdo the emotionality and a ballad can easily turn purple, dripping with the sentimentality that most jazz musicians spurn.

Just stating the melody is a crucial test for a jazz musician; it requires the skill in phrasing that only the greatest singers, such as Frank Sinatra and Billie Holiday, possess, and the rhythmic confidence to make it a truly jazz interpretation. Improvising at ballad tempo is one of the most difficult tasks in jazz. A jazz musician cannot just "play the changes" or rely on clichés or riffs and licks at this tempo, because his lack of invention will be far too obvious. He must at least try to improvise melody that is not too far from the ballad itself. Since jazz musicians have a knack for songs of great melodic and harmonic beauty, improvising melody equal to that of the tune itself is extremely challenging, a task that only the best jazzmen have truly mastered. Sonny is one of them. He can create melodic ideas at a slow tempo as well as any of the other great jazz improvisers—Charlie Parker, Lester Young, or Sonny's idol, Coleman Hawkins. His superior rhythmic conception gives his ballads an inner strength and a feeling of conviction rare in jazz or any other form of music. Rollins's improvisational conception in ballads extends even to his tone, which becomes less gruff and more rich than the sound he uses for up-tempo pieces.

Sonny reprises the melody, and it seems as if the ballad is coming to its end. But after the band lays out, Sonny plays an extended unaccompanied coda, which takes on a life of its on, becoming a musical statement within a statement. Such prolonged, unaccompanied improvising is truly playing without a net, and it is often the ultimate expression of Rollins's genius. Listening to this bravura performance, we in the audience are as filled with suspense as we would be during a particularly daring and difficult feat performed by a tightrope acrobat a hundred feet off the ground. When the unaccompanied coda finally ends, the crowd explodes into applause; we are awed, but also deeply relieved, as in that moment when the tightrope walker finally slides down the pole to the safety of the ground.

Following the ballad, Sonny changes the mood by playing a calypso, a genre associated with his name ever since his performance of "St. Thomas" (a calypso tune he heard his mother sing while he was a very young boy) on the masterpiece album *Saxophone Colossus*, recorded in

1956. Sonny's calypso improvisations are among the most joyous in all of jazz. This is where Sonny's rhythmic mastery becomes particularly obvious: he creates a rollicking, carnival-like atmosphere that rocks the audience to the point of ecstasy. Not to dance seems nearly impossible. At the end he plays a long cadenza, full of quotes from other tunes that seem to rise out of the flurry of notes like bubbles in champagne.

And then it is over. Sonny announces the names of the other musicians and then strolls off, casually but with almost imperial dignity. Inevitably, the crowd calls for more.

Sonny has a quite different view of his performance. Knowing and understanding his perspective should tell us a lot about both him and the nature of jazz improvisation.

For Sonny, live performance is the only genuine jazz experience, at least in terms of improvisation. He records because he must, but he lives for live performance. According to Sonny, an improvisation should be heard only once, at the time it has been performed, and then never heard again. This obviously makes the entire concept of recording in the studio profoundly antithetical to his musical philosophy. Being able to go back and redo a tune, or to edit out mistakes or overdub, runs contrary to the spontaneity that, to Sonny, is at the heart of the jazz aesthetic. In live performance, there are no second chances. Everything you play is for keeps, at least in that moment. According to Sonny (as well as most fans and critics), he only very rarely plays as well in the studio as he does live. He also doesn't play at his best when he is being recorded in an onstage performance (or, at least, when he is *aware* of being recorded). Being recorded makes him self-conscious and less able to let the music flow through him.

Sonny has become a master strategist in establishing the right set and setting for the creation of superlative musical improvisation. Bill Evans once said of himself that he had an inner switch that he could turn on so he could improvise whenever he performed. Responding to this, Sonny said, "Yes, I know what he is talking about. But I bet that Bill would also say that there were nights when he had no need to turn that switch on, and that the music just poured through him. That is what I live for."

Any performance is usually preceded by preparation, even a performance so based on spontaneity as jazz. This preparation for Sonny is minimal, at least now, in the latter part of his career. Sonny has always had to deal with the physical demands of playing in such a bravura style, and with the exigencies of improvisation itself. "I don't like to rehearse," he says.

I used to rehearse a lot, and I used to like rehearsing because I enjoy playing. These days I only work about fifty dates a year. If I worked more, I could work over new material with my band right on the job. I used to be able to rehearse four or five hours a day. Just playing, really. Refining things. A lot of it would be improvisation and finding ways to relate to each other while we are playing. I shouldn't say, actually, that I don't like to rehearse. I used to like to rehearse. But now I don't.

Sonny's former boss Miles Davis was famous for preparing his musicians as minimally as possible and for rarely holding rehearsals for his bands. He wanted his musicians to understand what he demanded of them through intuition and their own refined musical sensibility, not from his direction. Like Miles, Sonny rarely makes a point of directing his band members. Sometimes this poses a problem:

I was accused at one time by some of the members of my band of not talking to them and telling them what I wanted. My wife [his wife, Lucille, is also his manager] has accused me [of this] . . . because the band members would come to her and used to say, "Gee, if Sonny would just tell us what he wanted . . ." I have been accused of that. Miles Davis has been accused of doing the same thing.

So did Sonny learn this from his former boss? "No," replies Sonny.

It just seems to be a natural thing to do. But I am like Miles in that if a guy is up there playing with me, playing with this band, then he should be given the freedom to be himself. So if you've earned the right to be up there, I don't want to have to be telling you what to do. If you are playing on this level, playing with Miles or me, you should be able to handle this and know what I want without my actually telling you. I am mainly an intuitive player. And I guess I expect the members of the band to be kind of the same way.

Intuition, sensitivity, an ear for nuance, even a bit of ESP are necessary attributes for musicians who play with master improvisers such as Rollins and Miles.

A special problem facing musicians who play in Sonny's group is his immense repertoire. Rollins knows hundreds of tunes, many of them old chestnuts. Most bandleaders have a far more limited repertoire, relatively easy for the musicians to learn. Sonny rarely rehearses and while on the bandstand is likely to play any of the tunes from the vast number of songs that he knows and plays; isn't this a major problem for his sidemen? According to Sonny:

> Yes, this probably is a problem for my musicians. But, you know, I can't subvert my energies to the band. I can't try and think like one of my sidemen. I can't do that because then I will be diminishing what I am expected to do. But I suppose this is a problem at times.

On the bandstand, Sonny wants to feel completely free to go in any direction that his imagination takes him at that particular moment. And his musicians simply must have a sharp enough ear and sufficient technical facility to provide adequate support for Sonny no matter in what direction his muse wanders.

This is Sonny's single most important requirement for his band: it should never hamper his own freedom, never interfere with his playing at the transcendent level that is the greatest experience of his life—"better than sex," he says. He has a single agenda when he plays: creating "music that is truly Sonny Rollins, the music that comes out of who and what I really am."

In a piece written about Sonny many years ago, it was reported that he had hired a certain untalented trumpeter (nobody famous) because the trumpet man's playing was so bad that it made Sonny angry. And he played best when he was mad. Hearing this story Sonny, laughs and says:

I can't remember the particular situation. But when I am angry there is a difference in my playing. I've been told that, especially by my wife. I might be angry at my wife and go out and play better. But I hate to make these things a general rule because they are not always true. It's very complicated. But that story is not impossible.

As for Sonny's own preparation for performance, there is little that he can do to ready himself for playing at this level:

The way I prepare for it is to keep my chops up. Your tools have to be strong. After that, it is up to you or the elements or whatever it is that makes the music come out. But up to that point, that's my preparation. Because as much as I practice at home and all, there's nothing like actually being on the stage and playing. I can get a year's worth of results out of playing on the stage for half an hour. It would take me maybe two years of practicing in my studio to get that kind of musical thought. So there's nothing like performing.

After all these years, Sonny is no longer nervous about performing. But this has not always been true:

When I first started playing in public I was a little nervous. Now I would not use the word "nervous" for how I feel just before performing. I want to say "tense," but that is not the right word either. But I do get focused and ready for battle. You get ready to do what you have to do. Maybe I get slightly agitated, but not visibly so. There's a slight apprehension. But there is nothing of that sort of feeling once I start playing.

However, I do feel more confident about my performance if I get an opportunity to warm up. That is, if I get an opportunity to, say, prepare in the dressing room for an hour or so. But that does not mean strictly playing for an hour. You get interrupted. You have to do this or that, do a sound check or something. I need an uninterrupted hour before I go on the stand. If I have the chance to go over my music, get my chops up, and find a good reed I feel more comfortable when I go onstage.

Finding a good reed may seem trivial to those of us who do not play reed instruments. But at least for Sonny Rollins it is a crucial task:

> Finding the right reed is very important. I often go through several boxes of reeds before I find the right one [there are five reeds in every box]. If I find the right reed, it makes me want to play more and it affects what I play and my ability to play it.
>
> Usually a good reed will only last one concert. At the next one I have to go through this process all over again. But searching for the right reed is almost a mystical or magical experience for a reed player. Find the right one, and I know I have a chance to play really well.

Sonny points out that he is certainly not the only one obsessed with finding the right reed:

> I remember going to visit John Coltrane when he was playing at the Jazz Gallery many years ago. I went into his dressing room and he must have had fifty reeds that he had checked and rejected. You have to be a reed player to understand how profoundly important it is to find the right reed.
>
> Having some time to do these various things is important, but it does not mean I am going to have a great show. Or that I'm hot. I can never tell beforehand if I am going to be hot that night. In fact, about a year or so ago after a show everybody was saying, "Oh, gee, that was really great." And I was thinking about what happened before that show. I was trying to figure out "What did I do?" Because maybe I can do that every night! But actually I didn't do anything specifically different. There is really no way that I know what's going to happen on any night.
>
> Like some baseball players, I am a little superstitious about it. If I am wearing a shirt for the first time and I don't have a good performance in that shirt I tend not to wear it again. Then there are some things that you wear that you have a good show in. I always feel comfortable in them. I have that part covered.
>
> Except as I mentioned before, there's always times when you might be angry or something before a performance and that might

bring out something during the performance, which it has at times. But even if I am angry or something, that does not necessarily guarantee that everything is going to be great or it's going to be a hot show. If that was true I would find a reason to be angry every night! So there is nothing cut-and-dried. I wish it was.

When Sonny actually walks onstage he is aware of the audience, but his concentration is totally focused on the music. He is acutely aware of the unique position and paradox of a chiefly improvising jazz musician who is creating his art while in the act of performance.

When I first started out playing I felt the pull of the audience. The feedback of the audience can still have some effect on my performance. But I have always felt that it is up to the performer to find the audience. I guess I got that from going the Apollo when I was a kid and seeing some performers who were rudely received by the audience. The Apollo had some very raucous audiences. Sometimes the performer had to fight for his life up there. I always felt that it was up to me to reach the audience. I can't expect the audience to love me or give me the benefit of the doubt. All I can ask is that they meet me halfway. When I played the Apollo myself the first few times, I knew I had reached the audience. Then I knew that I had made it. So I have kept the philosophy that it is up to the artist to reach the people.

That being said, when I go out to play I try not to be influenced by the people. There are times that you are playing and you find these women wearing these short skirts in the first row. That kind of thing can be very distracting. You try not to notice these things, and [to] concentrate on the music. There are people who look at you as if you were an object. Once you are onstage, you kind of feel like you are a geek in a circus sideshow. I would often wear dark glasses when I played so I could close my eyes and nobody would notice it. Some guy was interviewing me not long ago and the first thing he said to me was, "Gee, you know you had sunglasses on when you performed the other night and you seemed not to be aware of the audience." So I said sarcastically, "Did you see me performing in an old pair of dungarees or with a dirty shirt? Of course I am aware of the audience."

You know the one thing I've always hated about European concerts is that they have the lights on really high. They like to have these bright white lights on the stage. It's always a battle with them to get more atmospheric lighting. I am always conscious of the audience. I guess I get that feeling from spending all my life going to shows at the Apollo Theater. I always liked it when the curtain opened up, the illusion of the stage as something magical. When I perform, I do have a sense of the fact that the people are going to be looking at us, and I do want to have some kind of impact on them. It is a very fine line. I mean, you do not want to go out there and lay down on the floor and play and all this stuff, which has been done. [But] I always feel a little sense of show business, if you want to put it in such a crass way. It's such a delicate thing to say this, and I want you to understand how delicate this is. Because I am not trying to turn out some kind of show for the people. But I also am not going to go out there wearing dirty clothes. I want to be cleanly dressed, and sharp if possible, and then play my music. That would be the extent to which I think about the fact that I am onstage and that I am not just playing around the house or reading a book. So I feel there is some responsibility on my part to bend a little to the audience, to give them something extra.

The point is, when I first start playing, I try not to really deal with the audience. I don't want to try to play to the audience. As the night goes on, then maybe a different sort of energy may be coming from them . . . that's different. Initially I try to be oblivious to the audience. I want to get into my own world and create my music. If the audience then comes in and likes it, fine.

Sonny does not decide ahead of time what tunes to play, or even which ones he'll use to open a set:

I don't have a playlist. Sometimes I like to open with a certain tune because it works with my unit. I am thinking as part of a unit rather than just a player. This is why as a bandleader you change as a player. You kind of have to be less spontaneous as a bandleader. I still do not have a set playlist. The closest I get to that is, although I can amend it a little bit, over the last few years or so I usually play a calypso at every concert. There are only two calypsos that I regularly play. I never play them in any order or anything like that.

Every time he performs, Sonny hopes that it will be one of those special nights when he feels he is creating on a transcendent plane. Those magnificent moments are, for him, the ultimate experiences of his life. Playing well is more than just a matter of pride; it is almost a religion to him. As with any spiritual experience, it is very difficult to put into words either what one feels or by what inner mechanism one reaches such an exalted plane:

> When I am really playing at my best, the music is sort of playing itself. I'm just standing there moving the keys. The music is coming, but I am not thinking about it. That is the state I try to reach— where I don't think about it.

Sonny seriously studied yoga as part of his spiritual search. But he discovered that playing was itself a form of yoga:

> When I am playing, I would say it is a spititual thing, in that the concentration is very similar to yoga. Because when I really concentrate while I am playing, I lose myself. Sometimes I feel like I am a whirling dervish, twirling around and getting into a certain state. It is truly an altered consciousness. That is what happens when I am really playing. You concentrate up to a point, and then you don't have to concentrate. *Then the other part comes in.*
>
> Every night I try to reach this level, and I succeed to a greater or lesser degree. My modus operandi at the start of each performance is the same. Often, when you begin playing, you have to begin thinking about things—what you are trying to do and so on. Early on, I often play well-known licks and riffs. I don't like playing licks and riffs. But just doing that gets me into it, gets me going.

When Sonny is playing at his best, he is known for his very long solos. Even a half-hour solo is not extraordinary.

> One night several years ago in a club I played a solo that went on for over two and a half hours. It didn't even occur to me how long it was.

I might have had a passing realization every now and then that we may have gone over the one-hour time usually allotted for a set so they can get a new crowd into the club and sell them whiskey. It was probably my record for a solo. I didn't think about "Well, gee, when should I stop?" That wasn't the point. The point was more "When should I start to get into this music? When will we really begin to burn?" When we'd reached a point where it was really satisfying, "Okay, we've finally gotten there." That night I never thought it got there.

That's how Coltrane felt, too. [John Coltrane was also known for his lengthy solos.] Knowing John, I have a feeling that he probably approached it from that way, too. He wasn't thinking "Well, gee, let's see. I've been playing for thirty minutes." He was trying to get to a certain musical place.

At this stage in his life, Sonny is no longer able to play comfortably at fast tempos. In earlier years, he was a master at playing very fast while being able to create coherent musical ideas, not just running the changes as many jazzmen do at such fiery tempos. Sonny recalls:

Several years ago, I played at a salute to Dizzy [Gillespie] at Wolf Trap [Massachusetts], not long before he died. I was talking to Dizzy about what we should play together. I suggested some things, but Dizzy said that he did not want to play anything fast. Of course Dizzy used to be so great at those kinds of tempos; he was famous for it! But in later years it becomes very hard to play like that, for just the mechanics involved.

So are ballads, then, much easier to play? Sonny laughs. "Well, ballads are hard to play, too. Everything is hard, I guess, at this age."

Despite Sonny's assertion that he no longer has the strength to play as he did when younger, he more than makes up for it with his long, brilliant solos. These solos sum up all the phases of his career—bebop, hard bop, free jazz, and funk—and at the same time point the way toward still more new directions. Despite their complexity and layers of nuance, his solos are coherent, complete, and powerful musical statements. Rollins's ability to use all that he has learned and explored over a half-century of playing gives his solos wisdom and depth.

After a performance, Sonny is physically and emotionally drained. Yet even on a good night, he seldom appreciates his own playing. "I wish," says Lucille Rollins,

> that Sonny would enjoy his own playing more than he does. Right after even a good night, he always says that for one reason or another he did not feel that he was playing the way he wanted or that the band wasn't giving him support, or something else. Even when everyone is telling him how brilliant he was, he doesn't believe it himself.

Sonny's humility arises from his belief that his creative genius comes from a higher source and that he is merely a vehicle for the music. His dedication to music is like that of a mystic or a monk, a lifelong devotion that gives him a belief in ecstatic transcendence.

For Sonny, playing before an audience is the hub of his life, the one thing, apart from his relationship with Lucille, that continues to bring him joy. Creating music that is heard only once, in the moment, and shared by the musician only with the particular audience that hears it has given this deeply sensitive and brilliant man hope and strength through the various struggles of his long life and astonishing career.

2

School Days

Perhaps it was ordained that Sonny Rollins would become a great jazz musician when he was born, on September 7, 1930. His family lived in the heart of Harlem, on 137th Street between Lenox Avenue and Seventh Avenue. The Harlem Renaissance was at its peak and the neighborhood was suffused with African American music. The Savoy Ballroom, the Apollo Theater, the Cotton Club, and many other venues were playing at maximum capacity.

The baby was named Walter Theodore Rollins, after his father; Sonny believes that he got his nickname to differentiate him from Walter Senior. Years later, when Sonny was a young man addicted to drugs and frequently in trouble with the law, he was unable to get working papers under his own name so he could appear in New York clubs. To get around this, he changed his name to Theodore Walter Rollins.

Both of Sonny's parents were from St. Thomas in the U.S. Virgin Islands. Sonny's mother's maiden name was Valborg, a Danish name (the Virgin Islands were owned by Denmark before the United States took them over), although her father was Haitian and Sonny believes that his grandmother was, too. Sonny's father was from St. Croix. One of Sonny's earliest memories is of his mother singing a traditional calypso melody that many years later he would record under the title "St. Thomas." Sonny's fusion of jazz and calypso is not his greatest innovation by any means, but it is probably the most personal.

Sonny became more aware of music when both his older sister and brother took up instruments and regularly practiced. "My sister played piano in church and my brother was a very good violinist."

My brother was going to play in a symphony orchestra when he got out of school. But then he changed his mind and joined the army instead. He and my sister were always playing music in the house. I always heard music in my home. I heard people like Fats [Waller] when I was quite young, six or seven, and I really liked him even way back when I was still a kid.

Because his mother worked, various members of his family often looked after Sonny. One of those helpers was his grandmother; her strong social and cultural views greatly influenced Sonny's lifelong interest and involvement in political and social issues:

Back in those days, everybody brought up the kids. My father was never around that much, because he was in the Navy, and my mother worked. I wound up spending a lot of time with my grandmother. She was very much socially conscious. She was a [Marcus] Garveyite—the "Back to Africa" movement. As a matter of fact, at that time she was also a Communist. So it was [she] who instilled in me that sense of equality. She was the most militant in my family. Black people [then] believed that the Communist Party had a lot of intriguing programs that we thought were beneficial. You have to remember that during that time, the 1930s, lynching was a big sport. People used to go to see the nigger getting lynched. . . . Because of this milieu, the Communists were able to make inroads with black people. Later we found out that the Communist Party was just as corrupt as any other political party. But that wasn't the point. The point was that they were offering black people some kind of semblance of dignity at a time when the mass culture was trying to keep us in subservient roles.
 . . . When I was a kid I went to a camp called Camp Unity. It was, I believe, a Communist camp, but it may have been a crossover.

There were a lot of progressive groups at that time that crossed over. This camp had a lot of black and white kids together. This was a very important experience for me as a black kid in America. That was how I was raised. We were always involved in what I would call the politics of equality.

Sonny developed strong ethical values even when he was very young:

> I was always a person who had strong feelings about the morality of life. I think I learned these values early on. When I was a kid we used to play on top of the roofs of some of the buildings. There used to be a shortcut through the back of some of the buildings so you could go between St. Nicholas Avenue and Ashcomb Avenue. I was on top of one of the buildings overlooking the shortcut, and they had these large hunks of plaster molding which we used to throw off the roof. So one time I saw this guy walking through the shortcut, and I wanted to scare this guy by throwing a large piece of molding near him. So I threw it off and suddenly this light flashed in my head: as it was going down it occurred to me that if the molding hit the guy it would probably kill him. That is when I first had an encounter praying to God. I prayed like I had never prayed before. I was so thankful when it missed the guy. So I had a strong feeling of right and wrong even when I was a little kid.

Sonny's intelligence was manifest early on; in elementary school he skipped a grade. At that time, though, his direction was not toward music: "I was first interested in the visual arts, painting and drawing. I actually thought of becoming a painter at one point." I don't think that it is a stretch to say that Sonny's interest in color and design would later play a role in his musical conception.

Sonny also spent a lot of time with his uncle, who would be among the first to open Sonny's ears to African American music:

> I had an uncle from Georgia, and he and his wife loved the blues. I spent a lot of time with them while I was growing up. They half-reared me. It was in their house that I first heard country bluesmen like Lonnie Johnson, Tommy McClannan, and those

other guys. I liked them. But I really loved Louis Jordan and his band, the Tympany Five. That is the first time I was exposed to the saxophone.

Louis Jordan played what was called jump music. Jump, an offshoot of black swing music (such as that of Count Basie or Jimmie Lunceford) and urban blues, was a forerunner of rhythm and blues. Jordan was very popular among African Americans in the late 1930s and 1940s; among his biggest hits were "Five Guys Named Moe" and "Nobody's Here but Us Chickens." With titles like these, it's obvious that this was unpretentious good-time music. Jordan spent most of his career playing the "chitlin' circuit" of small clubs featuring black entertainment. Although Jordan's only ambition was to create music that provided simple pleasure, he was a superb saxophonist. He probably could have become a fine jazz musician if he had been devoted to so-called pure jazz (although at this time—the late 1930s and early 1940s—the dividing line between "authentic" jazz and this kind of pop music was very narrow). Many years later, some jazz writers would criticize Sonny for writing and performing funk tunes. But for Sonny, that type of music had always been a key part of his musical universe.

Sonny first became interested in the saxophone early on because of Jordan; and not just because of the music itself:

> I loved the way that Louis Jordan's saxophone looked. But I liked his music first. Then I saw a picture of [Jordan] in a club across the street from my elementary school; he was posing with a King Zephyr alto saxophone. It is such a beautiful instrument! So all these things came together.

Sonny's mother, always supportive of her children's interests, bought Sonny his first saxophone when he was about nine years old. Because of his fascination with Jordan, it was an alto sax.

Although Rollins is largely self-taught, early on he did have some instruction:

> After I got my mother to buy me my first saxophone, she took me to a place called the New York Schools of Music. They were these

schools that were all over the city. They taught everything, every instrument from A to Z, from accordion to xylophone. I think they charged about fifteen or twenty-five cents a lesson. They had some private teachers, and that is where I took my first lessons. Later on I went to a teacher at the YMCA on 131st Street. That was sort of a cultural center at the time. This guy used to rent a little studio in there and I took lessons from him. In high school, I studied theory and harmony. I never went to college.

When Sonny was eleven, he was already interested in becoming a professional musician. He remembers an incident that increased his desire to make music his vocation:

I used to regularly spend summers with my father, who was stationed in Annapolis. I got this crush on a girl named Marjorie Brown who was older than I was and very beautiful. One time the Erskine Hawkins band came there to play, and I was crushed when I saw how interested she was in the musicians.

Sonny's childhood memories have had a specific effect on his later musical career. He is famous for his use of a huge repertoire mainly consisting of old pop songs. Many critics insist that Sonny is lampooning these songs, playing them with knowing sarcasm. But Sonny first heard many or most of them in the films that he adored as a child. Because of that, they have a special emotional resonance. That is certainly not the only reason he chooses the tunes that he plays; they have to possess some kind of melodic or harmonic element that intrigue him as well. Sonny has a particularly vivid memory of the first time he discovered the instrument that eventually would become the center of his life:

This guy came to my uncle's house and he had a beautiful, bright, and shiny horn and it was in one of those old-time cases that used to be lined with velvet. I just loved the way the tenor saxophone looked. To me it was just like looking at the Holy Grail. This was the first thing that drew me to the tenor sax. That and Coleman Hawkins, who became my idol.

Hawkins, who would remain Sonny's idol for the entirety of his life and career, was not just a key influence; he was also responsible for demonstrating what a richly expressive instrument the tenor sax could be.

Coleman Hawkins was known as the inventor of the tenor sax, because he was the first tenor saxophonist to develop a style uniquely based on that instrument's sonic properties. Hawkins was to the tenor sax what Louis Armstrong was to the trumpet. He was a true prodigy, playing at the age of five, taking up the cello at seven, and then the saxophone when he was nine. By the age of twelve, Hawkins was playing professionally. He first came to notice while he was a member of Fletcher Henderson's innovative big band. In those days, Hawkins's playing was crude and not unlike that of other early tenor players: he utilized "slap-tonguing," a technique of applying the tongue to the reed in a certain way in order to produce a highly percussive tone in which the notes literally sound as if they were "slapped," the standard approach of early-jazz tenor saxophonists, as well as a reedy waspish tone and a flatfooted rhythmic conception.

When Louis Armstrong briefly joined the Henderson band in 1924, Hawkins, like so many other jazz musicians, began to perceive the possibilities of improvising on his instrument. Certainly Armstrong affected Hawkins's rhythmic conception, just as the trumpeter influenced virtually every other jazz musician of the time.

By the late twenties, Hawkins had developed most of the elements of his style—the big tone with the fast vibrato, the focus on vertical, or harmonically complex playing, and the flow of highly inventive melodic ideas. Although Hawkins never played with the rhythmic fluidity of, say, Lester Young, he made up for it with a bravura operatic romanticism. His song "Body and Soul" became a big hit and made him famous beyond the boundaries of the jazz world. It has become the great test for tenor saxophonists. Virtually every great player since Hawkins has recorded it: Ben Webster, Chu Berry, Lucky Thompson, John Coltrane, and, of course, Sonny Rollins (who recorded an unaccompanied version of the tune).

Almost as important as his style itself was Hawkins's continual openness to fresh musical ideas. He was fascinated by the harmonic complexity at the heart of Art Tatum's playing. Unlike many musicians of his generation, he welcomed the revolutionary ideas of the bebop Young Turks of the 1940s. He held some of the earliest bop sessions, utilizing such key boppers as Dizzy Gillespie, Thelonious Monk, Fats Navarro, Oscar Pettiford, and Max Roach. Hawkins is clearly a key influence on Charlie Parker—and vice versa: elements of Bird's style can be heard in Hawkins's phrasing and rhythmic approach during this period. In the sixties, he demonstrated his interest in the playing of both Sonny and John Coltrane. He even successfully made a bossa nova album.

Yet Hawkins always remained resolutely and unmistakably himself every time he played, no matter how much he explored the latest developments in jazz. His big sound and bravura sense of drama owed much to opera, which he loved and to which he listened more often than any other music. His long career touched on virtually every development in jazz since the mid-twenties. It is hard to think of any other major jazz musician of whom this was true.

Sonny got to know Hawkins as a colleague much later:

> There was a time later on where I first got an inkling [Hawkins] had heard me play. I mean many, many years later, when I was a professional going around playing in clubs. I found out through somebody that he liked my playing or something, but there was no real contact between us until I began establishing my own reputation. Then I began to see him at different places, the bars where musicians liked to hang out. I remember Coleman playing at the Metropole [a now-defunct club in midtown Manhattan]. Hawkins would hang out at this bar across the street. Even before that, I would talk with him at times. But Hawkins was so far above me in both career and in age that he and I were never contemporaries.

When Sonny's family moved uptown to the affluent section of Harlem called Sugar Hill, he met a number of young neighborhood musicians who were as interested in jazz as he was. Sugar Hill attracted a number of men Sonny's age or a few years younger who became prominent jazzmen as part of the second wave of bop: alto saxophonist Jackie McLean; pianists Walter Bishop and Kenny Drew; the drummer Art Taylor; a young trumpet player named Lowell Louis; and Andy Kirk, Jr., the son of the bandleader Andy Kirk. They became a clique in high school, hanging out together and sharing ideas and enthusiasm for the burgeoning modern jazz scene. Sonny, looked up to by all of them, became their natural leader.

What was it about this neighborhood that seemed to attract so many young jazzmen?

> Sugar Hill was just a nice area, maybe you could even call it genteel. It attracted guys like Kenny Drew, who didn't really live on the Hill, but instead on the outskirts of what they called Down the Hill. We never got to know each other by playing with each other. Walter Bishop lived in what we called Greater Harlem. He came up on the Hill because he knew Andy Kirk, Jr., and Jackie McLean. It was just a nice area to hang out, unlike some other areas of Harlem. A lot of top-flight musicians lived in that area, like Coleman Hawkins or Oscar Moore, who was the guitarist with the Nat "King" Cole trio.

Because of the misgivings of some family members about his growing interest in jazz, Sonny's mother was not able to buy her son a tenor saxophone until his fourteenth birthday. She bought him a King model tenor sax, the same brand as Louis Jordan's alto.

Sonny was a reluctant student in elementary school; he even skipped a grade. He found high school oppressive and boring, especially because he had become so immersed in music. He became what is now known as an "underachiever."

His ability as a musician developed quickly. Sonny believes that his environment gave him a kind of "head start":

> When I started playing, I used to listen to a lot of music and, of course, I was born in Harlem and heard a lot of music around me as I was growing up. I got to recognize the saxophone as the instrument that I liked. I would listen to all these broadcasts, hearing how all these guys sounded on the radio. When I finally got my first saxophone, I already had a head start for playing it, in a manner of speaking. Pretty early on, I felt that there was nothing I couldn't play. During my career there were times where I felt I was up against a brick wall, even now. But that passes. But back in those early days, I never seemed to have any difficulty playing the horn. I came into it already prepared to play it.

During this early period, Sonny was giving long and deep thought to what it meant to be a musician. One incident, early in his high school years, has remained especially vivid in his memory and would affect his conception of an artist's social obligations:

> In about 1946, they opened a brand-new school on 116th Street and Pleasant Avenue. They wanted to fill it up so they had us bused down from Harlem in order to go to that school, Benjamin Franklin High School. It was right in the middle of an Italian neighborhood. We had to take the subway down to 116th Street and then take a crosstown bus to the school. So when we first started going down there it was like an invasion of black kids into an Italian neighborhood. This caused rioting. People would throw stuff at us as we walked down the street toward the school. We had to walk a couple of blocks and people were throwing not just insults at us, but objects. This became a big deal in the newspapers, with all these reports of "race riots" and that kind of stuff.
>
> Then Frank Sinatra heard about this and he came to the school and he gave a concert in the auditorium. He admonished the kids for fighting, especially the Italian kids. He said "Cut it out and learn how to be good neighbors." Then Nat "King" Cole came and he put on a concert. It was great, it was really great, and, it worked. The animosity stopped. We learned that you don't have to love everybody but you don't have to kill them either. I wound up becoming good friends with some of the Italian kids.

This was a crucial lesson for Sonny: that a musician has social as well as artistic obligations.

Despite Sonny's growing fascination with jazz as both a musical and a social force, his family had mixed feelings, at best, about jazz as a vocation:

> My family didn't like my playing jazz. My father was in the Navy and was always away. I was brought up by my mother, who would let me do what I wanted to do. She was in my corner. But my grandmother began to take over the job of rearing me and she was very, very much against my playing jazz. After I graduated from high school and began using drugs, she really got on my case. She linked it. She linked jazz and drugs and the whole thing. So at that forma-

tive stage I had a lot of opposition. But not from my mother. She had a lot of faith in me, although I really put her through the wringer. There were things I did, later on, to her and the family. But she had a mother's love and she had confidence that I would make something out of myself. Which was good, because she had a lot of faith in me when no one else did. Fortunately I was becoming successful at the time she died, in 1957. I had turned the page then, and . . . she saw that I was going to get my life together and make something out of myself.

As Sonny grew older, he became increasingly aware of the social and cultural issues sweeping the country, in particular those issues that especially affected African Americans. He was brought up to think like an iconoclast. This radical point of view would affect the course of his life in a number of ways. For example, his view of the military was very different from that of most young men at that time:

When the Second World War came I had to go down to Whitehall Street to be examined for the Army. I was already profoundly alienated from American society, to the extent that I did not want to go. We put pinpricks in our arms so we could say that we were drug addicts and be exempted. I guess the ordinary American kid was glad to fight in World War Two. But I was so alienated that I did not want to fight for this country. It was kind of like what Muhammad Ali said: "Ain't no Vietnamese ever called me nigger." It was just a fact of life. I knew what was happening as a teenager. I felt the cards were stacked against me. I felt left outside this country.

As Sonny grew older, his interest in jazz grew broader. The more he came to understand the nature of jazz, the more he began to realize that he had to expand his horizons beyond his earliest influences. Coleman Hawkins had been the dominant influence on tenormen since the late 1920s. But in the 1930s, another tenor saxophonist, Lester Young, gained notice with a style whose songlike lyricism was unlike anything else in jazz. (A possible exception was Bix Beiderbecke, a major influence on

Young.) "Prez" (short for "President of the Tenor Sax") played behind the beat, swinging hard but with great subtlety, true elegance, and restraint, almost like a great soft-shoe dancer. Many in the jazz world rallied behind either the Hawkins "school" or the Lester Young "school," but the best musicians listened closely to both players.

> I used to go around saying how great I thought Coleman Hawkins was. Everybody seemed to agree with that, but there was one guy who said that I had to check out Lester Young. So I bought the first Lester Young record I ever heard—"Afternoon of a Basieite," with Slam Stewart and Johnny Guarnieri. The first time I listened to that record—he was *tremendous!* Lester was playing in a style very different from my idol, Coleman Hawkins. I got to like him too, quite a bit, and I particularly was influenced by his ability to play legato.
>
> There was one particular period when you could say my playing was imbued with the spirit of Lester Young. No, I wouldn't say I was trying to play like him note for note, but I felt his influence pretty strongly. This was commented on. Somebody said, "There is the spirit of Lester Young in Sonny's playing."

Sonny discovered another one of his most important influences almost by accident. During the early 1940s, when he first began to study jazz, he listened closely to a number of tenormen generally of the "Hawkins school." Among the most prominent of these musicians were Chu Berry, Ben Webster, and, importantly, Don Byas.

> I thought that Don Byas was the most modern jazz player I had ever heard. I bought one of his records and on the "B" side was Charlie Parker playing "Koko." It was different from anything I had heard before. I didn't really understand what he was doing, but I did not dislike it, either. When I came across other Charlie Parker records I listened to those and I finally understood and appreciated what he was playing.

A few years ago there surfaced some recordings of Bird that he made privately in the early 1940s, the formative years of his style. On these sides, he plays tenor in a style not far removed from Byas's or Berry's. Although Parker is usually thought of as a student of Lester Young, his tenor playing in these incipient years was clearly influenced at least as much by Hawkins and his followers. Parker's harmonic sophistication was born, to a degree, out of his absorption of the styles of Hawkins and the tenormen he influenced, in particular Don Byas. Parker once said about Byas, "He played everything there was to play." It is significant that when Dizzy Gillespie performed with the first bebop band to play on Fifty-second Street, the saxophonist in his group was not Charlie Parker—he was unavailable—but Don Byas.

Sonny's ability to perceive the pivotal role between the swing era and bebop that musicians like Byas and Hawkins played is particularly significant, for he himself would later play a similar role between the bebop revolution of the 1940s and the free jazz revolution of the 1960s. That he immediately embraced bop was no doubt due to his fascination and close study of these crucial figures.

Charlie Parker's style was essential to Sonny's development because, among other reasons, Bird was at least as harmonically sophisticated as Hawkins or Byas, and yet was also as melodically inventive as Lester Young, and at least as rhythmically fluid. Bird and the other beboppers proved that jazz improvisation could be as harmonically dense as it was melodically inventive. In other words, the approaches of Coleman Hawkins and Lester Young did not necessarily cancel each other out. In addition, Parker was able to improvise rhythmically with as much invention as he brought to his flow of melodic ideas. One could listen to Bird just for his rhythmic message; Parker took the whole concept of swing to a new plateau of complexity and ingenuity.

Of course, Charlie Parker had not unilaterally "invented" bebop; a number of young musicians had been working toward a more sophisticated form of jazz over a period of years.

Bop had been incubated mainly in Harlem's after-hours clubs, such as Minton's and Monroe's. Forward-looking young musicians would share ideas, jam together, and challenge pretenders on the bandstand with complicated chord structures and bruising tempos. A great many musicians helped to inaugurate the modern jazz resolution, but many of them are now obscure. Among the most important innovators were the great guitarist Charlie Christian (who tragically died in 1942, when he was twenty-five, before the full flowering of bebop); Dizzy Gillespie; Thelonious Monk (known as the High Priest of Bop); Bud Powell, who lived near Sonny in Sugar Hill, and the key drum innovator of the movement, Kenny Clarke.

Besides producing their musical advances, these musicians were also trying to change the image of the jazz musician as simply an entertainer. This is not to say that previous jazzmen were not true artists, or that they did not view the music they played as genuine art. But the boppers wanted to separate themselves as far as possible from the expectations of the white audience. This, too, was of crucial importance to Sonny:

> We already felt like we were not part of the mainstream of American society. Then a music came along that was expressing this kind of view. Later on, John Coltrane and I were called the angry tenors. We were not angry, but we had strong views about American society. Bebop reflected our alienation from the mainstream. . . . My friends and I believed that bebop was the first musical movement to completely turn away from the minstrel image of most black entertainment. It was a complete opposite, and it was a new birth of freedom. It was more than music—it was a social movement, and we wanted to be part of it. We didn't want to be "entertainers," per se; we wanted to be serious musicians. That is one of the reasons why Charlie Parker was so important. Charlie Parker didn't joke around like Dizzy did. Charlie Parker would just stand up straight and play. It was just a complete change.
>
> In order to play jazz you have to be honest, honest to your audience and especially honest to yourself. Racism has no place in jazz. If you can play, *you can play!* That's what jazz is, really. Guys are playing with no consideration of color.
>
> Bebop was so great because guys were playing on such a high plane with each other. Everybody was trying to get *into the music.* The music itself was such a free expression. It's the greatest thing in the world to be able to create right on the spur of the moment, and to be able to get into yourself to that extent, you have to be honest. You really have to be a person of social awareness to do that. Maybe

it is not possible to live in America and not be racist to some degree. But to be a jazz musician you have to confront that more in your life. Because guys had to know that it was a matter of merit. The ability to play, to pursue this truly creative art form, is something that has nothing to do with racism.

The boppers' profound alienation was to spawn a hip culture with its own mores, ethics, and worldview. In many ways, this was a direct consequence of the horrors of Auschwitz, Buchenwald, Hiroshima, and Nagasaki. As Norman Mailer wrote in his famous essay "The White Negro: Superficial Reflections on the Hipster":

> The Second World War presented a mirror for the human condition which blinded anyone who looked into it. For if tens of millions were killed in concentration camps out of the inexorable agonies and contractions of superstates founded upon the always insoluble contradictions of injustice, one was obliged also to see that no matter how crippled and perverted an image of man was the society he had created, it was nonetheless his creation, his collective creation (at least his collective creation from the past) and if society was so murderous, then who could ignore the most hideous questions about his own nature?[1]

A great bop solo like Charlie Parker's "KoKo" or "Klacktovedestene" conveys a tragic view of life whose only hope is ecstatic transcendence. The contrast between these jazz performances and those of, say, Lester Young or Roy Eldridge is palpable. After the horrendous events of the war years, it was no longer possible to play music of boundless optimism.

Many of the young musicians in the Sugar Hill group, including Sonny himself, would be among the most important musicians of the second wave of boppers who continued the modern jazz revolution from the 1950s forward. For example, Jackie McLean became one of the most original—and often most strikingly brilliant—of the young alto saxophonists influenced by Charlie Parker. Jackie developed his own sound, a bronzed, searing wail quite unlike the tone of any other saxophonist in jazz. And—unlike many Bird-influenced altoists—he learned how to play with economy rather than hurling flurries of notes into the air. McLean went on to play with most of the important modernists, including Miles Davis, Art Blakey's Jazz Messengers, Kenny Dorham, and Donald Byrd, among others. His solos have always been searching and he has always been one of the most emotionally gripping musicians of his generation. In the 1960s, he was drawn to the music of Ornette Coleman and the "New Thing," and adapted his hard bop style successfully to the revolutionary ideas of the new band of Young Turks. McLean became an important composer as well as a consistently inventive and red-hot improviser.

Art Taylor became one of the most prolific drummers of the 1950s. He played and recorded with virtually every modern jazzman, from Monk and Bud Powell to John Coltrane (he is the drummer on Trane's classic *Giant Steps* album) and Miles Davis (he played drums on Miles's first classic orchestral collaboration with Gil Evans on Columbia, *Miles Ahead*). Taylor also moved to Europe in the early 1960s, but he came back to his home country for the last few years of his life.

But not all of this clique prevailed. Sonny remembers the trumpeter Lewis Lowell as being one of the most talented of this group. "We all liked Dizzy [Gillespie], of course. Lowell really liked Miles. He caught on to Miles for doing something different and he became one of the first guys to use Miles as an influence." Lowell eventually became mired in drugs. Andy Kirk, Jr., was another one of Sonny's earliest musical colleagues. Kirk's father was the famous bandleader, and Andy Jr. was a superb reedman who, according to Sonny, could play almost every reed instrument that he picked up. But Kirk, like Louis Lowell, was caught up in the drug epidemic of the late 1940s and early 1950s; he, too, dropped out of music. This clique of brilliant young musicians gravitated to the genius jazzmen living in or near to their neighborhood: Bud Powell, Thelonious Monk, and Coleman Hawkins. As Sonny remembers:

We used to follow Coleman Hawkins all around. He was my idol and just being in his company was thrilling for me. He lived in elegant style, driving a new Cadillac and always dressing really well. I admired his sense of style almost as much as I did his playing. We also used to follow Charlie Parker all around, from Fifty-second

Street to jam sessions in Harlem. We learned a lot about what it meant to be a jazz musician.

Sonny and his young colleagues learned more than music from following their idols, particularly Coleman Hawkins. There were lots of musicians in the late 1930s and 1940s, and almost all of them were dignified—John Kirby, Don Redman, Erskine Hawkins, and Jonah Jones. But Hawkins also seemed to project the air of a great artist.

Because of Charlie Parker, the alto saxophone was dominant in the early bop movement. But there would emerge some important tenor men:

> I listened to Dexter Gordon. But when I say that I listened to him, I don't mean that I tried to emulate him. I didn't go in Dexter Gordon's direction. I listened to Eddie "Lockjaw" Davis and I listened to Don Byas and I listened to Ben Webster. I listened to a lot of guys. I listened to Dexter because he was in Billy Eckstine's band. I heard him when he recorded "Blue and Boogie" with Dizzy Gillespie. Sonny Stitt was more relevant to me because he was playing regularly with Dizzy. But when I heard [Sonny Stitt] play tenor I was already far along with my own development.

These were heady, exciting times for the young Sonny Rollins. "Every day after school I would go to Thelonious Monk's place and practice with his band. He never really told me what to play, because I guess he respected my playing. But I learned a lot from Monk just hanging out with him."

Jackie McLean was two years younger than Sonny. He was a freshman in high school about the time Sonny was a senior (Sonny, as previously stated, had skipped a grade), and looked up to Rollins as a kind of older brother. As Jackie remembers it, "Sonny influenced everybody uptown playing every instrument. There were a lot of musicians in our neighborhood . . . and Sonny was the leader of all of them." Sonny formed his first band while in high school, the Countsmen. Sonny recalls:

> Kenny Drew was the pianist. I know that Art Taylor was in the band. And Lowell Louis. We played mainly dances. There were a lot

of little dance halls everywhere. There were almost no clubs where we could please. But there was one club uptown and it was sort of like a nightclub. It was called Brankers, and it was on 155th Street and Ashcomb Avenue. That was the first local club that we played in and it was a place where everybody played. I played there, Jackie played there, Lowell played there. People sat at tables and drank. It was mainly thought of as a nightclub in contrast [with] the dance halls where we played.

Even at this early period in his musical development, Sonny was such a prodigious player that he was recognized not only by the young talented musicians who were his friends but also by established jazzmen. For a teenage jazz musician to have among his admirers Thelonious Monk, Bud Powell, and Miles Davis was simply extraordinary. However, Sonny was still not convinced that he should devote his life to jazz. These were heady times for him, and probably would have been a peak in his life if not for one ugly problem: the heroin addiction that was rampant throughout Harlem, and not only among jazzmen. Sonny was becoming part of the jazz scene and he lived in the heart of Harlem; it was not surprising that he would become snared. His involvement with drugs turned out to have unexpected consequences, which profoundly changed the course of his life.

3

Blue Room

When Sonny graduated from high school in 1947, he was for all practical purposes a professional musician. He got gigs wherever he could find them, sometimes as a sideman and at other times as a leader. When he played with his own band, he usually used a trio—but not a pianoless trio like those he would lead later on. "Usually," Sonny recalls, "I would use a piano and drums or piano and bass but no drums. I just had to work with whatever guys I could get." Working with Monk and learning from Bud Powell, Sonny found himself noticed more and more by many in the bebop scene. The singer Babs Gonsales became the first to use Sonny on a recording.

Gonsales, who mostly sang nonsense songs that capitalized on the faddish aspects of bebop, knew and worked with some of the movement's best musicians. For example, his group often performed the arrangements of Tadd Dameron, one of the most important bop composers and arrangers.

Gonsales heard Rollins at one of the young saxophonist's gigs and hired him. As Sonny remembers it:

> I was playing gigs all around town and I began to get a reputation.
> Guys would be talking about some new guys that were playing up

town and so forth, and that is how Babs first heard of me. So he hired me to play some jobs all around town, and I got into that scene. Babs [had] all of these guys like [tenor saxophonist] Lucky Thompson and [trumpeter] Fats Navarro and [trombonist] Benny Green, all of the really top-notch people that were on the scene. Babs would do his little bit of singing and then all the guys would play.

I began doing jobs with Babs in Philadelphia and Boston and a bunch of other places before we made the records.

Gonsales gave Sonny his first chance to record. All that Sonny remembers from that date was how excited and nervous he was to be recording with the other boppers on the modern scene. Recently, he heard some of these recordings:

I was just casually listening to the radio and this guy was playing a record. It felt like the last time I had heard it was a hundred years ago. It caught my fancy. I said to myself, "Wait a minute!" It was me on my first recording with Babs Gonsales! It sounded very derivative. It was very much in Charlie Parker's bag. It was sort of, "Hey, who's that? Wait a minute, is that me?"

The trombonist J. J. Johnson had been in on the Gonsales date and had been impressed with the young tenorman. Johnson was given a recording date of his own by the Savoy label (which recorded much of the most important early bop, including Charlie Parker's first sessions as a leader), and he used Sonny. The opportunity to record with such an important musician was validation of Sonny's growth as a musician. Johnson also recorded a couple of Sonny's compositions that day: "Audoban" and "Bee Jay." Sonny's sound on the recording is unmistakable, as it had been with Gonsales. However, at this point his rhythmic conception was like that of most young boppers in its emulation of Charlie Parker's rhythmic advances.

In 1949, at the age of nineteen, Sonny played on a Blue Note session led by Bud Powell that produced some of the most exciting sides of the bop revolution. The brilliant bop pianist was at his peak during this period. Powell had been the first pianist to adapt the rhythmic and harmonic innovations of Charlie Parker and Dizzy Gillespie. (Monk was probably the first modern jazz pianist, but his playing owed little to the orthodox bop styles of Bird and Dizzy.)

It is interesting that Powell selected Sonny to play on this session because, at least up until this point, the two musicians had not been particularly close.

> I didn't hang out that much with Bud Powell. Jackie [McLean] was very friendly with Bud's brother, Richie. He and Richie were kind of in the same age bracket and they got kind of tight. I'm not exactly sure how I got to know Bud. I know that we used to go to his house like we used to follow Charlie Parker around or Coleman Hawkins. We used to go to his house and listen to him practicing. He was living on 141st Street off St. Nicholas Avenue back then. I guess he got to know me only after I started doing gigs.

Powell became inarguably the most influential pianist in jazz; it is difficult to imagine the jazz piano of the last fifty years or so without him. But, throughout his life, he had bouts of severe mental illness, which eventually caused great damage to his career. Sonny believes these problems arose, at least to a degree, from Powell's great frustration:

> I think if he had been white, and if they had recognized his genius, maybe the society would have protected him. He just would have been in a more privileged position in society, if he didn't have to put up with the normal treatment that minorities endure. Maybe his genius would have been treasured and therefore he might have been protected.

Powell used yet another modern genius in the front line with Sonny on the 1949 recording date: the magnificent trumpeter Fats Navarro. Navarro and Miles Davis provided Sonny with one of his most scintillating musical memories:

> One of the peak musical experiences of my life was listening to Miles and Fats Navarro play together. It was unbelievable—Miles

could play as fast as Fats and Fats could play with the same amount of soul as Miles.

Fats Navarro would also be the main influence on Clifford Brown, who was to play a very important role in Sonny's life, both personally and musically.

Even in this fast company Sonny held his own. The core of his musical personality was already in place—not just his style, but also his dedication to true spontaneity. As Martin Williams noted in his book *The Jazz Tradition*:

> The release of alternate takes from this session shows that Rollins was really improvising, offering a rather different solo on each performance of each piece. Most of the other performers had had experience with big bands. Rollins had not. . . . Big band work can teach lessons of discipline and terseness in short solos, and lessons of group precision and responsiveness. Rollins has learned some of these lessons but . . . he has surmounted not having learned others.[1]

Sonny has expressed some regret at having had no real experience in big bands. But, as Williams points out, he has the insight and sheer willpower to compensate for the lack of a musical experience that has been important in shaping many jazz musicians' conception and style.

During this period, the late 1940s, it was harder to be an apprentice jazz musician than it had been in earlier days. During the swing era of the 1930s and early 1940s, most jazz musicians had the opportunity to play in a big band and learn what it meant to be a jazz musician. This lesson went far beyond musicianship. Being a jazz musician entails a certain view of the world—an attitude and a particular strain of sophistication. The sensitivity to nuance and to the sensibilities of others borders on ESP. None of these key skills can be taught in the usual sense of the word. One simply has to "pay one's dues," by living the jazz life and being around jazz musicians, both as players and as human beings. In many ways, playing in big bands was similar to the experience of baseball players in the minor leagues; one could both hone one's skills and become imbued with the culture of one's chosen field.

The early boppers—Parker and Dizzy, Kenny Clarke and Charlie Christian—were the last generation of musicians to pay their dues mostly by touring in big bands. (Christian mainly played in Benny Goodman's sextet, which toured with the big band.) Although they would continue to offer this kind of experience to some young jazzmen, big bands later would be few and far between. Most jazzmen since the bop era have had to opt for playing in small groups led by established jazzmen, but those gigs were fewer than seats in the big bands had been in earlier times. So Sonny played whatever gigs he could get. He hung out with his idols, such as Hawkins and Parker, or just followed them around, absorbing the crucial lessons of the jazz life and becoming recognized as a colleague by a number of the more important modern jazz figures.

Sonny was growing as a musician at an amazing pace, developing every aspect of his playing. But this was not part of a curriculum or plan:

> Everything happened intuitively with me. After I started playing, I tried to learn as I went along. That's what I did then, and it is what I am still doing. There was no plan and no real method. I said, "Well, I'll do this and that." It just came in an intuitive manner. I was just getting knowledge as I went along.

> I know that some people will misunderstand this and try to make it seem that I am some kind of noble savage. There was a time when I worried about things like that, because I felt that I had to satisfy the majority culture, or reach their standards. Since that time I have appeared with so-called classical musicians, conservatory-trained musicians, and been around them. I have discovered that they are quite deficient in many things. . . . I do not see why jazz should have to be judged by the standards of western classical music. This is another way of keeping jazz musicians in their place. I don't care what people say in that regard, if they want to compare jazz and western classical music.

Most young jazzmen who had gained such recognition from established musicians would be thoroughly committed to a career in jazz by this point. But for Sonny, there were still doubts:

> My first love was painting and drawing, not music. So even when I started playing professionally I was never sure that music was going to be it for me. I knew I was good at it, at least comparatively, but it was always a kind of tug of war. When certain musicians, like Monk,

gave me their endorsement, it convinced me that, Well, maybe I *can* really make it as a musician. So maybe that was on my mind to some degree when I went into hiatus in later years. But I did always come back to the music.

Whatever his doubts, this was a very good time for Sonny. He was young and already he was beginning to establish a career in jazz. Yet despite—or possibly because of—his growing recognition in the jazz world, Sonny was soon mired in a nightmare that would continue for several years: drug addiction.

Sonny Rollins has never denied the drug addiction that plagued not only him but also many of his closest friends and associates. But he is very unhappy with the obsession of so many writers, jazz fans, and moviemakers with this aspect of the history of jazz, the lives of some jazz musicians, and his own life and career: "When some writers interview me they spend half the time talking about my drug addiction. That only lasted for a few years and it was a long time ago. But these guys seem obsessed with that part of my life."

There is no doubt that Sonny's life was greatly affected by his years of addiction. He was forced to discover what kind of man he was and what kind of human being he wanted to become. And, although he deeply regrets his years of addiction, Sonny believes that to an extent drugs were part of the boppers' radical social stance:

Using drugs was, in a strange way, a negation of the money ethic. Guys were saying, "I don't care about this, I don't care how I dress or how I look, all care about is *music*." Using drugs was kind of a way for the boppers to express what they thought about American capitalist values.

Sonny first started using drugs within a year of graduating from high school. "We all got addicted back then," Sonny recalls. "Me, Jackie [McLean], Art Taylor, Kenny Drew. Everybody was getting high."

Initially, Sonny believed that drugs had changed his life for the better.

When I was in New York and using drugs and playing my horn and beginning to get recognized as a young, up-and-coming player, I was really in a happy situation. I mean, before I got to the point where I had to steal and stuff to support my habit. I recall telling somebody that I would never stop using drugs because it felt good and it put me in the place I wanted to be, mentally and physically. I remember really being an advocate of drugs at one time.

At the time, heroin addiction was rampant; as Sonny's boyhood friend Jackie McLean remembers it:

In the forties it was just there. It was really being pushed on the scene. A lot of musicians used it and a lot of teenagers. . . . It was especially hard for musicians to exist in those days, so a lot of musicians sold themselves down the river under the influence of narcotics because they had to have that bit of money to get along.

Sonny believes that the reason he and his friends began using drugs had much more to do with their vocation than with what was happening on the street.

Dope was flooding everyplace at the time, but it was especially ubiquitous in the show-business life. I don't think that Jackie and Art Taylor and the other guys would have gotten into it if we had not been getting involved in show business. We were not the gang-bangers. We came from fairly middle-class people, with middle-class aspirations and all of that. So I don't think we would have got involved in that sort of thing if we had not been pursuing careers in show business. We started off with pot and then got involved with the heavier drugs. We greatly admired Charlie Parker and Billie Holiday, and maybe to some extent that affected us, too. So that is what got us into it, more than what was happening on the streets of our community.

In 1949 Sonny went to Chicago for the first time and stayed there for a while. A few years later Chicago would figure prominently in key changes in Sonny's life.

I wanted a chance to travel around and play, to go to different places and meet different musicians. I had gotten familiar with some of the musicians from Chicago—especially, guys in Louis Metcalf's band and Babs Gonsales used to play up there sometimes. There was a bass player named Al King who was playing with Louis Metcalf's band. Al had a white Canadian wife and he had just gotten this new car. I think it was a 1949 Mercury. So he said, "Hey, man, do you want to go to Chicago?" So both of us went along with his wife, which was a dangerous thing to do; two black guys and a white woman traveling across country. I do not recall any serious incidents along the way, just dirty looks and that sort of thing.

When Sonny got to Chicago he was already getting high, but he was not seriously addicted. "When I went to Chicago that first time I was involved with heroin, but I was not trying to escape anything. I didn't have a bad reputation or anything at that point." But it was as easy to score drugs in Chicago as in New York, and Sonny's habit got worse. By the time he returned to New York, his addiction had grown increasingly expensive. He soon found himself doing things he could never have previously imagined. Hanging out with the wrong crowd eventually caused disaster.

Around 1950, I got busted for armed robbery. I don't remember much about it, because I have blocked it out of my mind. But as I recall, there were two or three of us. We decided to go downtown and stick up some place. I don't think we had any specific place in mind. I think it was just an idea. It was such a *stupid* thing to do. But it wasn't like I was one of the guys sitting down and planning it. I was sort of the *dumb* guy who was just going along. I was the big dope who took the gun. I didn't really know anything about guns. I have never fired a gun in my life. So, being a big idiot, I took the gun and we went down and of course we got nabbed. Fortunately I did not shoot or kill anybody. There was really a wonderful intervention in my life by the Great Spirit. I easily could have done something even more stupid than holding the place up in the first place.

Anyway I got a one- to three-year sentence and I wound up spending ten months on Rikers Island before I was paroled.

After he got out, in early 1951, Sonny drifted back into drugs and his habit became even worse. Now began the ugliest period in his life.

   During this period I became a truly despicable person. I had no friends. I was really a rough cut. I stole all kinds of stuff from my own home. I stole other people's horns. If musicians saw me coming they'd go the other way.

   I went through some pretty bad times, you know. I was carrying the stick, as we used to say. "Carrying the stick" meant living like a hobo. Having no place to live. This expression comes from the old days when you would see these cartoons of a hobo and he would have a stick and his belongings would be tied up in a rag at the end of a stick. I was living that sort of an existence. This was especially true when I would go to Chicago or someplace. At least, in New York, my mother would never turn me away. When I was away from New York I really went through some very bad times. I was a really bad cat. I was doing a lot of stuff. I was pickpocketing and all this kind of thing. Hanging out with junkies and thieves, those kinds of people. When I stopped to realize what I was doing, it was terrible. I felt horrible about myself.

   I hung out with a guy who had a method for pickpocketing. There is kind of an art to pickpocketing. I would be the guy who distracted our mark. Then this guy would go to work. The person we stole from was usually some poor woman returning from a day job someplace. Maybe coming home to feed her kids. We'd be finding ways to distract her on the bus. And he would slip into her pocketbook. I've been through all these things. I wasn't proud of it. And I got away from that life as soon as I realized what I had become.

Sonny's short life in crime had a profound effect on him. It was a long time before he could really forgive himself. And if he has become a man of sterling integrity and even nobility, it is because he saw a side of life, and a side of himself, that contradicted everything he had learned about morality and ethics when he was growing up. Through iron determination, self-discipline, and hard work, he eventually became a man and an artist committed to deeply felt moral standards.

During the early 1950s, Miles Davis became increasingly important to Sonny's career. Sonny met Miles in the late 1940s, while jamming at a club in the Bronx. The short, striking, and charismatic trumpet player introduced himself to Sonny when the saxophonist walked off the stand. As Sonny recalls, "Miles just said, 'Look, man, I want you to join my band,' and just like that I was in his group." Sonny often played in Miles's group until his arrest.

After Sonny was released from prison, the scene had become much worse. Even Davis, who had remained clean during the time he was playing in Charlie Parker's group, was now addicted to dope.

> When I first met Miles in the 1940s, he was clean, but when I was released from jail the milieu had changed. Everybody was using drugs. Miles was using lots of drugs. We used to get high together all the time. We used to cop together.

Yet Sonny never stole from Miles, or any of the musicians he respected.

> I never ripped Miles off. I never ripped off Monk or Bud Powell. Ripping off is something I did, but only to guys who couldn't play, guys you might consider to be squares. I only ripped off people that were outside our life.

Miles was four years older than Sonny and, like him, had been a professional musician since he was a teenager. Born in Alton, Illinois, and raised in East St. Louis, Miles came to New York after being urged to do so by Charlie Parker and Dizzy Gillespie, who had visited St. Louis with Benny Carter's band. Although he supposedly had come east to study at the Juilliard School of Music, Miles spent most of his time hanging out on "Swing Street" (Fifty-second Street between Fifth and Sixth Avenues) with Charlie Parker and the other modernists. He first gained recognition as the trumpeter in Bird's mid-forties quintets, and quickly became part of the New York modern jazz scene, playing wherever he could at the various clubs on Swing Street and frequently jamming in clubs around the city. After Miles left Bird, he played with a number of important musicians of the period. In the late 1940s he led his first group, a nonet, which played one two-week gig at the Royal Roost and recorded a number of sides for Capitol Records. Eventually these sides were collected on an LP, *Birth of the Cool*. The title was more than hyperbole. Along with Lennie Tristano and, to an extent, Lester Young, the Davis nonet set off the "cool jazz" or "West Coast jazz" era.

Although Miles was a key founder of the cool movement, he soon moved in a different direction (a practice that was a constant with Miles throughout his career). Because of his drug addiction as well as the initial commercial failure of his nonet (the Capitol sides are now considered classic and essential recordings), Miles's career had fallen apart by the early fifties. In an interview around that time, he said: "I've worked so little I could probably tell you where I was working any night in the last three years."[2]

When Miles did get gigs, he hired Sonny, and when the trumpeter did his first recording for Prestige, he again used the young tenorman. As Sonny told the jazz writer Bob Blumenthal, "Miles was an idol of mine and we seemed to have a lot in common. Our styles blended. Encouragement from Miles, Monk, Bud Powell, and Art Blakey finally convinced me to not be so self-deprecating and try to make it."[3] Blumenthal wrote that "[in] Rollins's most impressive performances [for the Prestige recording session] he manages to string together ideas with a sense of continuity and authority that belie his 21 years."[4] (Actually, Sonny did not turn twenty-one until September 7, 1951, after the Prestige sessions.)

The contrast between Sonny's big sound and gruff, assertive phrasing and Miles's legato lyricism set a pattern for most of Davis's groups over the next several years, both with and without Sonny. When Miles formed his great 1950s quintet, John Coltrane played the same role, as an intensely driving tenorman who provided contrast to Miles's introverted lyricism. Many fans were initially disappointed that Coltrane, at the time a fairly obscure player, was in the Davis band instead of Sonny.

For the next few years, Sonny was Miles's choice as tenorman both for gigs and recording dates. Davis ignored the critics who complained about the "harshness" of Sonny's playing, just as later he ignored those who advised him to drop John Coltrane. It is not surprising that Miles realized Sonny's worth as a player well ahead of the rest of the world. This ability to discover and hire the best musicians, even long before they were genuine stars, is one of the things that made Miles so important in the jazz scene. As Sonny himself has said, "Miles is a star-maker." The same thing had happened to Miles. When Charlie Parker first hired him in 1945, he was very far from being a mature—or even competent—jazz trumpeter, and there were many who urged Charlie Parker to let the young musician go. But Bird was already aware of Miles's rough talent and basic musicality. In the late 1950s, after Miles had become a star jazzman, Billy Eckstine said to him: "You couldn't blow your nose, let alone your trumpet, when you first came to New York."

During Sonny's sessions with Miles, the trumpeter's laissez-faire attitude toward recording was already in place:

> I don't recall Miles ever telling me anything about what to play or what not to play. That doesn't mean it hasn't happened. Miles could come back from heaven and say, "Hey, man, didn't I tell you to do that or this?" Once Miles heard a person that he liked, I think that was it. If he liked something that a guy was playing, then he gave the guy the freedom to play because that is what he wanted to hear. He didn't want to tell you what to play. He wouldn't hire you if you were not playing something that he wanted to use.

Sonny showed up at the first session with Miles with a rope tied to his horn in place of the leather strap, which he had sold or pawned for drug money. This was during the height of Sonny's addiction and life was very rough for him. Nevertheless, his playing shows that he was already advancing steadily. His rhythmic conception had grown increasingly idiosyncratic and he was never at a loss for fresh melodic ideas.

Even on the ballad "Blue Room" (he plays only on the first take), Sonny's playing is amazingly mature. Playing ballads with authority is quite often tough going for novice jazz musicians; they are unable to rely on pure technique, and their lack of musical maturity is often obvious at ballad tempo. But Sonny is utterly convincing, amazingly so for a twenty-year-old saxophonist. It is clear that he was finding a way to meld his main influences: the big sound and harmonic sophistication of Hawkins; the long melodic lines of Lester Young; and the rhythmic innovations of

Charlie Parker. One can hear in almost every note Sonny's determination to evolve a personal style that, although obviously founded in bop, already exhibits an unmistakable musical personality.

At the end of the session, the pianist, John Lewis, had to leave because he had a job at a club. Miles asked Bob Weinstock, the owner and producer of Prestige, if Sonny could record a side on his own with Miles accompanying on piano. As Sonny recalls,

> I was anxious to do this because I was thinking of Dizzy Gillespie accompanying Charlie Parker on piano when he recorded "KoKo." This was following along the same lines. So I was thinking, "Boy, this is great!"

Weinstock agreed. Sonny recorded a themeless piece, "I Know," based on the chord changes of Charlie Parker's famous tune "Confirmation." "I Know" was later released on a 78, and it is key to Sonny's career for two reasons: it was the first record of any kind put out under his own name, and it impressed Weinstock enough to sign Sonny to his own recording contract.

Sonny—just twenty years old—was thrilled at being to be signed to a recording contract, but he was naive about business matters.

> These honchos [at Prestige] had an ear for guys that could sell records. Young, up-and-coming guys. I didn't know anything about the music business. I didn't know anything about royalties and copyrights for tunes—publishing.

The recording contract did not end Sonny's constant need for cash. Prestige was often referred to as the "junkie's label" because it paid musicians enough to score their dope, but not much more than that. For junkie musicians, whose main concern was ready cash, not future royalties, this policy encouraged them to record as often as possible. During this period, Miles would play a couple of tunes and then demand some immediate cash from Weinstock. If Prestige's owner wanted a few more sides, Miles would demand a little more money, and so on. It was mutual exploitation born out of desperation.

Sonny himself, in an interview he gave in the 1960s, described his frequent recording during this period as "promiscuous." Yet at the time he did not feel that way:

> I must have said the thing about "recording promiscuously" in hindsight, because at the time I was just there, doing things, and the opportunity was there to record. I was given the opportunity to record with Prestige, and I was also recording with Blue Note and then with Riverside. The opportunity was there and I saw no reason not to take it. I think it was later on that it seemed to me that I had been recording promiscuously, or, at least, very often. I know that some people might have thought that I was making up for the time I lost while I was incarcerated. Maybe I thought that, but I do not remember that. Basically, I was just taking advantage of all the opportunities I was given to record.
>
> There were no exclusivity rights involved, and there were economic reasons for recording during that time. We were glad when somebody offered us money to play. If [Blue Note's] Alfred Lion offered us a chance to make a record, we made some records! This was true for almost every musician I knew. Maybe Miles was different, at least after he went with Columbia. But in the 1950s, most musicians would record anytime they had an opportunity.

The tracks from Sonny's earliest recording sessions were tailored to the length of single 78s, about three minutes or so. The LP had gone on the market in 1949, but it was initially used only for classical recordings. Weinstock had recently started to record for long-playing 33¹/₃ rpm records; the Miles Davis date of October 1951 resulted in one of the first long-playing jazz albums.

Miles assembled a band for this date that, besides Sonny (who had just turned twenty-one), included the tenorman's high school pal Jackie McLean and the pianist Walter Bishop, as well as bassist Tommy Potter. Both Potter and Bishop had played and recorded with Charlie Parker. Also on the date was an up-and-coming drummer: Art Blakey. In some ways, this session was a progenitor of the hard bop movement of a few years later.

Miles Davis was a key figure not only in the advent of cool jazz but also in hard bop. But for years afterward, and even after his death, Miles was continually referred to in the popular press as a cool jazzman. However, the "cool" or "West Coast" jazz was for the most part associated with white jazzmen:

> When Jackie and I played with Miles, it was sort of an antidote to Miles's playing with Gerry Mulligan and Lee Konitz and that "West Coast" style. So when Miles used us in his band, it was sort of a sharp break with that direction and some people drew this analogy of "black jazz" and "white jazz."

Aside from the historical significance of the "Dig" session (named after one of Miles's tunes for the date), the music is fascinating and, even now, still fresh and vigorous. Now that jazzmen were finally able to stretch out on records, listeners could hear performances far more like those typical of live jazz. This session was Jackie McLean's recording debut and he sounds mature and accomplished; although the influence of Charlie Parker is obvious, one can hear the bluesy wail that would give his playing a deeply emotional resonance, a sound that is already recognizably his own.

Sonny is as convincing as a fresh individual voice here as he was on the first Miles session, but he seems to have technical problems, squeaking throughout the session and even playing out of tune. At times his playing seems unfocused, and it is easy to guess that he was being affected by "personal problems," a favorite euphemism in the jazz press of the day for drug addiction or alcoholism. However, other factors may have had more immediate effect on Sonny. For one thing, Charlie Parker was present, and Sonny was nervous playing in front of his idol; dissatisfied, he dropped out after one chorus.

Despite his problems, Sonny never seem to run out of ideas and it is clear that his phrasing is becoming increasingly speechlike, one of the cornerstones of his mature style.

Two months after the Miles Davis "Dig" session, Sonny recorded his first complete date under his own name. The backing group for his quartet comprised yet another high school pal, Kenny Drew, the bassist Percy

Heath, who was the bassist for the Modern Jazz Quartet, and, again, Art Blakey. The tunes were a mix of Rollins originals and standards, a pattern that has held for virtually every Rollins album since. The standards included some songs rarely, if ever, performed by jazzmen: "Time on My Hands," "Shadrack," and "A Slow Boat to China" (a tune that Charlie Parker occasionally liked to play). Unorthodox or unusual pop tunes have been a trademark of Rollins's performances, both on record and in person.

One of the originals on the date is "Mambo Bounce," whose presence is the first indication of Sonny's interest in Latin-influenced music. The mambo was a dance fad at the time and, as with the bossa nova a decade later, musicians were urged to record mambos. According to Ira Gitler, who supervised this session, a conga player was supposed to play on this tune, but he was unable to make it to the session. Although the group plays the theme as a mambo, the rhythm section switches to straight-ahead 4/4 swinging when Rollins takes his solo. A similar tactic is used in a much more celebrated performance from a few years later, the original "St. Thomas."

Sonny's playing on this date is far more confident than in the Miles Davis "Dig" session. So many components of his mature style seem to be falling into place: his big sound, his use of tonal coloration, the unceasing flow of melodic ideas, the lack of cliché and easy lick, and the idiosyncratic rhythmic conception. Perhaps at this point he did not feel self-assured enough to take the harmonic risks of his later playing. But—and this is most important—he is obviously his own man now, with an individual sound and style. He is not just the young bebopper of his earliest recording dates. He is clearly a young musician with an exciting future ahead of him.

Despite his increasing success as a musician, Sonny was in deep trouble personally. Unable to kick dope, he knew it was just a matter of time before he was arrested and once again sent back to Rikers Island—this time, perhaps, for much longer. And by this point, Sonny no longer glamorized drugs. His addiction had become a nightmare that seemed to have no end. Sonny's intense self-awareness made it completely clear to him how dope was ruining his life; drugs were also ruining the lives of many of his friends and associates. Perhaps Sonny's insight derived partly from devoting himself to improvisation, which forces the musician to look deeply into his own soul for inspiration. For whatever reason, Sonny knew that he had to change this part of his life. And he had to change soon, before it was too late.

4

"Oleo"

Nineteen fifty-two was a dark year for Sonny Rollins. Early in the year, he was arrested for violating his parole; he had been caught using dope. He spent the rest of 1952 on Rikers Island; it was obvious that drugs had become the primary focus of his life. He was not released until January 1953. The imprisonment was a terrible blow to Sonny's career, which had seemed to be moving ahead with great momentum in 1950–51. Few leaders or club owners wanted to hire a junkie jailbird who seemed to be unable to stay away from trouble, which is what Sonny had become.

Sonny had convinced himself that he had to be high just to play on the level he was trying to attain. He could not imagine his life, or his music, without dope. In addition, he and the other young musicians were very skeptical about the hypocrisy of American moral standards. After all, people were being put in jail for the crime of getting high while at the same time bigotry and corruption pervaded American culture. Black people and other minorities rightly assumed that American justice was really white justice and that they could never get a fair shake in a society so imbued with racism. Though not an excuse for addiction, this was a factor that led to the tightness of the jazz subculture and that affected its mores and values.

Sonny's career had become a tragic paradox: he had made great strides very quickly, at a very young age. But his personal life had gone off-track to the extent that many thought his career was permanently sidetracked.

In the early 1950s, drugs had already destroyed many promising jazz careers. The great jazz trumpeter Fats Navarro (whom was described by Miles Davis as the greatest of all modern jazz trumpeters) had died from drug-related causes in July 1950. Most of Sonny's high school musician friends were badly addicted and two of the most talented, Lowell Louis and Andy Kirk, Jr., had to give up their musical careers altogether because of their drug addiction. Many junkie musicians were losing the cabaret cards that permitted them to play in New York clubs. Those clubs were at the heart of the jazz world; not being allowed to play in them was disastrous. Charlie Parker himself was becoming increasingly erratic; by 1952–53 he was obviously beginning to pay a price for his excesses. (He would die at the age of thirty-four in 1955; the doctor who certified his death was certain that Bird was at least in his fifties.)

Quite simply, drugs were ravaging the jazz world. *Down Beat* ran articles claiming that only a handful of jazzmen had drug problems, but those close to the scene knew that the situation was far worse than many would admit.

When Sonny was released from Rikers Island in January 1953, he had decided that he wanted to end his addiction, but he very quickly fell back into his old ways. What turned him around and gave him the impetus to get off drugs for once and for all was, ironically enough, an encounter with Charlie Parker.

A few weeks after his release, Sonny played in his first recording session since the "Mambo Bounce" session of December 1951. It was another Miles Davis date; Miles used Sonny's old friends the pianist Walter Bishop, Jr., and Percy Heath, the Modern Jazz Quartet bassist. Also playing was an up-and-coming drummer, Philly Joe Jones (he called himself Philly to distinguish himself from Count Basie's great drummer, Jo Jones). This was the first time Miles recorded with Jones, who two years later became part of Miles's first classic quintet with John Coltrane. Sonny was not the only saxophonist on the date: Charlie Parker played tenor (instead of his usual alto) in tandem with him.

It was an infamously chaotic session. Parker arrived at the studio with a large bottle of gin and proceeded to drink all of it himself. The friction between Miles and Bird was acute; their relationship had been complicated since Miles first met Parker in St. Louis. As I described the session in my book about Miles Davis, *'Round About Midnight*:

> Ira Gitler, who was supervising the session for Bob Weinstock, quickly saw that he had his hands full. Bird . . . fell asleep in the middle of the studio, much to Miles's displeasure. "I never did that to you when I was on your recording dates," he complained after waking [Bird]. Parker simply smiled. Miles's irritation showed in his playing and Gitler came out of the control booth and told him "You're not playing shit." Miles immediately began packing his trumpet back into his case. "What's he doing?" asked Bird. "This motherfucker is telling me I ain't playing shit," Miles replied.
>
> "Come on, Miles. Let's play some music," Bird insisted.
>
> After this [contretemps] the session proceeded smoothly. . . . At the end of the session, Bird fell asleep again. "Wake up, motherfucker," Miles steamed. "Yes, Lily Pons," said Bird, using a favorite sobriquet. As Miles stalked out of the studio, Parker called after him, reciting aphorisms in his fake British accent, "To produce beauty, we must suffer pain. From the oyster comes the pearl, Miles."[1]

This turned out to be the last time Miles and Parker recorded together, so simply for that reason it was a dramatic reunion. For Sonny, it would be a turning point:

> At the time of this session, I was on parole but I knew that I was probably headed right back to Rikers Island because I was still getting high. Charlie Parker asked me something like "Well, are you okay now?" or something of that nature—"Have you straightened yourself out?"—because he was always a very avuncular figure to me. That's when I told him, "Oh, yeah, I'm straight now." But there was somebody on the date with whom I had just been getting high before the date, and he spilled the beans to Bird.
>
> The guy may not have told Charlie Parker this in order to hurt me, so there is no blame to go around. I never told anybody, "Well, look, man, don't say anything." So it wasn't malicious. But after Bird

found that out he became very cold to me. Not just cold to me, I could see in his face that once again he had been confronted with the fact that all of his young protégés were messed up on drugs. So once again this was in front of him. I could see that in him at that session and I got the realization of how he must really feel about it. I realized then that I really wanted to get off drugs. I thought, "Okay, this is the impetus to get off drugs and I'm going to come back one day and show Bird that I actually did get off drugs. And this time it will be true." I saw the pain in his face that day. And then it all made sense to me.

Many people have described Charlie Parker as a man without a conscience, who did not care about the terrible example he set for young jazz musicians. James Lincoln Collier called him a sociopath. Sonny, however, disputes this.

> I guess my views [of Bird] would not have much currency. Because the man that I knew was not the picture that they usually use to portray him. But every time people ask me how I got off drugs, I always tell them that story—that Bird got so upset by seeing me lying to him and knowing that I was another protégé of his messing up again. I actually saw it on his face. He wasn't so mad at me as he was upset about this whole thing he was engaged in.

Neither Parker, Miles, nor Sonny was in top form for this date, but the music they recorded is particularly revealing about Sonny's musical direction at this time. Because Charlie Parker was playing tenor for one reason or another (apparently Miles wanted a "deeper" sound), it is easier to hear both the similarities and the differences between his style and Sonny's.

It is obvious from close listening to the music from this session that Parker is an important influence on the twenty-two-year-old Sonny Rollins. It is also clear that Sonny is is in the middle of developing a style and conception that are all his own. The flow of his ideas and, in particular, his rhythmic conception are obviously rooted in bebop, but these aspects of his playing are evolving in a rather different direction from that of classic bop. For one thing, Sonny's big, sinewy sound is quite dissimilar from the thinner, airier tones of many (although certainly not all) of the boppers. Clearly, the powerful influence of Coleman Hawkins and the "Hawkins school" was as least as important to Sonny as that of Charlie Parker.

It is undeniable that Sonny had by now gained enormous maturity as a musician. Perhaps most important is his creation of a personal and totally idiosyncratic sound. Sound is at the heart of the musical conception of great jazz musicians. Miles Davis once said to me: "Sound is the heart of my music. Ideas are a dime a dozen, but creating a sound all your own is most important." And in a brief discussion I had with Alice Coltrane after a concert, she said that her late husband had said basically the same thing. Coltrane's sound was so powerful that even when he played a ballad with little or no improvisation the searing emotionality created simply through his sound moved listeners deeply. Sonny agrees with his former friends and colleagues.

> I think that sound is the overall biggest component. It's more important than ideas, really. My experience has been that a production of a certain sound supersedes what you are actually playing. Over the years I have found that sometimes ideas can help generate a sound. That can happen if you have a definitive style, that your ideas are usually part of the sound itself. But sound itself supersedes ideas in general.

Sonny's faith in the primacy of sound would be borne out throughout his career. For example, his famous forays onto the Williamsburg Bridge challenged him to find and create a sound despite the wind, the traffic noise, and the sounds of the river itself. Later on in his career, he would walk around the club or stage and even wander out to the street while playing because he was fascinated at how different his sound was in various locations.

The idea that production of a sound is the most profound aspect of musical expression has roots deep in some fundamental concepts of human spirituality. According to an Eastern tradition, everything that exists comes from the utterance of the word "Om." In the Bible, the physical universe is born after the utterance of "the Word." The Sufi writer Hazrat Inayat Khan has expressed the spirituality of pure sound perfectly:

> Why is music considered the divine art while all the other arts are not so called? We may certainly see God in all arts and all sci-

ences, but in music alone we see God free from all forms and thoughts. In every other art there is idolatry. Every thought, every word has a form. Sound alone is free from form. Every word of poetry forms a picture in our mind. Sound alone does not make any object appear before us. . . . Sound is the perceptible activity of all pervading art. Different sounds differ in their outer expression, but within it are one and the same activity which directs all sounds.[2]

The creation of a personal sound—and all the elements that go into the production of that sound—defines the individuality of musician, particularly a jazz musician, more than any other element. The difference between a jazz musician and one trained in the European musical aesthetic is that jazz has no single tradition for playing an instrument. The ability to create a personal sound is more important—far more important—than sheer virtuosity, or playing with technique that is acceptable according to tradition. Thelonious Monk, Miles Davis, Chet Baker, Pee Wee Russell, Ornette Coleman, and many other jazzmen may not possess what is considered in the European tradition to be authoritative "formal" technique. Their greatness lies in their ability to project the core of their being into their music and in their development of an idiosyncratic technique to do that. In other words, each musician in jazz is his own academy—or at least, every major player is. The rhythmic, melodic, and harmonic features of music are secondary to the sound itself, that wail from the jazzman's heart, that stylized noise which reflects his innermost soul.

Nineteen fifty-three was another bleak year for Sonny. Despite his decision to go straight after the encounter with Charlie Parker, he was still using drugs, and although he got gigs here and there with Miles and, even more rarely, with Thelonious Monk, many musicians were reluctant to hire someone as strung out and out of control as Sonny. This lack of trust was beginning to affect his ability to work. So despite the recognition Sonny was receiving from so many great jazzmen, his life continued to be a mess.

In October 1953, Sonny recorded the second session to be released under his name (the third, if you count the single title "I Know" from the

Miles Davis session of January 1951). It was a collaboration with the group that had defined "chamber jazz" for the modern idiom, the Modern Jazz Quartet. Although all five of the musicians on this session were superb players, the mix with the freewheeling Sonny Rollins never quite jelled, either on this session or on those Sonny would play with the MJQ in the future.

The MJQ was born out of Dizzy Gillespie's big band of the 1940s. Dizzy would let the four members of his rhythm section (although originally Ray Brown was the bassist) play a short set in order to spell the rest of the band. John Lewis, Gillespie's pianist, was a sophisticated and well-schooled musician, interested in developing arrangements for a small group far more intricate and fully fleshed out than those of most small jazz groups, whose arrangements often amounted to little more than the main theme and a series of solos. Lewis, the MJQ's chief arranger and composer, was also a wonderful jazz pianist, especially in the blues; he has been vastly underrated. His playing has a singing, seemingly simple melodicism that reveals a gift for subtle wit and a particularly lucid sense of form. But the MJQ's star soloist was the vibraphonist, Milt Jackson, who was one of the most melodically inventive and hard-swinging soloists in modern jazz. The rhythm section consisted of the bassist Percy Heath and Kenny Clarke, one of the most important architects of modern jazz, particularly for drums. Clarke had taken some of the techniques of Jo Jones, the great Count Basie drummer, and adapted that style to the special demands of modern jazz. Without Clarke's innovations, Parker and Gillespie would not have had the freedom to greatly extend the rhythmic boundaries of jazz. However, Clarke left the MJQ after a few years because, according to him, John Lewis was more interested in classical music than in jazz.

Lewis was fascinated by the European classical tradition, and in particular by Bach. But Lewis was also committed to genuine improvisation and the blues, thus mitigating his classical tendencies with elements central to the jazz tradition. Not only were the members of the MJQ excellent improvisors in their own right, they also had the ability to genuinely improvise as a group. Lewis's interest in giving form to small-group jazz and Jackson's commitment to the blues and straight-ahead improvisation created a fascinating tension organic to the MJQ's makeup.

On the surface, there would seem to be a problem in Sonny's playing with the MJQ. While Lewis and Jackson had found a way to integrate the vibist's commitment to bluesy, swinging improvisation with Lewis's formal tendencies, the group's dynamics were tight and enclosed. There was no real place for a hard-driving saxophonist like Rollins, who has always thrived in those musical situations where he has the most freedom. That he did not fit in was true both of the 1953 date and on future occasions when Sonny played with the MJQ. Or at least, so it might seem; Sonny does not remember many problems:

> I felt comfortable playing with them, because I had played indi-vidually with them before. So I was not particularly threatened by the tightness of the group. Of course, this was early on in their career and maybe they were not as tightly knit as they were later on.

Sonny plays well enough on this session, but there is something unfo-cused about his soloing, as if he were wishing he were somewhere else, or at least playing in a different format. Still, the music is interesting in that Sonny sounds as if he has been working toward a more legato, more lyri-cal style. Perhaps this was the time when Lester Young had more influence on Sonny's style than did Coleman Hawkins. Or it may have reflected his way of adjusting to the demands of playing with the Modern Jazz Quartet.

His next recording session would be led by a musician at least as sin-gular and original as he: his guru, Thelonious Monk.

During the late 1940s and early 1950s, Thelonious Monk was an underground musician, ignored by many jazz fans and derided by others. However, this opinion of Monk was not shared by the Young Turks of this period. They recognized his genius both as a composer and as a pianist. Playing with him was a tricky proposition; Coltrane said that when he played with Monk he often felt as if he had walked into an empty elevator shaft. For Sonny, the association with Monk was perhaps even more important than that with Miles Davis, at least for his growth as a soloist.

Part of the problem with Monk in these early years was that he never fit into any of the convenient slots that jazz writers and fans create. Although he was undoubtedly one of the architects of bebop, his own style can hardly be considered bop, at least not the classic bebop played by such central fig-ures as Charlie Parker, Dizzy Gillespie, and Bud Powell. Monk did not rely on the kind of multinoted virtuosity we associate with the great beboppers. He stubbornly tended his own musical garden, creating music that seemed to embrace the entire jazz tradition while at the same time sounding like nothing anyone had ever heard before. Monk's stubbornness in sticking to his singular vision caused those who only heard the outer shell of his music to call both him and his music weird, bizarre, and eccentric. If these people had listened at a deeper level, they would have discovered that Monk's music was profound, beautiful, wonderfully humorous, and always imbued with Monk's off-kilter but perfectly worked-out logic. If Monk was stubborn, it was a stubbornness born out of his commitment to be exactly who he was. Monk was more than a great musician; he was also a visionary, and that is why great young musicians, like Sonny Rollins and Jackie McLean, were drawn to him.

Thelonious Sphere Monk was born on October 10, 1917, in Rocky Mount, North Carolina. Four years later his family moved to New York City, where he remained for the rest of his life, venturing out of the city only when he had to tour with his band. Early on, he played piano for church gospel groups. He took on jobs as a sideman with various musicians and then became the house pianist at Minton's, a Harlem nightclub that catered mainly to musicians who loved to jam. It was at Minton's that Monk and some of the other advanced jazzmen, such as Dizzy Gillespie, the key bop drummer Kenny Clarke, and, early on, the guitarist Charlie Christian, worked on advanced harmonic sequences. They would use these sequences to discourage musicians who were not their equals from getting on the Minton's bandstand and sitting in. To Monk, what was happening at Minton's was organic. There was no organized commitment to musical revolution:

> I was just playing a gig, just trying to play music. . . . I had no idea that anything new was being built. It's true that modern jazz probably began to get popular there, but some of these histories and articles put what happened over the course of ten years into one year. They put people all together in one time and place. I've seen practically everyone at Minton's, but they were just playing. They weren't giving any lectures.[3]

But although Monk was not consciously trying to foment a musical revolution, he did hear a certain kind of music in his head, and in order to create that music he had to expand the harmonic and rhythmic vocabulary of jazz. By serendipity, other like-minded musicians were going through the same process; to find their own way, they realized that they had to boldly take jazz in directions it had never gone before.

Monk was developing a technique for playing jazz piano that owed virtually nothing to the European model of pianistic technique. He was, in effect, reinventing the piano, discarding assumptions about the "correct" or "proper" technique in order to create his own highly personal sound and expression. Monk often seemed to be improvising his own rules as well as the music itself when he played. That is why those who could only conceive of the European tradition for playing piano insisted that he had no technique. Monk's extreme individuality also got him branded as somebody too strange to be taken seriously. But Sonny never felt this way: "There was nothing strange or weird about Monk. He was like anybody else. He was just a guy and a great musician. An average Joe."

Monk survived years of obscurity in the 1940s, more famous in the jazz world for his unusual name than his music. For a while, he was a prolific composer, writing tunes that sounded like nothing else in jazz literature. In later years, he only rarely composed new pieces. It is as if he had constructed a complete, insular world with his body of work and felt no need to add anything extraneous to its perfection. Some of his pieces, such as the blues "Misterio," have the pretzel logic of a Zen koan. Others, like "Brilliant Corners," challenge even the best jazz musicians (including, as we shall see, Sonny).

In addition to being one of the great jazz composers, Monk was also a magnificent improviser. His technique was, to say the least, individualistic. He ignored the dictum given to all novice pianists to use the tips of the fingers. Instead, he deliberately played with the flats of his fingers, producing a chunky, percussive, but immediately recognizable sound. Monk would at times, pound on the piano with his elbow and slam out totally dissonant chords with the flat of his hand. Monk always respected the melody, deconstructing a tune as if he were taking it apart to discover how it worked. This aspect of Monk's playing had a strong effect on Sonny's. Monk also used space, sometimes creating great suspense by refraining from playing at unexpected points throughout the solo.

As iconoclastic as Monk's music was, it had roots deep in the jazz tradition. Listen closely and you can hear echoes of Jelly Roll Morton, Fats Waller, Earl "Fatha" Hines, and, most importantly, Duke Ellington (both as a composer and pianist). Nobody understood more profoundly than Monk the necessity for a musician to find his own idiosyncratic voice. Anyone with even a passing knowledge of his music can identify a Monk tune or piano improvisation after hearing just a few bars. The ability to do this—to create music that reflects one's own mind, heart, and soul—was of immense importance to young musicians.

Monk was known as the High Priest of Bebop for a number of reasons; the fact that he was one of the founders of modern jazz was just one of them. He was also a kind of guru to young musicians who were learning the often arcane language and technique of bop. Charlie Parker brought the youthful Miles Davis to Monk; Miles learned from him the importance of using space in improvisation, which became one of the hallmarks of his style.

Monk also demanded that those playing his music use the melody itself when they soloed, not just the chord changes. This lesson was profoundly important to the growth of Sonny Rollins's mature style. Monk did not lecture Sonny—or anyone else, for that matter—about these principles. Like many master jazzmen, he taught by example and through a subtle language of musical gesture and facial expression, with a word or two that carried several layers of significance. At times, this communication bordered on the psychic.

Perhaps the single most important thing Sonny got from Monk was the pianist-composer's encouragement that he could make it as a jazz musician. As deeply introspective as Sonny was (and still is), he did not feel he had the objectivity to decide if he had anything important to offer the world as a musician.

But of course, Monk did more than encourage Rollins; Sonny learned a number of lessons from him. Although they only recorded together a few times, what they did produce offers some fascinating insights into their musical relationship. The two had been playing together since the 1940s, mostly in private sessions; Sonny recorded with Monk for the first time in November 1953. The three tunes recorded at this session were all Monk's: "Think of One," "Let's Call This," and "Friday the Thirteenth." The session was held on Friday, November 13; as befitted the date, there were several minor disasters. The cab in which Sonny and Monk were riding to the session had a collision, so they were late. Also, the front line was originally supposed to be Sonny and the trumpeter Ray Copeland, a favorite of Monk's. But Copeland had come down with the flu. As a last-minute replacement Monk hired Julius Watkins, who played an instrument not usually associated with jazz (particularly as a solo instrument): the French horn. Copeland was already familiar with the tricky tunes Monk was using for the session, but Watkins had to figure them out on the spot and adapt them to his horn.

The result should have been a mess, but it has weathered the years very well. The front line of Julius Watkins's French horn and Sonny's tenor saxophone produced a pleasing sonic texture, similar to that of tenor and trombone (a pairing that Sonny would often turn to, especially in the groups he has led during the 1990s). But it is somewhat more full-bodied and sonically pleasing. However, the French horn is not an easy instrument to improvise with, especially on tunes as harmonically gnarled and melodically paradoxical as Monk's. Although he struggles valiantly, Watkins is clearly hampered by the limitations of his instrument. Many jazz musicians playing far less cumbersome instruments have had their problems both playing Monk's tunes and being accompanied by Monk.

Monk's comping has often caused even brilliant players difficulties. Perhaps the most famous example is Miles Davis. When he recorded for Prestige with Monk, Milt Jackson, and what was at the time the Prestige house rhythm section, Percy Heath and Kenny Clarke, Miles admonished Monk not to accompany him when he soloed because his comping was confusing. You can actually hear the musicians arguing on the record that they produced; at one point Monk went to the bathroom while Miles soloed. They finally compromised by agreeing to let Monk comp behind Miles only on his own tune, "Bemsha Swing"; he did not comp for Miles on the rest of the session, but he did comp behind Milt Jackson, who enjoyed it. Perhaps the problem for Miles was that the trumpeter's own strong musical conception simply did not jibe with Monk's. When Monk comps, he does much more than give the soloist harmonic guidance. He shapes the improvisations in such a way as to give the entire piece a direction that reflects his musical sensibility. That is why it takes greatly skilled musicians to play Monk's music the way he insists it should be played, and especially to comply with his constant admonitions to the soloist to "use the melody" and not just play on the chord changes of a tune.

While always sounding completely like himself and nobody else, Sonny seems to thrive when playing with Monk. For a twenty-three-year-old to have such a profound understanding of Monk's musical conception is truly extraordinary. The tunes on the session, Bob Blumenthal writes, "were as difficult as any compositions by Monk, and yet Rollins manages the material with an ease and sense of propriety that belie his relative inexperience. . . . Such is the case with 'Friday the Thirteenth,' a ten-minute rendition of a repetitious bi-tonal chord pattern—as provocative an exercise as anything in Monk's repertoire."

Especially in that tune, the music Monk and Rollins were creating here was already several steps forward from orthodox bebop. Here, way back in 1953, they were beginning to explore musical paths that lead in the direction of the next jazz revolution several years later. "Friday the 13th" flirts with polytonality and dissonance. The tune sounds like something Ornette Coleman could have written several years later. And Monk's comping, and the way that Sonny responds to it, make it clear that both men were looking ahead.

Nineteen fifty-four was an important year. In January, Sonny played on a date led by the great trumpeter Art Farmer, one of the most lyrical players in jazz. In addition to his melodic talent, Farmer is a master of improvisational form. The session is fascinating because it presents two young jazzmen on the verge of great careers; their styles are still forming, yet one can hear key elements already in place.

More important, at least from Sonny's point of view, was yet another recording session with Miles Davis, in June. Sonny's reputation as an important jazz composer began to develop with this session. According to Sonny, composing was not a new wrinkle in his career:

> I started composing when I was pretty much a youngster. Long before I got into really professional playing, I started composing. But I would say I probably began composing when I first started playing, which would be around nine years old, I guess. Around that time, songs would come to me, or melodies would come to me, or sketches of melodies, and I would try to compose.
>
> I like to compose. As record producer Orrin Keepnews once

told me, "You know, some horn players are really the best composers, because the stuff they compose are things that are really suited to them, 'cause they're improvising also." So a lot of guys that play also compose; it's composition, but it's also geared to their playing, and that's the vehicle for them to extemporize. And I guess that makes sense with me, too. I mean, a lot of these songs I was playing, I composed, though I didn't compose them to play specifically. In fact, there's a song I composed for which I found it very hard to play the melody. I had a lot of trouble playing the melody. So I didn't really think about soloing, by composing. But you know, the two are so close together; they're very, very close, composing and playing.

All three of the tunes that Sonny brought to this Miles Davis session date became jazz standards: "Dozy," "Airegin," and, especially, "Oleo." None of the tunes were written expressly for the session, according to Sonny. "At the date, Miles asked me if I had any tunes that we could use. So I showed him what I had and we wound up doing them. That is the way things were back then." In this era of overproduced albums, it seems immensely ironic that such casual spontaneity so often led to the production of classic records that still sound wonderful today.

"Dozy" is an appealing, funky little tune that sounds like something Horace Silver might have composed. "Oleo" is based on the chord changes of "I've Got Rhythm"; what makes it a fascinating vehicle for improvisation is the arrangement. "Airegin" is interesting for a number of reasons, starting with its title, "Nigeria" spelled backwards. Was Sonny consciously injecting his sociocultural concerns?

Absolutely! Most of the young black guys playing modern jazz were aware of these issues and we wanted our music, at least to an extent, to make a statement. And don't forget that my grandmother was follower of Marcus Garvey. I heard these things expressed while I was very young. I meant "Airegin" to be provocative.

Marcus Garvey preached black pride and argued that African Americans should return to Africa, the Motherland, leaving the country where they were enslaved and then treated as second-class citizens. In 1954, to proclaim black pride even in the subtle way that Sonny was doing was a brave and radical act for a young man trying to make it in a racist society.

As a melody, "Airegin" is not particularly African in any obvious way, but it is an extremely unusual tune for this period. It gives further evidence that Sonny, like his colleague and occasional employer Miles Davis, was working to push modern jazz further away from orthodox bebop. As Bob Blumenthal writes:

> Like Thelonious['s work, Sonny's] compositions make use of both space and accent, qualities that would not escape notice from Miles. "Airegin" actually embodies progressive characteristics of time and space that would become identified with the trumpeter for the rest of the 1950s and with his imitators ever since.[4]

Sonny's playing on this date gives convincing evidence that, despite the chaos of his life, he was advancing as a musician. Particularly noticeable is his increasingly personal rhythmic conception.

In jazz, the ability to develop a personal rhythmic conception is as important as any other aspect of an idiosyncratic style, such as tone or melodic invention. The primacy of rhythm—the use of rhythm as a kind of language—is, of course, part of the African legacy that is so central to the jazz tradition. The dominance of rhythm in jazz is often misunderstood by those grounded only in the European, "classical" tradition; the driving force of rhythm and the prominence of drums in jazz are considered "vulgar" by those who do not make a serious attempt to understand the music on its own terms. In jazz, rhythm itself is a powerful form of expression.

Rhythm is probably the most visceral element of music. We feel rhythm as much as we hear it; our reaction to strong rhythm is primal. As the Sufi writer Hazrat Inayat Khan puts it:

> There exists in all people, either consciously or unconsciously, a tendency toward rhythm. . . . Rhythm in every guise, be it called game, play, amusement, poetry, music or dance, is the very nature of a man's whole constitution . . . the whole mechanism of the universe is based on rhythm.[5]

When classical music snobs criticize jazz for its emphasis on rhythm, they do so because they believe that the emphasis on rhythm is somehow crude and obvious. It is true that our reaction to strong rhythm is, at least to an extent, elemental. But a great artist, like Louis Armstrong, Charlie Parker, or Sonny Rollins (or a great drummer, like Max Roach or Elvin Jones), can twist rhythm at will, suspend it, turn it around, and lift us out of our seats with its power.

Sonny's rhythmic conception is tied to his speechlike phrasing; that is, he accents notes in a way that resembles the patterns of speech. Perhaps the best way to define Sonny's rhythm and make it comprehensible is to compare it to that of the great nineteenth-century British clergyman and poet Gerard Manley Hopkins. Hopkins used "sprung rhythm" in much of his best poetry.

In sprung rhythm, according to the *Merriam-Webster Encyclopedia of Literature*, "the line is measured by the number of speech-like syllables, the number of unstressed syllables being indeterminate." In other words, although sprung rhythm is a much freer and more natural rhythm than, say, iambic pentameter, it is not a completely free rhythm, such as that of Ezra Pound and many other modern poets. Hopkins used marks to accent usually unstressed syllables in order to break the rhythm into patterns that were close to colloquial speech. He did not consider himself to be the "inventor" of this system. He maintained that it was based on common English speech.

The comparison to Sonny is obvious. Sonny's phrasing is also speechlike and he uses rhythmic patterns that are unusual (at least for jazz) and that naturally fit the phrasing. Sonny took the rhythmic conception of Charlie Parker and the other boppers a step further. This is one of the reasons why listening to him is often similar to hearing a great raconteur. Certainly his rhythmic conception was a huge influence on the free jazz men, who constantly used speechlike effects and who had an even freer rhythmic attack. There are great differences between poetry and music, but there are also important similarities. One of those similarities is the innate power of rhythm. It is through rhythm that the artist connects with the reader or audience, through the deepest recesses of their nervous systems.

In October 1954, Sonny would record again with Monk. But this time Sonny was the leader for the date. It is a marvelous session. Sonny and Monk are so tightly attuned to each other throughout each piece that one might have thought that they had been working together on this music for a long time. As Sonny recalls, Monk was not even the pianist he originally wanted on the date:

> Monk came in at the last minute for that session. I was going to use Elmo [Hope] and I think that Elmo got busted and couldn't make the session. Elmo and I had been working on some stuff and playing together, but when Elmo got busted at the last minute, . . . I got Monk. It was great that I could call Monk and get him to come down and do it, which he gladly did, and he did it as a sideman. Later they put it out on a record called *Thelonious Monk and Sonny Rollins* but it was really my date. The fact that he did it was great.
>
> Actually, I was initially a little nervous to approach Monk. It is something that I would not have initially done. Not for musical reasons but because of his position in the jazz world.

Besides Monk, the group included bassist Tommy Potter, and the formidable Art Blakey, who had the same kind of musical relationship with Monk that Sonny had with Max Roach. None of the tunes were originals. Rather, Sonny pulled some old chestnuts out of his prodigious musical memory— "I Want to Be Happy," "The Way You Look Tonight," and the ballad "More Than You Know." It is too bad that the group only recorded three tunes because, at least in my view, this is easily Sonny's best early recording. The two up tunes are both played at a bouncy tempo and are among the most purely joyous music Sonny has ever recorded. This kind of ecstatic celebration has always been at the heart of the jazz aesthetic; just think of Louis Armstrong playing "Sweethearts on Parade" or Dizzy on "Groovin' High," and the jazz tradition of unalloyed joyousness becomes obvious. Rather than an obstacle, Monk's accompaniment prods Sonny to play with an energy and purpose unheard on his previous recordings. In addition, Monk constantly acts like the force of gravity by keeping Sonny grounded in the melody which is in play throughout the tenorman's entire solo.

Sonny's improvisation on the ballad "More Than You Know" could have been composed by Chopin. Sonny seems so assured on this date, so confident in playing the entire range of his saxophone and continually developing new ideas it is hard to believe that he is only twenty-four years old.

Perhaps his self-assurance on this date was related to the presence of Monk. At times, the two seem to be conversing, much as Charles Mingus used to converse with Eric Dolphy; they would take a conversation they had been having backstage and continue it musically when they performed. Monk clearly prodded Sonny through his comping to play at the top of his game. It is unfortunate that these two giants, who were so finely attuned to each other, would only record a few more dates together.

Both this session and the Miles Davis "Oleo" session clearly showed that all the elements of Sonny's mature style were finally cohering. In addition, the three tunes that Sonny contributed to the Davis "Dig" session proved that he was coming into his own as a composer, too. His future might have looked bright if it were not for the continuing nightmare of his personal life. But, after the saddening incident with Charlie Parker, Sonny finally realized what drugs were doing to him. He was now determined to do something about it.

5

Work Time

Sonny was increasingly desperate to kick his drug habit. After his encounter with Charlie Parker at the Miles Davis recording section, he had decided that he no longer wanted to continue using heroin. But, as he points out, "Once you are addicted, it is not easy to quit it even if you want to. You just can't walk away from it." Quitting heroin was especially hard for a jazz musician, because, as has been mentioned, drug use was rife in the jazz scene.

Sonny was in a paradoxical position. He had recorded with some of the most important modern jazzmen—Miles Davis, Charlie Parker, Thelonious Monk, Art Blakey, Horace Silver, Bud Powell, and the Modern Jazz Quartet, to name but a few. But his reputation was in tatters. "I was a disreputable person back then. People knew to stay away from me." He had become a pariah in the jazz world while simultaneously establishing himself as one of the most important musicians of his generation. It was an intolerable situation.

At the end of 1954, Sonny decided that he finally had to do something about his drug addiction, especially with the threat of further prison time hanging over his head:

> I knew it was just a matter of time that I would be picked up for
> parole violation since I was still using drugs. I would have to spend

the rest of my sentence, two more years, in jail on Rikers Island. That would have been tough. So I found out about this institution in Lexington, Kentucky, which was a federal institution for drug addicts. A lot of guys went there—Dexter Gordon, Sonny Stitt, Tadd Dameron, lots of others. So I went to Chicago. I wanted to first get out of New York. I played a couple of gigs, but then I finally went to Lexington. They called their treatment the cure, and it took four and a half months. They treated drug addiction like an illness, not a crime, and you felt more like a patient than a convict. It was very compassionate treatment. They used dolophine, which was an early form of methadone. It gave you more of a chance.

The humane treatment at Lexington deeply impressed Sonny. It was a stark contrast to the way that American society as a whole dealt with drugs:

The police spend too much of their time going after some poor dummy doing drugs while the real criminals are committing murder and rape and other violent crimes. It is obvious that there is a more humane way to treat the drug problem, but America is not about "humane." America is about "puritanical" and "punitive."

When Sonny left Lexington in May 1955, he returned to Chicago. Now he faced a more difficult ordeal than kicking his habit: successfully avoiding drugs.

I was constantly worried about going back to using dope. I knew that I had to build up my willpower. Finally I went to a club, just to test the waters. I had this whole scene, with all the drug dealers offering me drugs, free drugs. And you know, that was hard, man. I had some really sweaty palms there. On a couple of occasions I almost went to get high. It was very close. It was really a tug-of-war between going back to my old ways or trying to get myself together. It was an epic battle. It was something like the scene in that movie *Cabin in the Sky*, the fight between the devil and the angels trying to get Little Joe to do one thing or another. I lived that. Being back in that ambience, the temptation was so great. I fought it, man. As I said, I was sweating; but I fought it and I was able to turn it down.

Another night I went back to the club again, and the temptation was still there. But that time it was a little easier to withstand the temptation. That really strengthened me. If you can finally defeat that, it really makes you a stronger person. Because that is a rough one.

Sonny knew that he was not yet ready to return to the jazz world as a player, although he planned to continue his career in music: "I never seriously thought about leaving music. I always knew that sooner or later I had to go back to it."

But instead of returning immediately, he got a series of menial jobs to tide himself over and to build himself up mentally and physically:

> I knew I had to get a job and I took whatever was available. It was all physical work. I did not literally do construction work, but I got jobs like janitorial work or loading up trucks. I was just trying to get my life back together.

When Sonny finally realized that he had defeated his addiction, and that he had the inner strength to avoid temptation, he became eager to once again pursue his career as a musician. He had one new worry: what if his ability to improvise was predicated on his use of drugs? Could he still play well straight? Of course, Charlie Parker had claimed that he played best when straight, but for Bird those were rare occasions. Sonny's concern was genuine. To Sonny's great relief, his musical ability was noticeably sharpened and it continued to improve after he finally kicked his addiction.

While Sonny had been battling with his drug addiction, there had been some major shifts in jazz, shifts that would accelerate Sonny's rise.

Charlie Parker had died of general dissipation. He was only thirty-four, and his death seemed to herald the end of the bop era. However, the advances of bop had taken hold of the music and there was no going back. Jazz would continue to evolve in new and surprising ways. Cool jazz, or West Coast jazz, had dominated the scene since the early 1950s. Many on the West Coast experimented with some of the most fundamental elements of jazz. They often used elaborate arrangements that borrowed heavily from classical music, attempted counterpoint, wrote suites, eliminated the rhythm section, and used instruments usually associated with European music, such as the flute, French horn, and oboe. Many of the more pretentious works of Stan Kenton had only a tenuous connection to jazz.

West Coast musicians were not the only ones to experiment in this way. Nobody employed aspects of classical music more than the Modern Jazz Quartet did. Moreover, Yusef Lateef, a prominent East Coaster, often played oboe, and Julius Watkins, as we have seen, played French horn. There were several West Coast players as dedicated to straight-ahead playing as any East Coast jazzmen: Art Pepper, Hampton Hawes, Chet Baker, and Stan Getz (who really did not belong to either East or West Coast jazz, although in the early and mid-1950s he was assumed to belong to the latter). Hampton Hawes, the bassist Leroy Vinnegar, and the tenorman Teddy Edwards, to name just a few, were black West Coast players. But despite them, and despite the central importance of Miles Davis, Lester Young, and Charlie Parker to the movement, cool jazz was thought of as a mainly white phenomenon. There was a growing feeling among many musicians that jazz was losing its black sensibility and aesthetic and was becoming less and less relevant to black lives. There was also a feeling that the music needed to return to its roots while at the same time maintaining the progressive changes brought on by the bop revolution. This new, "rootsier" modern jazz would be dubbed hard bop.

Hard bop made the blues central to jazz expression again and gave a more prominent role to the drums. The music became both more funky as well as harder-driving and more polyrhythmic—in emulation, at least to a degree, of the complex rhythms of African music.

Two of the key musicians in founding of the Hard Bop movement were the pianist-composer Horace Silver and the drummer Art Blakey. Silver was the pianist on the Miles Davis record session in which Sonny's compositions "Airegin," "Oleo," and "Doxy" were first recorded. Perhaps more important to the hard bop movement was another recording session of Miles, the so-called "Walkin' " session. On this date Miles led a group that included J. J. Johnson and the wonderful saxophonist Lucky Thompson, as well as Silver and the Prestige "house rhythm section" of the time: bassist Percy Heath and the bop pioneer and drummer Kenny Clarke. The group recorded two blues, the medium-tempo "Walkin' " and the faster-tempo "Blue and Boogie." Silver's style was even more in evidence here than in the "Oleo" session: blues-drenched and highly percussive, the intensity of his attack seemed to make the keys sweat.

The "Walkin' " session has been called by some the true beginning of the hard bop movement, but another 1954 session was even more crucial. That session was recorded for Blue Note Records and it was the debut of a group called the Jazz Messengers. Silver and Art Blakey, as well as the trumpeter Kenny Dorham and the tenor saxophonist Hank Mobley, made up the original Messengers. The first album, simply entitled *Horace Silver and the Jazz Messengers*, included tunes written by Silver that became hard bop standards: "Doodlin' " and, most important, "The Preacher." Blakey's dominating drums and Silver's modernized honky-tonk piano were at the center of the Messengers, giving the music its unrelenting drive and fin-ger-snapping funk. Dorham and Mobley were wonderfully inventive and richly lyrical players, but their lyricism was bluesier and grittier than the pastel, airy lyricism typical of most of the West Coast cool musicians.

There was a conscious effort among the members of this band to revive for the mainstream of jazz some of the earthier elements of black music. Referring to "The Preacher," Silver explained in the original liner notes to the first Messengers album, "We can reach back and get that old-time gutbucket feeling with just a taste of the backbeat."

Ironically, much 1990s jazz is a return to hard bop that is viewed by many critics and fans as an alternative to the rock/funk/jazz fusion of the 1970s. The original hard boppers were consciously attempting to use sub-tle elements of rhythm and blues in order to give their music greater cur-rency among African Americans, many of whom had lost interest in jazz during the cool era. Hard bop was an attempt to create music relevant to the lives of black people instead of what was viewed by some as the elitist, rarefied, and experimental jazz that at times seemed more European than African American in its sensibility. The intention of the hard boppers was to accomplish this while not sacrificing the gains of the original bebop-pers—neither pandering nor sacrificing the great intelligence of the music nor surrendering its lofty aesthetic goals.

The particular moment when Sonny finally felt strong enough, both physically and mentally, to safely return to the jazz scene was propitious.

Since the late 1940s, he had been developing a style that fit perfectly into the new currents of jazz. "Doxy" would easily have fit into the repertoire of the Jazz Messengers; his style of improvising was clearly rooted in African American musical tradition.

It is too pat and easy to state that Sonny was a member of the hard bop movement, or any other movement, for that matter, other than that of modern jazz itself. Sonny feels that terms like "hard bop" are mainly the inventions of writers trying to create pat explanations and pigeonholes, and there is much truth in that. Sonny had his own agenda throughout his entire career, and his music has always been far too personal and idiosyncratic to give it any kind of convenient appellation. At times it jibed with what was going on in the jazz scene, and at other times it did not. Sonny has always been too independent a thinker (and not just in terms of his music) to care much about being fashionable.

During this period, Miles Davis's career, too, had taken a new turn. Miles had kicked his addiction under his own auspices in the previous year and, not unlike Sonny, he found his fluency and conception greatly improved after he became clean. Miles was the hit of that year's Newport Jazz Festival, especially for his rendition of Monk's " 'Round Midnight." Miles had evolved beyond the "cool" of his earlier recordings; there was now a greater emotional depth at the core of his playing that was profoundly poignant and moving. This was due, perhaps, to the dark years of his addiction and the effect they had on his career. Whatever the reason, the performance so impressed the producer George Avakian that he signed Miles to a contract with Columbia, then the biggest and most prestigious record company in the country.

Miles now wanted to put together a permanent group that he could tour with, and Sonny was high on his list of potential band members. "I never knew that Miles wanted me to join his new group. I never had signed a contract with him or anything like that." When Miles was putting his group together, Sonny was off the scene. A couple of members of Miles's new band suggested to him that, since his first choice was not available, he choose instead a journeyman tenor saxophonist with whom he had played briefly a few years earlier: John Coltrane. Although fans were upset at first that Sonny had been replaced by such an obscure figure, that opinion would, of course, change; the group was eventually considered one of the seminal combos of modern jazz.

It was perhaps best for Sonny that he did not join the Davis quintet. Every member of that group, with the exception of Miles himself, was a drug addict and the group would become notorious for that; it was even given the nickname the Booze and Dope Band. Sonny needed not only great musical latitude but also as clean an environment as possible. Through incredible luck, that environment became a reality just at the moment when Sonny was ready.

In late 1955, Sonny felt strong enough to return to jazz full-time. By a wonderful serendipity, he got the chance to restart his jazz career with one of the greatest bands of the hard bop era.

During the period of Sonny's pursuit of sobriety the bebop drummer Max Roach put together a group co-led by the young trumpet player Clifford Brown. Brown had become something of a sensation in jazz; he was an amazing virtuoso, yet his playing was especially warm and sinuously melodic. He also had a gorgeous golden tone that was a perfect match for his indigo lyricism. Brown's best playing expressed a sunny joyousness equaled only by that of Louis Armstrong. The Brown-Roach band, and especially Brown himself, would have far-reaching importance to both the life and career of Sonny Rollins.

Clifford Brown was born in the same year as Sonny, 1930, and first started playing trumpet at thirteen. His technique developed amazingly quickly, to the extent that his talent was recognized by Charlie Parker and Dizzy Gillespie while he was still a teenager. He befriended Fats Navarro, who became his most important influence. When Navarro died in July 1950, Brown was clearly his heir apparent. However, unlike Navarro and so many other young modernists, Brown never got involved with hard drugs and never drank heavily. There seemed to be nothing to dim his rising star. Despite his great gifts, Brown was a truly humble man with an ebullient and gentle disposition; he was almost universally beloved. While it is not always true that a jazz musician's style directly reflects his personality, with Brown this was so.

Brown's career shot skyward until 1950, when a terrible automobile accident sidelined him for several months. In retrospect, this misfortune seems like an omen of the tragedy that came a few years later.

After several months of recovery, Brown resumed his career, touring Europe with bands led by Quincy Jones and Lionel Hampton. He also began recording under his own leadership and that of others, both at home and in Europe. At one of his sessions in 1953 for Blue Note, Sonny and the pianist-composer Elmo Hope brought him a composition called "Carvin' the Rock," which they wrote while serving time together (the Rock was what prisoners called Rikers Island). Hope had been a good friend of both Bud Powell and Thelonious Monk, and his style seemed like a missing link between these two bop piano geniuses. This was the fateful first meeting for Sonny and Brown.

In this same year, 1954, Clifford Brown played trumpet in a group formed by Art Blakey that also featured Horace Silver. The group would not last long, but this first collaboration between Silver and Blakey led to the formation of the Jazz Messengers in the following year. In that same year, 1954, Max Roach, who at the time was playing at the Lighthouse club in Los Angeles, heard an album that Clifford Brown had recorded under the leadership of J. J. Johnson. Like many others in the jazz world, Roach was amazed by Brown's technical mastery and improvisational inventiveness, so he contacted the young hornman, who went to Los Angeles for the purpose of forming a band with Roach. They tried several musicians to fill out the group, including Sonny Stitt, Eric Dolphy, the pianist Carl Perkins, and Teddy Edwards. The L.A.-based tenorman Harold Land was chosen as their reedman, and fellow Angeleno George Morrow became the group's bassist. Roach chose Richie Powell as the group's pianist.

While Roach and Brown dominated the group, the other players made significant contributions. Richie Powell was Bud's brother and was continually overshadowed by the genius of his sibling, but he himself was a fine pianist. He was also the group's chief arranger for the group. During his tenure, he seemed to be developing as a skillful and inventive arranger for small-group jazz. Despite the geographical location of his home, Harold Land's style was heated and blues-oriented. He was and is one of those players constantly designated "underrated." Land did manage to hold his own alongside the soaring virtuosity of the group's leaders. The Clifford Brown–Max Roach quintet was inarguably one of the classic modern jazz groups even before Sonny joined it.

For Sonny, the element of serendipity arose when Harold Land had to leave the group in Chicago in late 1955 because his wife was giving birth to their child back in Los Angeles. This was exactly the time when Sonny felt that he had built up enough inner strength to resume his musical career. The Brown/Roach group provided a perfect ensemble for a great young virtuoso like Sonny Rollins since its founders were also two of the greatest virtuosi on their instruments. And joining the Brown-Roach group was propitious for Sonny at this time.

> I had just come out on the Chicago jazz scene. I had begun sitting in at a couple of clubs and stuff, but I wasn't . . . back into the business yet. Then they [the Brown/Roach group] came through town and I was about ready to go back to New York [where the quintet was headed]. I felt I had sort of got myself strong enough to be able to come back and face the big city again. There was the fact that everybody in that group was clean, or at least none of them were junkies, which was clean enough for me.

Sonny acknowledges that had he been in New York at the time, he might have joined Miles's new group. But he did not join the Brown/Roach group on the rebound.

> I didn't join Max's and Brownie's band because I had turned down Miles. There just weren't that many gigs around and people took gigs wherever they could find them. When I joined the Brown-Roach band it was just another gig. I played with them because I was in Chicago and because I could go with them back to New York. I had already started sitting in, doing some blowing at the clubs. They just happened to be there at the time. I had no idea how long I would stay with them. Circumstances just had me there and in that spot and I went with them.

At this point in his life it was of great importance to Sonny to be playing in a band made up of musicians who were not junkies. Clifford Brown provided Sonny a model that gave him additional strength at this crucial juncture in his life.

> I had overcome the really big battles against returning to drugs by the time I joined Clifford and Max's band. I was going to be okay as

far as drugs were concerned. What Clifford Brown did do is enforce my feelings about staying clean, because he was a very clean-living guy. He sort of epitomized the kind of guy who could really play but who was clean-living. You didn't have to be such a rake in order to be a great jazz musician.

Most guys back then drank a lot. All of those guys that I knew when I was growing up, Hawkins and all those guys spent a lot of time at the bar. What Clifford showed me was that you didn't have to drink a lot and be super-macho and have a big head and all that, to be a great player. I got a lot out of knowing Clifford. Although I already knew that I wanted to stay away from drugs at that time, he reinforced the idea that you don't have to be a drug addict to play this music.

Clifford Brown had another, more profound effect on Sonny:

Clifford was a big influence on me and not just musically or [because] he was clean-living. Before I met Clifford, I had never met anybody who was such a good player and yet was so self-effacing and humble. This was new to me. I had always been around guys who were pretty full of themselves. Clifford was just a very humble guy for being such a prodigious talent. I had never encountered anything like that. If anybody could play as much as Clifford, you would expect him to have certain idiosyncrasies, to be more cocky, which I would excuse, of course. I would accept that. But Clifford was the first person with that kind of talent that was such a humble person. That struck a light in my head. I said to myself, "Well, gee, you don't have to try to act like you're so great. I mean you could really be down-to-earth." At that time I wanted to be humble, but nobody else around me was. I was certainly not as humble as I wanted to be. I think I felt more natural being a humble person; I think that was my nature. I was not following my nature and I was acting, well, arrogant.

I remember in particular when I realized how arrogant I was. I was telling [pianist-composer] Herbie Nichols something that was sort of putting him down, acting like what he was saying wasn't important. He called me on it and I realized, "Wait a minute, I'm acting kind of arrogant here." This was when I had just come back to New York with Max and Brownie.

This was a deeply spiritual lesson that I got from Clifford. The career of Sonny Rollins is really irrelevant, unless it can do something larger than be just that. It is not about Sonny Rollins, and if that was it, it would be ridiculous. If it *is* about Sonny Rollins doing something that means something for the enlightenment of other people or whatever it is supposed to be, then it means something. Then it's okay. That is what I got from Clifford. He helped me crystallize a lot of these thoughts.

Sonny was equally committed to changing as a person as he was to changing as a musician. Sonny has always been a deeply introspective man, and what he had gone through had changed him.

After you get away from the drug lifestyle, you have to look in the mirror and say "Well, who am I now? I'm not that guy, the guy I used to be. I don't want to be that guy. So am I?"

It's a metamorphosis. You've got to really catch ahold of yourself and face a lot of things that you used to deal with before. You have to deal with them in a different way. So it's a big moment in a guy's life.

Like his friend John Coltrane, Sonny became deeply involved in a spiritual search that was tied directly to his musical vision. Undoubtedly, the seeming paradox of Clifford Brown—an incredibly gifted musician who was also genuinely humble—was the very beginning of Sonny's spiritual pilgrimage. He had begun to understand that his gifts had value beyond his own success and well-being. It was a major revelation.

Sonny, in turn, had a strong effect on the Roach/Brown group. Harold Land is a superb player, and he fit very well into the Brown-Roach quintet, but after he left and Sonny joined the band, the group seemed to expand its prodigious virtuosity even further, and to reach new heights of improvisational glory. Everyone in the band knew that they had something very special and they worked to grow, both as individuals and as a group, with great dedication.

When I joined the band we used to rehearse a lot. Of course, I was a new member of the group and I had to deal with the music. Brownie and I used to rehearse a lot together, playing out of our exercise books and all that. We were a working band and always went over things while on the job, either before or after we played. We would even practice while still in the hotel.

On the bandstand, Rollins and Brown goaded each other to greater achievements every time they played. The group was also evolving continuously, getting tighter within a relatively short time. Sonny's playing advanced quickly for two reasons: he was no longer addicted to drugs and could now spend far more time on his music and his technique; and he was in a band that forced him to play at the top of his game every night it performed. The group enthralled the jazz world.

Another energizing force for Sonny was Max Roach himself. Only a handful of drummers have been able to give Sonny the rhythmic support he needs, and Roach is at the top, or certainly near the top, of that list.

Max has always been among the best drummers for me. I need a drummer that is really strong and secure in establishing a beat and who knows where he is at all time because I am a very rhythmic player. I have the rhythms already. I need a drummer that I can interface with and who can trade choruses with me. Max has all those qualities. More than that, we had such a close rapport that we could almost read each other's minds.

Shortly after he returned to New York with the Roach-Brown band in December 1955, Sonny went into the studio for Prestige and recorded his first album since leaving Lexington.

I was worried that I could not play as well as I used to without drugs. What if I needed drugs in order to play well? I felt much better when I realized that I could play just as well without drugs as with them.

I've been high and I've been straight. I have never been sure how getting high affected my playing. After I stopped using narcotics I used to drink a little vodka before performing and that would help me get comfortable before I went on stage. It helped free me of my inhibitions or whatever alcohol does for people.

During the formative years of my career I was using drugs. So it's hard for me to look back. I would probably have developed the same way if I had not taken drugs. At least, I hope that would be the case. Since I was using drugs up until the mid-1950s, I don't know what part drugs played in all of that. When I recorded *Work Time* I was trying to confront that question. I wasn't sure. I was hoping that I could make a record as fulfilling as I had when I was high. When I finally started making some records that I thought were good, or better than, the stuff I had done when I was getting high, I heaved a sigh of relief because I was not sure if getting high helped me play better. I am not sure of this, but I do not think so.

Sonny's first album since kicking his addiction demonstrated that he had nothing to worry about. The *Work Time* album is telling in the high level of its cohesive, continually inventive, exploratory yet brightly optimistic improvising.

The album's title, like those of several other Rollins albums, was an autobiographical reference. Sonny had been working as a menial laborer for several months and this album was his return to his most important work. For Sonny, although inspiration and one's heart and soul are crucial to the creation of music, what's necessary is also simply work, hard work. And the idea that music is simply hard labor was a way to prevent himself from developing any sense of pretention or self-importance. The more he worked at improving his physical ability, the greater his feeling of freedom on the bandstand; having the mechanical dexterity to play anything that came through his mind and heart gave him the wings to soar as far afield as his imagination and vision could go.

The first tune on *Work Time* is an example of Sonny's ability to use unlikely vehicles for jazz expression: Irving Berlin's "There's No Business Like Show Business." Although Sonny chose this tune, like all the others he uses, mainly for legitimate musical reasons, he also had in the back of his mind a more personal association:

"There's No Business Like Show Business" was a song I had been rehearsing in Chicago after I had been rehabilitated. I had been rehearsing that tune with the trumpet player Booker Little and with other guys around Chicago. *Work Time*, in a way of speaking, was my entrée back on the scene and that is why I thought about using the tune.

Despite Sonny's serious dedication to his art, there is something about showbiz that has always amused and, in some odd fashion, even attracted him. His use of Jolson tunes, and the importance to him of old movies and radio shows and, especially, old tunes associated with Broadway shows, cinematic confections, and vaudeville, demonstrate the affinity he feels. Much like his mentor Thelonious Monk, Sonny always delights in turning sentimental ditties inside out and making them relevant to the world that he, as an artist, knows and lives in. He and Monk seem to take special delight in choosing tunes from a dated popular culture, dripping with honeyed Americana, and through musical alchemy turning them into a vehicle for cultural iconoclasm (for example, Monk has performed a solo rendition of "There's Danger in Your Eyes Cherie").

No matter the reason, Sonny turned this unlikely tune into a convincing, fast-tempo bebop cooker. Although such unusual choices have long been a hallmark of Sonny's repertoire, he has no conscious humorous or satirical purpose:

I never choose a tune just as a joke. I never approach any of my material in a light-hearted way. There is always something musical about the tune that I like or which interests me. I am serious about everything that I play. If it is a funny tune that everybody has associated with the pop world, or whatever, there are musical elements to the tune that intrigue me. I am not just playing it because it is a funny tune. There is always a musical reason why I choose a tune like that.

Some people accuse me of being sardonic. Since I am a deep thinker about a lot of social issues, I cannot completely dismiss that as having no foundation. So that if I play a song like "There's No Business Like Show Business," maybe in the bottom of my consciousness I am trying to make a statement. But on a conscious level, I just saw it as a musical vehicle; I wasn't aware of any double entendres.

If some guy says that I was trying to make a statement about music, I can't deny that some of that is present in my work, since I play a lot of songs that some people might think are unusual. I play most of those songs since I first heard them as a child.

But I can't deny that there may be some kind of sarcasm, especially when playing a song like "Rockabye Your Baby." I knew that Al Jolson had sung it. That was a little closer to being a parody. But even then, I chose it mainly because I thought it would be a good tune to extemporize on.

And there is another reason why Sonny sometimes chooses tunes that are rarely covered by other jazz musicians.

Playing different tunes brings on different challenges and it makes it harder just to fall into clichés or easy licks. That would be a part of why I choose unusual tunes. I'm like Miles in that I hate clichés. I think that is the difference between competence and playing at a level beyond competence.

The undoubted highlight of *Work Time* is a lengthy version of the ballad "There Are Such Things." This performance could almost function as a textbook on how to play a ballad. Sonny never double-times, as so many lesser jazz musicians do with a ballad, nor does he resort to facile blues licks, or any other easy response. His variations flow directly and logically out of the tune itself. Given a melody as lovely as this one, that is an amazing feat. This performance alone is convincing evidence that Sonny has come of age as an artist; it is the work of a confident, mature jazzman. With this album, Sonny moved to the front ranks of his generation of jazz improvisers. His hard work was paying off.

The high quality of Sonny's playing on *Work Time* was an enormous relief to him. Now that he was playing with one of the finest groups in jazz, there seemed to be nothing that could hold him back.

In January 1956, the Brown-Roach group recorded its first album with Sonny, *Clifford Brown and Max Roach Quintet at Basin Street East*. The title is deceptive because it implies that the band was recorded live at the Basin Street East club in New York. In fact, this was a strictly a studio date. The band had had a successful engagement at the club and perhaps chose the title for that reason.

Forget about the title; this album is simply one of the great jazz albums of the past fifty years. Brown and Roach are at the top of their form, and Richie Powell's arrangements are continually ingenious and obviously stimulating to the players. But it is Sonny's contribution that pushes this record into a special category. He plays with an extroverted élan unlike anything he had ever previously recorded. Clifford Brown's irrepressible ebullience obviously sparked him to play with such a feeling of celebration. He is able to keep pace with Brownie, no small achievement, playing with great inventiveness even at the brightest of tempos.

Critics have overused the word "brilliant" to write about great artistic achievements. But "brilliant" perfectly describes the sound of this band, on this album. The music has a golden, burnished hue that dazzles the ears as the gleam of the sun affects our eyes. It is a shadowless music that seems to light up even the darkest corners.

The future for Sonny's new band seemed limitless.

Nineteen fifty-six was the single most crucial year in Sonny's career. He would participate in seven recordings (the *Work Time* session occurred in late 1955), several of which are considered modern jazz classics. They cemented Sonny's reputation as one of the greatest saxophonists in jazz history and a master improviser, as well as an important jazz composer. Now that he was sober, he was clearly committed to making up for lost time. The high quality of most of his recordings justifies his prolific output; even the least of them (such as his first Blue Note album) has more than its share of moments of innovative and inventive playing. All this while he was only twenty-five. He turned twenty-six in 1956.

Sonny recorded with Miles again in March 1956, for what would turn out to be the final time. It is unfortunate that they only recorded three tunes, because both musicians had finally matured into master jazzmen. Miles had broken up his famous quintet; the problems of dealing with a group of junkies had become too burdensome, especially because he himself had cleaned up. Miles might also have wanted to tour with the group he put together for the recording session (Sonny; pianist Tommy Flanagan; Paul Chambers, the bassist from the former quintet; and Sonny's boyhood pal Art Taylor). The three tunes they recorded were Dave Brubeck's "In Your Own Sweet Way"; "No Line," which true to its name is simply a set of chord changes; and "Vierd Blues," which is self-explanatory. Sonny's playing on this last is a preview of his "Blue Seven" improvisations, which would later gain great critical notice. He uses elements of the blues line itself to create his musical statement rather than just using the tune's chord changes; undoubtedly, he was remembering Monk's admonition to "use the melody." Like this entire session, this piece seems tentative, a preview for a great Davis-Rollins album that was, unfortunately, never made.

Sonny's own evolution as a player was now tied directly to the dynamics of the Brown-Roach band. His musical conception had developed in the context of that group, so it was natural that the next album he recorded under his own leadership would use the members of that band. The album's somewhat misleading title, *Sonny Rollins Plus Four*, was not Sonny's idea.

Musicians did not have control over things like that back then. That is the title that the guys who ran Prestige wanted to use. I am pretty sure that never sat right with Max. After all, it was his and Brownie's band. But I had nothing to do with it. A little later Max himself put out a record called *Max Roach Plus Four* [on which Sonny also played].

This is a valuable album because it and *Basin Street East* are the only two albums the group produced with Sonny in the saxophone chair. The most interesting thing in Sonny's playing on this album, recorded in March 1956 (two months after the *Basin Street East* album) is the effect of this band on his conception. His playing seems more extroverted than on his albums without the Brown-Roach group. Roach's support and his virtually psychic rapport with the drummer gave Sonny the confidence to break out of himself. And it was undoubtedly the presence of Brown that enabled Sonny to play with such brassy optimism.

Almost as significant as Sonny's improvisations are his compositions on *Sonny Rollins Plus Four*: "Pent Up House" and "Valse Hot." The latter was unusual in that it was in waltz time instead of the straight-ahead 4/4 swing that had been virtually the only meter jazzmen used since the last years of the New Orleans era. With rare exceptions (like Fats Waller's "Jitterbug Waltz"), virtually all jazz performances since the beginning of the swing era were in 4/4. By the late 1950s, many musicians, including Miles Davis, John Coltrane, Charles Mingus, and Dave Brubeck, began to explore a variety of meters.

Sonny once again returned to the studio late in May 1956, to record *Tenor Madness*. The album includes another remarkable choice of pop tune, "The Most Beautiful Girl in the World," as well as some Rollins originals such as "Paul's Pal." As just a Rollins quartet album, it would probably not be considered particularly important. However, the title cut makes *Tenor Madness* essential: it is the only recording of Rollins and John Coltrane playing together. This was not an extraordinary event, for the scene was much more casual back then.

Back in those days, musicians would hang out together a lot more than now. I remember going to other guys' dates all the time. Things were much more casual. . . . Coltrane was just hanging out during that date; I did not even know that he had brought his horn with him. When I found out that he had, we decided to do this song together. After that he was always saying, "We should do another date together." But unfortunately, that never came about.

Coltrane was still struggling to carve out a career in jazz at this point. Many fans thought his tone was ugly, and at times he seemed to be struggling just to play coherently. However, in hindsight it is clear that Coltrane was struggling with the birth pains of a style that would eventually cause momentous changes in the evolution of jazz.

The tune "Tenor Madness" had origins that probably stretched back to the early swing era. It was one of those riffs that jazzmen find easy to improvise on, and it was perfect for a "tenor duel." However, this performance was more a duet than a duel. The two musicians were already good friends and they did not feel competitive toward each other (their relationship grew a bit more complicated for a short period later). At this point, Sonny is more accomplished technically than Coltrane, and his style is far more mature. Coltrane's own style is still in its embryonic period. Within a year, after kicking his addictions to heroin and alcohol, he would finally attain stylistic maturity. For Sonny, Coltrane was always a unique voice.

Coltrane was always Coltrane to me. He was unique when I heard him in the early 1950s and then later when he was in Miles's groups and his own group. He was always Coltrane to me, just as Monk was always Monk. Even in his later years, his music always was Coltrane. It's you writers who divide up careers into stages. For me, great individuals like Coltrane or Miles always sounded unique.

Apart from its one extraordinary track, *Tenor Madness* is a fine enough album, but it does not have the sense of discovery and love of playing audible in some of Rollins's earlier recorded work. This had partly to do with Sonny's changing attitude toward recording. Around this time, he had begun to feel increasingly uncomfortable about recording. His musical conception deepened, as did his commitment to the philosophy of improvisation:

I was much more comfortable playing before an audience. That was a position that had changed over the years. Originally, when I first started recording in the 1940s and early 1950s, we didn't have the luxury to think about whether we were scared or too cautious or any of that. We just had a couple of takes and that was it!

In later years, having the luxury of being able to do a lot of takes and that kind of thing, then the artificiality of the studio became even more pronounced. Then I began to develop this real unease in the studio. Since I have to make studio recordings, I try to overcome that feeling. I guess that it is a fact.

Sonny is not perverse in his attitude toward recording. His commitment to the art of improvisation is rooted in his belief in the profundity of music being created for and of the moment. He is not the only jazz musician to feel this way, but probably no one has a more deep-seated, constitutional commitment to the concept of truly spontaneous music than Sonny. His most important spiritual beliefs about the music he creates are directly tied to this concept of genuine spontaneity. In its ideal state, a jazz improvisation should be heard only once, at the time it is actually created. It is miraculous how many brilliant recordings Sonny has produced over the years despite his unease with the recording of improvisation, especially recording in the studio.

There are two main schools of thought about recording among jazzmen. The first tries to keep the music as spontaneous as possible by playing only one or two takes. That is how Miles Davis recorded. The other school does take after take in order to find a performance as close as possible to perfection. That was the method of John Coltrane. Sonny sees value in both philosophies.

I guess I would fall into the "do a lot of takes" philosophy. But after I was given the freedom to make all these different takes, I discovered that when I listened to them back, it was often the earlier takes were the better takes. Not all the time, but enough that it caused me to question whether a lot of takes were necessary.

So it's a dilemma. Unfortunately, it is not always the rule that the first or second take is the best. I tend to nitpick. It's very difficult to use my ears and listen and really tell which is best. At times I have to depend on other people's ears and I would rather depend on my own.

This brief period in Sonny Rollins's life was a golden one, especially for someone only a few months short of his twenty-sixth birthday. He was off drugs and he was back full throttle in the jazz world. He was playing with one of the most exciting and popular groups, where he was given plenty of freedom to evolve as a musician. He had recorded some brilliant albums under his own name and that of the Brown-Roach group. He was becoming increasingly thought of as the most important tenorman of his generation.

This was a wonderfully happy time for him. Besides enjoying a bright musical career, he was also evolving as a human being, becoming the kind of person he had always wanted to be. His growth as a man was increasingly reflected in his music as he continued to look deeper into himself. But one of the greatest tragedies of Sonny's life was lurking right around the corner.

Saxophone Colossus

It was harvest time for Sonny Rollins. He felt that he had a mission and that that mission was tethered to his musical career. Intuitively, he understood that music was not just his savior, it was also his destiny. Now he was ready to make definitive statements as to who he was, both as a man and a musician. Believing that the world must change for the better, he realized that his best weapon for change was his horn. Maybe music could save others, just as it had saved him.

On June 22, 1956, Sonny recorded *Saxophone Colossus*, his fourth album since leaving Lexington. It was his third under his own name, and many consider it Sonny's masterpiece. A tour de force, it presents Sonny in a variety of moods and tempos. All of it is superior work. Sonny, however, does not think of *Saxophone Colossus* as an especially important album: "I know that a lot of people think it was an especially great album. But it just seemed like another record when I did it. I don't have any special memories about making it." Despite Sonny's own lack of enthusiasm (at least in retrospect), *Saxophone Colossus* would permanently establish Sonny on the first tier of great jazzmen and as one of the greatest of all tenor saxophonists.

The format is a quartet, which includes the exquisitely lyrical and subtle pianist Tommy Flanagan (at an early stage of his career), the Jazz Messengers bassist Doug Watkins, and Max Roach, who by now was so attuned to Sonny's musical sensibility that the two often seemed to be sharing the same mind. These three musicians made up about as solid a rhythm section as jazz could produce at this time. Their strong and inventive support is one reason why Sonny plays at such a high level.

The first tune on the album is the calypso "St. Thomas," Sonny's single most famous and popular piece. Although he is given writing credit, it is, as Sonny recalls, actually one of the first tunes he can remember hearing as a child:

> "St. Thomas" is a song that my mother used to sing. It's a traditional tune. Its etymology is very interesting. I called it "St. Thomas" because it was just a tune that I knew and since my mother was from St. Thomas I called it that. In the Virgin Islands, it had different names. The Virgin Islands were Danish. And there was a Danish song I heard sung by Lauritz Melchior in an old Hollywood movie. So I just arranged that tune and gave it the title "St. Thomas." It actually originated as a Scandinavian folk song.

The tune—it opens the album—begins with Max Roach playing a jazzed-up calypso rhythm. Sonny enters and plays the catchy tune, then improvises around a little two-bar riff. Roach then takes a solo that begins in calypso rhythm but ends in "swinging" 4/4, as Sonny returns with a straight-ahead solo, followed by a typically lyrical Flanagan solo. Sonny then reprises the tune in straight-ahead rhythm, which changes back to the original calypso rhythm. The difference between this, Sonny's first calypso, and those that he would play later is that this one segues between calypso and straight-ahead swing and the others remain in calypso rhythm. "St. Thomas" is a remarkably refreshing and successful fusion of jazz and calypso.

The next tune on the album is the ballad "You Don't Know What Love Is." This is a classic Rollins ballad and a particularly powerful performance. His playing here is at least as good as on the more celebrated pieces on the album. One thing that Sonny learned from his idol Coleman Hawkins was the use of drama. Sonny's sense of drama here is so strong that he is able to create genuine suspense, tension, and release, riveting the listener as if he is telling one of the great mysteries Sonny loved to hear on the radio when he was a boy. Sonny's mastery of improvised form was becoming increasingly obvious. He had now learned not only what to play, but also what not to play, which is an element of art that is usually not mastered until the artist is fully mature. The most striking aspect of Sonny's playing on "You Don't Know What Love Is" is its emotional depth. He plays as if bleeding every note. Perhaps, like Lester Young, he was thinking of the lyrics while he played. The emotion of this performance is that of an ardent lover desperately pleading with his beloved.

The next tune is "Strode Rode," a fast-tempo Rollins composition that would become one of his more widely played tunes. There is a sense of tension and suspense in Sonny's solo, particularly in his first improvised chorus, which he plays only accompanied by Doug Watkins's swiftly walking bass. Such stark accompaniment is particularly challenging at such a swift tempo; listening to it for the first time, one holds his breath until the rest of the group enters and the tension is released. Sonny's eloquence at this tempo gives the listener the illusion that he is able to manipulate time itself, bending and twisting it at will. It is an extraordinary technique, yet one never has the sense that Sonny is simply showing off his virtuosity for its own sake. It is clear that he is a man with important and profound things to say and an unfaltering ability to communicate with us on the deepest of levels.

"Moritat" (the German title for "Mack the Knife") comes next, played at a swinging medium tempo. For many, this is as important a piece as the famous one that follows it. Sonny obviously loves the melody, which is never totally discarded during his improvisation. He seems to take such delight in taking this melody apart, then reassembling it in new and inventive ways, that the word "play" takes on a double meaning; this is surely the mind of a genius musician at play.

The final piece, "Blue Seven," has been called both a masterpiece by some and highly overrated by others. The tune is a basic blues line that has an intriguing harmonic ambiguity. Sonny takes this slight melody and deconstructs it, turning it around, inside and out, creating a series of new and ingenious patterns with the same melodic thread. It is a classic example of thematic improvising. That is, instead of simply ignoring the melody and creating an improvisation based solely on the harmonic structure, the musician improvises with the melody itself as well as with the harmony. It is likely that Sonny picked up this technique from Thelonious Monk, but he believes that this kind of improvising can be found throughout jazz history. Wherever Sonny got it from, it is easily understandable even to a jazz novice. Improvisation in which the melody of the piece is ignored and which is based totally on the harmonic structure has often confused neophyte jazz listeners, who wonder, "Where's the melody?" (to quote a title of a book by the jazz critic Martin Williams). Thematic improvisation, in which the original melody or elements of it are always in play, is a concept that seems on the surface quite simple.

Well, not so fast. "Blue Seven" became the subject of one of the most influential and controversial pieces of musical interpretation in all of jazz history. This article also had a strong effect on Sonny himself. That in itself illuminates why a jazz musician's musical sensibility is so different from that of the conservatory-trained "classical" musician.

The piece was written by Gunther Schuller who, along with the MJQ's John Lewis, figures crucially in the "third stream" movement, which attempted to fuse jazz with the tradition of European classical music. Schuller had briefly played French horn in Miles Davis's *Birth of the Cool* nonet and later composed several works, including some third stream pieces such as "Variations on a Theme by Thelonious Monk" ("Criss Cross"). Schuller has gone on to become an administrator at the New England Conservatory of Music and has written a series of books analyzing the evolution of jazz from its inception to the present.

His analysis of Sonny's "Blue Seven" improvisation was written for the now defunct *Jazz Review*. Established in 1958, it was edited by Martin Williams and published only in-depth analysis of jazz and jazz musicians, covering the gamut of jazz history from Jelly Roll Morton to Ornette Coleman.

Gunther Schuller's "Sonny Rollins and Thematic Improvisation" states, "Today we have reached another juncture in the constant evolution of improvisation and the central figure of this present renewal is Sonny Rollins."[1] In the late 1990s, it is clear that Schuller, writing around 1957–58, has proved to be far more correct than he realized.

As noted earlier, it is clear that Sonny was a pivotal figure between the bebop revolution of the 1940s and the free jazz revolution of the 1960s, just as his idol, Coleman Hawkins, was a crucial figure bridging the innovations of Louis Armstrong and his generation in the 1920s and those of Charlie Parker and the other boppers in the 1940s. Schuller was unaware of the jazz revolution in the 1960s when he wrote this piece. But he and others with their ears to the ground sensed that jazz was about to go through another major shift forward in its evolution.

In his piece, Schuller points out that all of the great jazz instrumentalists have expanded the music's frontiers, or helped to define them. Sonny Rollins's great contribution to jazz, according to Schuller, is his ability to create unifying form throughout his improvisations. Schuller states that there had previously been two distinct approaches to jazz improvisation—that of paraphrase or ornamentation (which dominated the early development of jazz) and that of chorus improvisation, improvisation in which the melody is usually ignored and only its harmonic structure is used as a basis for the solo. This latter approach had become dominant in jazz, and because of that, according to Schuller, despite the increasing sophistication of jazz improvisation since the advent of the bop era, most jazz solos lacked the kind of "unifying force" of form that gives the greatest music direction and purpose.

In other words, most solos are just a string of unrelated licks and melodic ideas whose relationship to the original tune depends solely on its harmonic structure. According to Schuller, a performance that is only a series of solos that otherwise have no connection to one another or the piece of music on which it is based lacks the cohesion of music, and art, at its greatest. This concept of giving unifying form to jazz has been a central problem throughout the music's history. Jazz composers from Jelly Roll Morton and Duke Ellington to Charles Mingus and Thelonious Monk have attempted to give jazz performance a form that nonetheless utilizes the individual expression of the players. Can a truly improvisational music also embrace form and cohesiveness? Or does that mean inevitably limiting the players' freedom to create solos that are personal and idiosyncratic?

Form and structure must be dealt with one way or another as jazz becomes an increasingly sophisticated art form and less and less a folk art, even if the idea of form itself is deliberately abandoned (as in much free jazz). Making the music as random as possible is one way of dealing with the problem of form.

Schuller shows that not only does Sonny Rollins's playing on "Blue Seven" demonstrate that an improvised solo can have form, but also that it is possible for a piece of music consisting primarily of improvised solos to have true musical unity. Schuller continues:

There is now a tendency among a number of jazz musicians to bring thematic (or motivic) and structural unity into improvisation. Some do this by combining composition and improvisation; for instance, the Modern Jazz Quartet and the [Jimmy] Giuffre Three; others, like Sonny Rollins, prefer to work solely by extemporization. . . . "Blue Seven" is the best example of this so far. . . . It is at the same time a striking example of how two soloists [Sonny and Max Roach] can integrate their improvisations into a unified entity.[2]

Schuller transcribes part of Sonny's solo (actually Sonny makes three solo statements in the piece, separated by solos from Flanagan and Roach) and analyzes it in great technical detail. He concludes:

This then is an example of real variation technique. The improvisation is based not only on a harmonic sequence but also on a melodic idea as well. . . . He has come to expect from the composer who spends days or weeks writing a given passage. It is another matter to achieve this in on-the-spur-of-the-moment extemporization. . . . Such methods of musical procedure as employed here by Sonny and Max are symptomatic of the growing concern of an increasing number of jazz musicians for a certain degree of intellectuality.[3]

Schuller also points out that Max Roach's drum solo uses thematic devices not all that different from Sonny's, and he proves that a drum solo can be musically valid and not "just an unthinking burst of energy . . . but instead an intrinsic element of a complete, albeit improvised, musical statement."

Schuller's study of "Blue Seven" is an example of what serious, scholarly jazz criticism can be. It had a strong but unnerving effect on Sonny. He had never thought about his playing in the terms used by Schuller, and reading the piece made him so self-conscious that it was hard to relax on the bandstand and just play.

I am a naturally intuitive player, so I just do what comes naturally. I mean, I don't have any guideposts, nor do I say to myself, "Gee,

I'm going to do this and this," or that I am going to go into this or that which is going to give me resolution—all of that sort of stuff. For a while there I kind of said, "Gee, I'm never going to read this stuff again. This guy's going to have me going off the wall here." Fortunately, that didn't last long. I just want to play, you know?

That is my modus operandi: I study, but then when I am onstage, I don't have to concentrate. So I don't have to think about which chord goes here and how this chord is run and all this kind of stuff. Then the music gets to the point where it plays itself, so to speak.

The story of how Schuller's piece affected Sonny has become famous—perhaps regrettably, because it is misleading and fits too snugly into the whole conception of the jazz artist as a "native genius"—a jazz musician does not create his music out of an intellectual process, but rather through a mindless instinct devoid of intellectual depth: this is the standard tack that racists take concerning the musical ability of black jazzmen (and maybe of some white jazzmen too).

Sonny Rollins and the other great jazz musicians conceive their music with the same intellectual depth as any conservatory-trained classical composer, but their conceptual mode is simply on different terms. To at least some extent, Sonny picked up the idea of thematic-oriented improvisation from Thelonious Monk. Although Sonny did not record much with Monk, they did practice and rehearse together a good deal while Sonny was still very young, and he clearly absorbed much from the "High Priest of Bop." Just listen to any typical performance of a Monk group. He is constantly reminding the soloists of the melody through his insistent accompaniment. He makes the soloist use the melody by never letting the soloist forget what that melody is. When Sonny recorded *Saxophone Colossus*, he had mastered what Schuller calls thematic improvisation, which for Sonny was merely the idea of using every element of a tune, not just its chord changes.

This same point applies to Max Roach's apposite drum solos. Roach had been developing a more melodic and musical approach to playing drums, both in general and for the solo. The melodic and rhythmic elements of a piece had been for a long time a key to Roach's conception for his drum solos. Coming from a different angle from Schuller's, Sonny and Max Roach had created a piece of music, "Blue Seven," that the critic analyzed from his own, different point of view, one no more or less profound than that of the jazz musicians. Sonny has very strong views on this subject:

> Just the other day I was reading a book of short interviews with a lot of different horn players. In one of the interviews, Coltrane was talking about something that I really agree with. He was saying that he studies and practices up to a point. But, he said, after that point it is you . . . it is something else. I mean, you first do your preliminary stuff when you are actually performing, then *you forget it.* That is how I would describe it.

Wynton Marsalis contributed one of the best retorts to the notion of the "native genius." Referring to Louis Armstrong, Marsalis pointed out that if Armstrong had just happened to play such brilliant music, how was he able to create such magnificent musical statements over and over again? He simply had to have worked very consciously and deliberately to develop his musical modus operandi (as Sonny calls it) or he could never have produced so many solos of unquestioned genius.

Sonny himself is puzzled by the brouhaha over "Blue Seven." He would later use the same concepts to create far more complex solos using thematic improvisation. This is not to detract from "Blue Seven," a remarkable improvisation that brings great pleasure to any careful listener, but rather to point out that he later took the concepts discussed by Schuller and developed them far beyond the felicities of "Blue Seven." As Al Jolson himself might have put it, "You ain't seen nothin' yet!"

In June 1956, Sonny and Max were back in Chicago for a club appearance with the Brown-Roach band. They had gone to Chicago early and were waiting for Clifford Brown and Richie Powell to join them from Philadelphia. Brown and Powell never made it to Chicago; they had a car accident and both men were killed. Sonny will never forget the moment he heard the news:

> When Max told me about the deaths of Clifford and Richie, all I could do was go back to my hotel room and practice all night long. I was so stunned that at first it did not seem real and the only way to deal with it was to practice for the rest of the night. When Max and I went to the funeral we cried like little babies.

Clifford Brown seemed like an unlikely candidate for such an early death. He was only twenty-six, a clean-living musician who had already been in a bad automobile accident. Jazz history is replete with early deaths, but the loss of such a prodigiously talented man, who was just beginning what should have been a magnificent career, was truly tragic.

The loss of Brown was particularly sorrowful for Sonny. More than anybody else, Brown had been a model of sobriety for him, a greatly talented musician who was able to stay clean and sober and whose ego was not inflated. His dedication to his art was complete. Brownie undoubtedly had been a key factor in Sonny's ability to reenter the jazz scene without falling prey again to the demons of addiction, self-delusion, and arrogance.

Max found it difficult to decide how to proceed with his career after Brown's death. He had put together probably the hottest small band in jazz, and suddenly his co-leader—a man whom he not only respected as a musician but also loved as a brother—was dead. The group's pianist and arranger, Richie Powell, was also gone. His arrangements for the final Roach-Brown album, *Clifford Brown and Max Roach Quintet at Basin Street East*, showed how adept he had become at creating arrangements and tunes suited to this particular group.

A number of dates were scheduled for the band, however, and Roach had no choice but to hire another trumpet player and pianist and go on. Sonny, for a number of reasons, chose to stay with Max.

> I had a commitment to the band and to Max. Although I originally joined the band to fill in for Harold Land, while the band was together I had built up a relationship with Brownie, Richie, and Max. I felt a loyalty to Max in trying to keep up whatever semblance of what we had built up. Of course, that didn't last long,

because there wasn't enough to build on. I don't think that Max was particularly interested in keeping me as a sideman. He did keep the band together, first using Kenny Dorham as the trumpeter and later Donald Byrd. But I don't think that Max was interested in really keeping a band after Clifford died. Now all we had was, well, just another band. It wasn't the idea or the spirit of that band with Max and Brownie. When Brownie died, we were really on the verge of taking the music to an even higher level. It was really getting off into something different. The music was there. It was music of high quality, and I liked playing with Max, who is a great drummer for me. It was just that Max's concept of the group with Brownie was something that he could never get back.

The groups that Roach went on to lead after the tragedy may not have been equal to the band with Clifford Brown and Richie Powell, although they were all on a musically high level. But with its galvanizing virtuosity, the Brown-Roach band had been, during its brief existence, probably the definitive small group of its time and one of the most fervently exciting of all jazz combos from any era.

Perhaps it was the loss of Brown and Powell that caused Sonny to record even more "promiscuously" than ever before. In the second half of 1956, he recorded an amazing seven times. What is even more astonishing is the level of accomplishment heard on most of these recordings, on every one of which Max Roach performed too. Most A&R men knew about the amazing empathy between Max and Sonny. It was the recordings of this period, including *Saxophone Colossus*, that defined Sonny Rollins's place in the jazz firmament.

Sonny's first album after *Saxophone Colossus* was a salute to Charlie Parker, who had died the previous year. *Sonny Rollins Plays for Bird* is dominated by a medley of tunes associated with Parker (only one—"My Little Suede Shoes"—was actually composed by him). As on *Sonny Rollins Plus Four*, the personnel was basically that of the Roach group of that time. Neither Sonny nor the other horn on the date, trumpeter Kenny Dorham, has much opportunity to stretch out, but Sonny plays one superb solo on "Star Eyes," a favorite tune of Bird's.

The most interesting cut from this session did not appear on the *Plays for Bird* album and had nothing to do with Charlie Parker: "The House I Live In." The song's lyrics celebrate America's multiracial society. It was originally sung by Frank Sinatra for a film short that promoted racial harmony. Sonny had undoubtedly recalled Sinatra's concert at his school, during which he encouraged the Italian and black kids to forgo their racial animosity. Sonny never forgot the social commitment of Sinatra and Nat "King" Cole. Throughout his career, he has been committed to using his genius for social good.

Sonny continued to record as part of the Max Roach group, now just the Max Roach Quintet or "Max Roach + Four." They made two albums in 1956 that were innovative and exciting in their own right. For a number of years Sonny would mention his solo for the Roach group's version of the George Russell classic "Ezz-thetics" as his own favorite solo on record.

An astonishing improvisation that has not received the attention it deserves, it is more "traditional" than, say, the solo in "Blue Seven," but Sonny has rigorously constructed it, each phrase logically leading to the next. The solo takes form not from any particular principle, but rather through Sonny's ability to create a cohesive statement out of logic and discipline. His playing has the emotional bite and a feeling of purpose that we associate with the very best jazz solos. It resembles the best solos of Lester Young, in that it tells a story through melodic invention and tonal coloring.

The next Roach album was a rather daring and innovative project—an entire album of tunes in 3/4 waltz time. Sonny had already composed one waltz for the Roach group ("Valse Hot" on *Sonny Rollins Plus Four*), but doing an entire album of tunes in 3/4 was unprecedented. However, Dave Brubeck, Charles Mingus, George Russell, and others were expanding jazz's rhythmic frontiers during the 1950s, and it was logical for a drummer as innovative as Max to see if he could make waltz time as compelling as straight-ahead swing. The results (rather predictably titled *Jazz in 3/4 Time*) are decidedly mixed; an entire album of jazz waltzes is a surfeit of a good thing, but with musicians of this caliber it's compelling nonetheless.

Sonny's next recording project turned out to be a classic, but a rather pixilated one: Thelonious Monk's *Brilliant Corners* session for Orrin Keepnews's Riverside label. It was on this date that Sonny first met Orrin Keepnews; that alone made it a key milestone in Sonny's career. Besides Sonny and Monk, the band consisted of the alto saxophonist Ernie Henry (who was unable to participate in the third session, for which he was replaced by the trumpeter Clark Terry), the bassist Oscar Pettiford, and, once again, Max Roach. The album was recorded over three sessions; as Orrin Keepnews, who produced it, recalls:

> The first session went very smoothly and I thought that doing this session would be easy. But the second session, during which the tune "Brilliant Corners" was performed, was chaotic. It was a very difficult tune with tricky rhythmic passages. I don't remember that Sonny had any problems, but Max and Oscar Pettiford did. It almost caused a fistfight between Pettiford and Monk. Monk was a forgiving guy, but after that session he never mentioned Pettiford's name.

Sonny had never had many problems playing with Monk, but recording "Brilliant Corners" was a nightmare. The tune is so bizarre and difficult that it seems almost as if Monk composed it to test the abilities of even great musicians to play it correctly. It goes through a series of tempo changes that carries over to the actual solos. Despite the high level of musicianship, it required several takes, none of them completely successful. Keepnews managed to create a complete performance by pasting together sections from a number of takes.

Also on the date is Monk's "Pannonica," for which he plays a celeste. Given Monk's approach to the piano, the notion of his playing the sweet and delicate celeste may seem more than a little strange, but somehow his playing is eerily poignant and affecting.

Making this album was rough sledding for Sonny and the other musicians, but it was worth it. *Brilliant Corners* is one of the best examples of Monk's misterioso worldview and the self-contained, oddly specific musical landscape that is his alone.

On the same day in early December as the third and final *Brilliant Corners* session, Sonny also recorded a session for his first album under his own name since *Sonny Rollins Plays for Bird*. *Tour de Force* (the title is apropos) is almost as bizarre, in its own very distinctive way, as *Brilliant Corners*. Two of the tunes, "B. Quick" and "B. Swift," are played at such fast tempos that they seem to be intended for the *Guiness Book of World Records*, under the heading "Fastest Tunes Ever Recorded." These tunes were clearly meant as a challenge to all concerned, at least according to Sonny:

> We used to do that quite a bit. It was one of those things we used to do if a guy wanted to come up and sit in with the band. We would always test them by seeing how fast they could play. And then we would play something at breakneck speed in order to separate the men from the boys, so to speak.

In contrast to these tunes, Sonny recorded two romantic ballads with the singer Earl Coleman. There were rumors that Sonny wanted to do these tunes with a romantic crooner because he was in love. The reason was rather more prosaic: "Well, romance is an emotion which is not foreign to me. But the main reason I hired [Earl Coleman] for the date was that he had recorded with Bird. It was another tribute to Charlie Parker."

Sonny made yet another album under his name a couple of weeks later. Its significance is not the music itself, which is fine if not essential Rollins, but rather the label, Blue Note. Blue Note was owned and operated by Albert Lion and Francis Wolff, two German émigrés who fell in love with jazz in the late 1930s. After attending the famous "From Spirituals to Swing" concert at Carnegie Hall, they created Blue Note Records in order to record the boogie-woogie pianists Albert Ammons and Meade Lux Lewis. Early on they recorded classic jazzmen, such as Sidney Bechet, George Lewis, and Albert Hall. But by the late 1940s, the tenorman Ike Quebec became their principal A & R man, and through him they became increasingly involved in modern jazz. Thelonious Monk's first recordings under his own leadership were made for Blue Note, and Bud Powell recorded some of his greatest sides for the label. Sonny had been in the front line at one of those sessions, and undoubtedly Lion and Wolff kept the young tenorman in mind. Inevitably Sonny wound up making some of his best albums for the label.

Blue Note became famous for treating musicians with great respect and recording them with care. Unlike most labels, they paid the musicians to rehearse their music before they actually recorded it. In addition, the label was known for what many referred to as the Blue Note sound. Lion and Wolff worked very carefully with their sound engineer, who was the legendary Rudy Van Gelder for most of Blue Note's great period (the 1950s and 1960s), to record not just the music but also the ambience. Francis Wolff was a photographer, and he had an amazing knack for capturing atmospheric shots of the musicians. If you want to have some idea of what this golden age was like, the covers of Blue Note albums perfectly catch the mood of the jazz scene of that time. It is no surprise that many musicians made their finest recordings for this label. Sonny's first Blue Note album, unpretentiously titled *Sonny Rollins Volume One*, was certainly not among his great recordings. But his later work for the label would be quite a different matter.

A few months after Clifford Brown's death, Nat Hentoff interviewed Sonny for *Down Beat*. He began his piece by calling Sonny "the first major influence on a significant number of young tenors since Stan Getz of the late forties and early fifties."[4]

The comparison is worth some thought. The two men's sounds are so unlike that that they may as well be playing different instruments. It is far too facile to say that Getz's creamy, lilting lyricism reflects a white view of the world as contrasted to the harsher, more intense, and rhythmically more compelling black worldview of Sonny Rollins. But there is little doubt that the sensibilities reflected in the styles of these two great tenormen are worlds apart, and yet viewed against the backdrop of American society in the 1950s, they perfectly complemented each other, Getz's dreamy yin to Rollins's explosive yang.

At the time of the Hentoff interview Sonny was still mourning his friend's death. Discussing the experience of playing with Clifford Brown, he told Hentoff:

> It was a pleasure. There was never any kind of conflict at all. In fact, there were times I wished there was something I could be mad at him for—he blew so much. He was perfect all the way around.

We were just starting to achieve a sound when the accident happened.

On our last job we played together, all of a sudden we both heard it. We were phrasing, attacking, breathing together. That's a very difficult thing for two horns to make in unison playing. It's easier playing harmony. In unison, for one thing, the intonation of both horns has to be exactly the same. That's why I think all groups that get together should *stay* together. It's the only way for them to achieve what they want to.[5]

Sonny also discussed with Hentoff certain plans that would not bear fruit for a few more years:

Next year I may take time off, go back to school, and stay away from the scene completely until I'm finished. I've continued studying off and on by myself and with teachers. I've just started. I've just scratched the surface. That's an honest appraisal of myself. I don't dig this being an influence. I'm not trying to put myself down or anything. Being considered an influence admittedly is more of a challenge because people look for me to produce. But that bugs me too, because I really don't feel I'm as great as they think I am. Being considered that good creates a mental thing too. . . . I've got a lot of work to do, a lot of work.[6]

At the end of the interview Sonny makes a comment rather surprising for someone who had been playing and recording with many of the greatest names in jazz since the 1940s:

I've been really serious about music for about two years. Music is the main thing now. It's a commitment—that's stronger than a decision—to make it a career. . . . I'm not satisfied with anything about my playing. I know what I want. I can hear it. But it will take time and study to get it.[7]

Because of such self-disparaging remarks, some critics and fans believe that Sonny has an inferiority complex. This is a profound misunderstanding of the man. Partly because of the weathering of intense experiences,

Sonny had gone through a sea-change since the days when he was an arrogant young tenorman. His commitment to music had become not just a career decision but also the core of his life—his religion, so to speak, as well as his vocation. It was not his life experiences alone that had changed him; his realization of the awesome vastness of his musical universe had also humbled him. If music truly was an "open sky," then he was just one man looking up at the infinity of stars.

7

A Night at the Village Vanguard

If 1956 had been a key year in Sonny's life and career, the following year would prove even more monumental. He was now ready to go out on his own as a leader. After years of apprenticeship, playing and recording with most of the greatest names in modern jazz—Miles Davis, Thelonious Monk, Charlie Parker, Bud Powell, the Modern Jazz Quartet—Sonny had paid his dues as a sideman and was now ready to become a leader himself. For the early part of 1957, he remained in the Roach band, though he was getting increasingly restless to go out on his own.

Between December 1955 and the end of 1956, Sonny had "promiscuously" recorded several albums, a few of which are considered classic jazz records. In addition to becoming the most important young tenor saxophonist in jazz, he was also one of the most influential musicians of his time. Sonny was affecting even the way the saxophone was being played.

Up until the mid-1950s, cool or West Coast jazz saxophonists such as Stan Getz, Bill Perkins, Gerry Mulligan, and Lee Konitz dominated the jazz scene. Their main influence was Lester Young, although they had absorbed the sophisticated harmonic conception of the beboppers and, in particular,

Charlie Parker. Their style was chiefly associated with white jazzmen, although there were a few important black players in the movement.

When Sonny became prominent in the mid-1950s, many young saxophonists, particularly those on the East Coast, began to pursue a more intense, bluesier, rhythmically compelling kind of jazz. This included Hank Mobley, Clifford Jordan, John Gilmore, J. R. Monterose, and the young Philadelphian John Coltrane. Even if Sonny was not a direct influence on them, his fiery, dark-hued, rhythmically complex style had an enormous effect on most saxophonists. Even some of the cool jazzmen toughened up their style, playing with less limpid lyricism and more grit. By the late 1950s even Stan Getz, the king of cool, developed a more intensely driving style. This was an indirect reaction to Sonny's work. And after the important West Coast reed player and composer/arranger Jimmy Giuffre visited New York and heard Sonny play, he went back to California deeply shaken about his direction as an artist.

Although Sonny has asserted that his style has developed "intuitively," he was certainly consciously attempting to bring jazz back to its black roots. He had been brought up in a household where he was instilled with a profound awareness of his black heritage. Sonny brought his experiences of the mean streets of Harlem into his playing; there was a cutting tension in his improvisation that was rarely heard in the playing of those in the cool jazz movement with the exception of a few, such as the starkly emotional alto saxophonist Art Pepper.

Sonny was not alone in attempting to take his music in this direction. During this period jazz musicians were much more closely knit than they are now; they were a tight subculture, with its own jargon, values, mores, and history, and they evolved together both as musicians and as human beings. It was a golden age, according to Sonny:

> We were really a brotherhood back then. It is gone now, but the reason why this was so back then was because there was a smaller, more intelligent audience; a much more insular audience, I would say. Everybody knew everybody else; everybody played the same clubs. It was just different. Now it is no longer a small group of people with a mission. Now there are a lot of guys playing, and some of them are pretty good, but then you played for

the love of it, and didn't expect to get anything. And we didn't get anything.

Many critics complained about Sonny's "harsh" tone and the lack of surface prettiness in his playing. He was accused of being an "angry" musician whose playing reflected his dark rage. To those attuned to Stan Getz's or Bill Perkins's cool melodicism, Sonny probably did sound coarse and strident. It would take a while for many jazz fans and writers to accustom themselves to his musical sensibility. Most did so eventually, and that sensibility, or at least variations of it, would dominate modern jazz from the mid-1950s on.

In 1957, with his career in high gear, Sonny married for the first time. His wife was a model, dancer, and actress named Dawn Finney. The marriage lasted only about a year; Sonny later explained, "I just wanted to get married. So I looked around and found somebody, and I did." Coincidentally, 1957 was also the year in which Sonny met Lucille Pearson, who remains his wife today. Earlier in his life, while he was a junkie and self-described "despicable person," marriage had been out of the question; for one thing, he was frequently homeless. He viewed marriage as another way of anchoring himself and creating a stable domestic life after so many years of chaos.

In 1957 Sonny was increasingly recognized as a major star in jazz by fans and critics alike. He was named the "New Star" tenor saxophonist in the *Down Beat* critics' poll and was increasingly looked upon as a bandleader in his own right.

Early in the year, Sonny traveled with the Roach group to California. This, his first trip to the West Coast, would turn out to be crucial for him and his musical direction. But he was initially taken aback by the ambiance of Los Angeles: "It was really a completely new experience for me. It was a tremendous culture shock going out there. Coming from the East, it is just very different in Hollywood."

Les Koenig, who owned the West Coast label Contemporary Records, had a broad appreciation for jazz other than the cool jazz he mainly recorded. For example, he recorded Ornette Coleman's first two albums. When he heard that Sonny was in California, he decided that it would be a great opportunity to record the tenorman with some of the best West Coast musicians.

I was approached by this guy Les Koenig, who was a very ethical guy. He ran Contemporary Records. I think he had been in the movie business but then he was blacklisted in the 1950s. He was one of the most honest record people I have ever known, just a really nice guy, a real honest guy.

Since this was his first visit to the West Coast, and since he'd grown up enthralled with "B" movies and serials, particularly Westerns, Sonny came up with the idea of giving the album a Western theme.

I loved the old cowboy movies I saw as a kid, Tom Mix and Ken Maynard and Hoot Gibson. They were never about shooting Indians or anything. There were always a lot of bad guys in those old movies but they were never extravaganzas about beating up the Indians. They used to call them two-reelers, and most of them didn't even have music. Just the sound of hoofs. I still love to watch those old films. I can't remember for certain, but I am pretty sure that the Western theme was my idea. And it was also my idea for the cover, in which I am dressed like a cowboy.

The album was titled, aptly enough, *Way Out West*, and the cover photo alone is worth the price. Sonny is in a Western setting with sagebush and cactus, dressed in cowboy clothing, holding his sax like a six-shooter. Among the tunes on the album are two songs associated with the West but never, never with jazz: "Wagon Wheels" and "I'm an Old Cowhound." The title tune was written by Sonny himself.

This may all sound like kitsch, like a typical gimmick album of little musical value; the actual results were amazingly enough, sublime. *Way Out West* is one of Sonny's greatest achievements in the studio, a constantly fascinating, timeless jazz album. Sonny associated the West with freedom and new frontiers, and this album was the first one he recorded with what he refers to as the classic trio. He had been thinking for a while of playing accompanied only by bass and drums, because without a pianist or guitarist comping for him, he would have an unprecedented freedom from the tyranny of harmonic structure. Although he had led trios early in his career, he had always used a chording instrument such as piano or guitar.

It is clear from such performances as the famous "Blue Seven," with its harmonic ambiguity and emphasis on thematic development, that he was becoming restless with the exigencies of rigid harmonic structure and was interested in exploring a new kind of melodic freedom. Playing with only bass and drums gave him an opportunity to take his music to places that had previously been out of reach.

The rhythm section consisted of probably the two best players on their instruments available on the West Coast—drummer Shelly Manne and bassist Ray Brown. Manne had played with virtually every important musician on the scene, from Coleman Hawkins and Charlie Parker to Ornette Coleman on his first album for Contemporary. Ray Brown had first gained fame playing in Dizzy Gillespie's 1950s big band, and at the time of this recording was with Oscar Peterson's trio. Sonny could not have chosen better players to support him in his first daring attempt to play in this format.

Sonny remembers that the session was unusual for more than one reason: "We recorded in some very strange place, and very late at night, after guys had been working other gigs."

Although all three musicians had been playing earlier that night, they had not been together. Manne had been performing with his own group; Brown had been playing with Peterson; and Sonny had been at a club with the Roach group. All three were already warmed up and still in the mood to play. Most recording sessions are held in the daytime, and musicians have to switch on their creative juices in the cold environment of the recording studio. This was especially troublesome for Sonny because of his strong feelings about recording jazz in general, and especially about playing in the artificial environment of the recording studio.

The album begins with Shelly Manne playing a clippety-clop like the sound of a horse's hooves (which undoubtedly reminded Sonny of the sound effects in the radio Westerns he listened to as a kid); when Sonny starts playing the melody of "I'm an Old Cowhound," it is almost impossible, at least at first listen, not to wince and wonder if this could possibly be as trite as it seems. But as the group begins to swing, and swing hard, such thoughts evaporate.

The most immediate impression is made by Sonny's tone. It is less gruff, more cellolike, with a new power that grabs the ear. His sound is now charismatic; his improvisation, once again, is basically thematic. The melody, or rather elements of the melody, are constantly in play. It is clear that this has became a prime method for shaping his improvisation with a sense of unifying order and logic while always creating "in the moment." The thematic organization of "I'm an Old Cowhund" is more complex than that of "Blue Seven," which proves that, whether intuitively or consciously, Sonny was working on further developing this aspect of his playing. But the highest praise for Sonny's playing on this track is that he completely dispels one's incredulity about the use of "I'm an Old Cowhand" as a jazz vehicle.

Sonny makes further use of thematic improvisation on an even less likely tune, "Wagon Wheels." This tune also opens with Shelly Manne's sound effects. "Wagon Wheels" is far less interesting melodically than "I'm an Old Cowhound," but the very simplicity of the tune makes it, at least for Sonny, perfect fodder for thematic development. Without the gravity of a chording instrument he is free to use melodic motives, rather than just the song's chords, to structure his solo. As in "Blue Seven," Sonny's thematic improvisation is *not* the same thing as the paraphrasing of melody associated with earlier eras in jazz. He does not just repeat the melody with embellishments; rather, he takes elements of the tune, deconstructs them, and then reconstructs them into a cohesive musical statement.

Sonny's playing on the album's ballad, "There Is No Greater Love," and especially on Duke Ellington's "Solitude" provides further evidence of his maturity. At this slow tempo, accompanied only by bass and drums, he creates a shimmering, beautifully worked-out improvisational statement. Without a piano to guide him and give him melodic "hints," improvising at this tempo is perhaps the most difficult kind of jazz improvisation.

The highlights of the album are "Come, Gone" and "Way Out West." The former is credited to Sonny, but it is actually themeless. According to Koenig's notes, after they felt their way through the first couple of tunes, all three musicians felt fired up to play (by this time it was probably five in the morning). That fever is particularly obvious on "Come, Gone." This up-tempo piece seems to summarize all the aspects of Sonny's latest direction in a display of fervent improvisation whose structural logic places his solos on the highest level of achievement.

"Way Out West" is even more fascinating. Played at a medium tempo, the tune has a slightly Monkish flavor, but Sonny's compositional style clearly has a personal and idiosyncratic as his improvisation (this seems obvious, since as we have seen, for Sonny, one is born out of the other). This is clearly the same composer who wrote "Oleo," "Doxy," and "Blue Seven." The master version of "Way Out West" is another example of thematic improvisation, far more complex than "Blue Seven." An alternative version of this tune has been released that is so different in its basic structure and direction it could almost be the work of another musician (of course, Sonny's tone is unmistakable). A comparison of these two takes makes clear Sonny's devotion to true creative spontaneity.

Listening to these solos, especially their rhythmic thrust, offers us the exhilarating illusion of riding a sonic roller coaster in which we are made to feel as if we are floating in air, gravity defeated. His use of tonal inflection gives his solos variety as well an earthy grit and a heartfelt soulfulness. This is one of Sonny's few studio albums in which one can clearly hear his "holistic" approach to improvisation, the ability to play in the moment a complete solo statement that is greater than the sum of its components.

A number of critics were beginning to notice the ramifications of Sonny's innovations. One of these critics was Whitney Balliett. Balliett had at first disliked Sonny's playing, especially his tone and gruff phrasing. But he, like many critics, gradually became aware of Sonny's expanding musical landscape. In a piece for the *New Yorker*, he wrote:

> Rollins fashions choruses that are—regardless of his persistently goatlike tone and his abrupt, cantankerous phrasing—a clear indication of a striving toward an improvisational approach that is revolutionary, for it is based on a remarkable use of polyrhythm and it wrestles continually with a new, elastic phrasing that completely reshapes the measure-by-measure chorus which Charlie Parker was the first to break down.

It is clear with *Way Out West* that Sonny was continuing to break away from bebop orthodoxy, attempting to reconceive a new modern jazz that fit the contours of his own personality in a manner not unlike Thelonious Monk's. Like Monk, he seemed to be improvising with musical orthodoxy as well as his solo itself when he played. It is not surprising, therefore, that Sonny was immediately intrigued by the work of two musicians he met in Los Angeles who would later set off the next jazz revolution.

Ornette Coleman was an alto saxophonist whose main career before he moved to Los Angeles was playing in various rhythm-and-blues bands in his native Texas. Coleman had been forging his own ideas in jazz that would eventually have an enormous effect on the music. He wanted to be able to freely improvise without the "gravity" of harmonic structure. He played music that came out of his deepest feelings, unfiltered through the prism of European harmony. His playing disturbed some and exhilarated others, but nobody could doubt his originality. He and his close colleague, the trumpeter Don Cherry, were consolidating their ideas and in 1958 would record their first album, aptly titled *Something Else*, for Les Koenig's Contemporary label.

Through other musicians, Sonny met Coleman and Cherry; he was immediately intrigued by their musical ideas. Sonny was drawn to Coleman's music because it was a direction that he had been going himself in the previous few years. Two years later Coleman and Cherry went to New York and shocked most of the jazz world, but not Sonny.

When Sonny was in California, he practiced with Ornette on the beach. Sonny recalls that because of the wind and the crash of the waves, the beach was a perfect challenge to their ability to create a strong sound. He also practiced separately with Cherry, who, a few years later, would play in Sonny's band. The acquaintance Sonny formed at this time with the two men's musical principles would have great significance after Coleman and Cherry came to New York and shocked the jazz world.

The experience of playing with just bass and drums on the *Way Out West* sessions was a revelation for Sonny. He had been groping toward a greater freedom and he now discovered that eschewing a chording instrument was useful in doing just that. Within a year or so, he produced his three most important recorded achievements, all of them now considered classics, without piano or guitar in accompaniment. On one track recorded in 1958, he played while accompanied only by drums.

It was becoming increasingly obvious to Sonny that his musical conception had become so idiosyncratic that he simply had to lead his own groups. He also realized that in order to develop in the increasingly expansive direction to which he was committed, he needed a group without other horns or a chording instrument. Although he has not played while accompanied by just bass and drums very much in recent years, he still believes that this kind of group is genuinely liberating:

With the right musicians, there really are no limitations playing with just bass and drums. There might be a piano player, like Wynton Kelly, who might play something [when he is comping] that would be very moving and very apt and inspiring. The one limitation of a piano-less trio is that sometimes a pianist might play something that is really quite helpful. But too often a pianist ends up limiting me. From the point of view of looking back on a long career playing jazz, I do believe that my playing with a bass-and-drums trio is more expansive. When I was playing mainly with a trio it really freed me up. However, playing in that format is very physically demanding and at my age it is easier to play with a pianist.

At a recent concert I was forced to play without my pianist because he was in Japan at the time. It was the first time I had played without a piano in a long time. It was really very liberating and I enjoyed it. I was kind of skeptical about it because I hadn't been feeling very well and also I was having some work done on my horn, experimental work. I was a little bit anxious about the job because we hadn't played lately. Anyway, there was no piano player and actually I am used to that. My whole history is playing *without* a piano. I think everybody played better. [Bassist] Bob Cranshaw had to step up and really play much, much better than he's been playing. You kind of get used to playing with a piano and you kind of just get in a kind of rut, but he had to really play like he used to play, and it was great. Playing without a piano gives me more of a chance to *be myself*. I never really had to play with a piano player. I mean, you don't want to be egotistical and I realize that jazz is supposed to be a collective thing. But you don't want to feel constricted.

Back in New York, Sonny made another unusual album, this time for Blue Note. Sonny's second album for the label was given the obvious (if not very imaginative) title *Sonny Rollins Volume Two*. It was something of a mixed bag. The rhythm section was one of the best that jazz could offer: the ubiquitous Paul Chambers, Miles Davis's favorite bassist for this period, Horace Silver (recording with Sonny for the first time since the

Miles Davis "Airegin" session three years earlier), and Art Blakey, who had last recorded with Sonny in an even earlier Miles Davis session, the "Dig" session of 1951. Also on hand was J. J. Johnson, who, years before, had been one of the first jazz musicians to hire Sonny for a recording.

The tracks with these musicians are fine enough, since these are some of the greatest of all modern jazzmen. The music is not particularly special, but two tracks are genuinely fascinating. On Thelonious Monk's ballad "Reflections," Monk himself replaces Silver; the continuing chemistry between Rollins and Monk makes the track riveting. Another Monk tune, the blues "Misterioso," is even more extraordinary. Monk and Silver both play on this track; Silver accompanies Johnson, but he is replaced by Monk when Sonny begins to solo; Monk then plays his own solo and takes the tune out. If it sounds confusing, it works out beautifully.

There are a number of similarities between Silver's style and Monk's. Both men are percussive pianists whose playing, although unequivocally modern, is based in the roots of jazz. Both of them have worked out styles for the piano that owe very little to the European pianistic tradition. But part of the power of this performance is created by the disparity between the two "teams": Johnson's and Silver's styles are closer to orthodox bebop. By this point, Sonny's playing is as sui generis as Monk's; both of them had created their own orthodoxies, their own insular musical worlds. Some of the greatest music created by either Sonny or Monk has been that of unaccompanied solo.

Monk, as always, seems to energize Sonny and make him reach for fresh ideas. Some jazz musicians have found Monk's comping at times eccentric and distracting. Nobody felt more strongly about this than Miles Davis. He expressed his views on Monk's comping quite vividly in a *Down Beat* "Blindfold Test." Leonard Feather invented this feature, in which records are played for a jazz musician who is not told the personnel or any information about the music. During this test, Feather played "The Way You Look Tonight" from the 1953 session in which Sonny was accompanied by Monk. It is a wonderful track, a true classic. But Miles did not agree:

I don't see how a record company can record something like that. You know the way Monk plays—he never gives any support to a rhythm section. When I had him on my date [the 1954 *Miles Davis and the Giants of Jazz* session], I had him lay out until the ensemble.

I like to hear him play, but I can't stand him in a rhythm section unless it's one of his own songs. . . . I can't understand a record like this.

The Rollins session Miles is discussing is beloved by many jazz fans and writers. Sonny himself has never found playing with Monk difficult:

Monk's comping never bothered me. As I have often said, Monk was my guru, so I would not even think about questioning Monk's comping. It didn't seem to bother me. I was a straight-ahead guy who knew what he wanted to do, and was trying to do it. So my playing was not dependent on anyone's comping. I wasn't playing with them so much as I was just playing by myself, in a manner of speaking. I think my playing was more in that vein than maybe Miles's was. I was just playing my music. I don't know if that is negative or positive, but that is the way I played.

Sonny's playing at this time makes it clear that he was consciously striving toward the new jazz that Whitney Balliett was referring to in his review of *Way Out West*. Sonny never thought of himself as creating a new jazz revolution. His own goal, as we have already noted, was to play the music closest to his inner, true self, creating music that was genuinely Sonny Rollins.

No longer was Sonny struggling for his very existence. He was now able to focus completely on developing his musical conception, to put all his concentration into expanding his musical vision:

Around this time, I was really working on my music. Before I went to a job at a club, I would form an idea of what I wanted to work on. I would be working on ideas and choosing songs with the idea of seeing what I could do with a particular tune. I would work toward getting into a certain mode of thinking and choosing tunes which would help me do that. Now when I do a concert, that *before* is a little bit different. I mean, I am not always thinking in those terms. But back then, I would get into something that I would try to work on that night. I don't mean that I would prearrange anything.

For example, I would work on a certain rhythmic pattern or some kind of tonal pattern that would develop as I tried to elaborate on it.

Sonny continued to record frequently. He played on *Jazz Contrasts*, led by Kenny Dorham, his colleague in Max Roach's quintet. Along with Roach, he recorded *It's Him*, led by Roach's then-wife, the singer Abbey Lincoln. He also recorded *The Sound of Sonny* under his own leadership for yet another small independent jazz label, Orrin Keepnews's Riverside. Like Blue Note, Riverside treated musicians with great respect. Keepnews ran virtually every aspect of the company and established close relationships with the musicians who recorded for him. He recorded many great and classic albums. Riverside was the first label to record Bill Evans as a leader, and it recorded what is considered by many as Thelonious Monk's best work. Keepnews vividly remembers his negotiations with Sonny:

> We offered Sonny a flat fee as an advance for two albums. And we told him that he would be given some royalties, too. But Sonny told us that he wanted just the flat fee. My partner and I told him that the royalties were in addition to the fee, that the fee would remain the same whether or not he was also given royalties. But Sonny insisted that he wanted only the flat fee. The reason, he told us, was that he looked on us as friends and, as he put it, "Sooner or later I am going to be suspicious that you are cheating me. And I do not want to feel that way about friends." That is the kind of thing that makes Sonny such a special person.

Although it was the only time Sonny recorded with the superlative pianist Sonny Clark, the *Sound of Sonny* album is fairly perfunctory, despite many marvelous moments. Once again, Rollins chose some out-of-the-ordinary tunes, such as "Mangoes" and yet another Jolson tune, "Toot Toot Tootsie." (I once suggested to Sonny that he record an album titled *Sonny Plays Jolson*; with his tongue firmly in his cheek, he said it was a great idea.) There is one significant track on this album: Sonny plays "It Could Happen to You" completely unaccompanied. He had been working toward this for a while, playing unaccompanied codas. Years later, concerts and albums by unaccompanied horn players, including Anthony

Braxton, Jan Garbarek, and Sonny himself, would become fairly routine. While Sonny was not the first jazz musician to record a piece unaccompanied—Coleman Hawkins had done it several years earlier—it was still a bold move. In addition, it gave credence to some of Martin Williams's contentions in a piece published in his collection *The Jazz Tradition*. In "Sonny Rollins—Spontaneous Orchestration," Williams writes:

> A great deal of extended soloing in jazz has had the air of an endurance feat—a player tries to keep going with as little repetition as possible. But when the ideas are original and are imaginatively handled, such playing can have virtues of its own. However, a hornman's best solos are apt to be continually developing linear inventions. Sonny Rollins has recorded long solos which in quality and approach go beyond good soloist's form and amount to spontaneous orchestration.[1]

Sonny is not unaware of this aspect of his playing:

> There are times when I feel like a one-man orchestra, where I had to be my own rhythm section and all the other parts of a band. When I play solo, completely by myself. I have had a few experiences playing like that—a few times on record and several other times when I was playing live or practicing by the oceanfront or places like that. I have developed a way of accompanying myself maybe to a higher degree than other players. About twenty years ago I was playing without accompaniment in Toronto and this bassist told me, "Sonny, you're the whole band. You play all the parts." So I am aware of what Martin Williams is talking about.

Sonny is a "holistic" improviser; he is able to approach a solo from several angles at once while creating spontaneously. By so doing, he forces musicians to address the most basic notions of jazz performance. Is it necessary to have a rhythm section whose primary function is to just keep time? Are solos just strings of melodic ideas in a particular harmonic structure? Is the accompaniment of a chording instrument really necessary? Does a piano or guitar aid the soloist or interfere with his melodic freedom?

A few months after "It Could Happen to You," Sonny recorded another unaccompanied solo, this time of "Body and Soul" (which Coleman

Hawkins had used both for his small-band masterpiece—which went a long way toward making him a jazz star—and also for his own unaccompanied solo). This unaccompanied solo is far more successful. Sonny clearly is more confident playing in this mode; he is far bolder. These early experiments were the precursors of Sonny's legendary solo concerts a decade later.

For the first few months of 1957, Sonny remained in Max Roach's band. Although he liked playing with Roach's group, it was no longer the tight, thrilling band it had been when Brownie and Sonny challenged each other to reach greater heights of virtuosity and Richie Powell was creating his perfectly suited arrangements for the group. The musicianship was still on the highest plane, but the spirit of the old band was gone.

Sonny's ideas and musical conception were growing increasingly idiosyncratic; it was clear from his own albums, especially *Saxophone Colossus*, that he was heading in a direction that would change the course of jazz itself. By the fall of 1957, it was obvious that he was ready to go on his own, and with Max Roach's blessing he finally did so. He had become the leading East Coast tenorman and one of the most admired musicians in jazz. His musical conception had become increasingly personal and he could no longer remain comfortably in somebody else's group.

As Sonny has pointed out, being a leader was nothing new for him:

Don't forget that I was leading my own band in high school. After that, I played around town in my own trios—usually piano, bass, and sax, or piano, drums, and sax, not the classic trio of sax, bass, and drums. So I already knew about being a leader and it was not a difficult leap for me.

Sonny decided to record a live performance as a way of launching his career as a leader. Alfred Lion agreed to record him, and Max Gordon agreed to hire Sonny for two weeks at his club, the Village Vanguard in Manhattan's Greenwich Village.

In 1957, the Village Vanguard was not exclusively a jazz club. The entertainment ranged from comedians such as Lenny Bruce and "Professor" Irwin Corey to folk groups such as the Kingston Trio to jazz acts like Miles Davis and Thelonious Monk. This recording would be a first. It was the first time any jazz musician recorded at the Vanguard.

Following Sonny's sessions, a number of classic albums were recorded there. Among the most famous sessions were those of Bill Evans, recorded with his trio just a couple of years later. Coltrane recorded at the Vanguard in 1961 and then again in 1966. Some of his best-known work was first recorded there: "Chasing the Trane," "India," and "Impressions."

Max Gordon had been aware of Sonny's work for a while; he was eager to have him perform at the Vanguard as a leader. The two-week engagement gave Sonny the time to put together a band he felt comfortable with. For the first several days he experimented with various combinations of musicians—a quintet, a quartet, and, finally, a trio like the one that recorded *Way Out West*.

Sonny chose the stripped-down sax, bass, and drums trio that gave him the greatest freedom, since freedom was what he was primarily seeking by going out on his own. Yet in many ways it was a daring decision, especially considering the kind of player Sonny is: a "pure" improviser, who relies on the inspiration of the moment. The best pianist accompanists, such as Wynton Kelly, John Lewis, and even Monk (in his angular way), could suggest ideas through their comping if Sonny suddenly hit a creative brick wall. Sonny's trio left him without other front-line soloists to take over if his imagination flagged. To play set after set accompanied only by bass and drums, especially for a player who eschewed easy licks and memorized solos, was a brave way to both launch his career as a leader and to record his first live album.

Even after Sonny had decided on the format and Blue Note was ready to begin recording, he was still uncertain about which musicians to use. His biggest problem, one that has plagued him throughout his career, was finding the right drummer. There was probably nobody equal to Max Roach. He needed a drummer whose playing well complemented his own increasingly polyrhythmic style.

The Vanguard had a matinee show on Sunday. Blue Note decided to record Sonny during both the matinee and the regular nighttime show and then choose the best performances for the album. Sonny selected the bassist Donald Bailey and the drummer Pete LaRoca. LaRoca (whose real name is Pete Sims) is a strong musician whose work was suggestive of the innovations of certain drummers who emerged in the 1960s, such as Tony Williams or Jack DeJohnette; Bailey was a fine enough bassist, if something of a journeyman. It was an excellent group, but even on the day of recording Sonny was not satisfied, so for the evening performance he hired Elvin Jones and the bassist Wilbur Ware. Didn't this game of musical chairs make Alfred Lion, who was producing the session, nervous? If so, Sonny could not be concerned. His obsession with his music overrode everything else:

> I wasn't worrying about Alfred Lion, I was worrying about the music. I had played with Elvin Jones and Wilbur Ware before. I did at least one job with Elvin and I had played with Wilbur back in Chicago. As I recall, I was trying to get them for the entire session but they did not arrive until after the matinee had ended. The real tightrope I had to walk across was trying to keep up the confidence of these other players [LaRoca and Bailey] and still tell them, "Well, look, I want somebody else to play on this one." As a leader, I had to be very diplomatic. But in those days I was not concerned with the niceties of life or refinements. I was just really trying to get a sound, a certain sound, and I didn't care about what I had to do to accomplish that. I used to hire guys and fire guys on the same night. I was pretty ruthless in that respect. Not that it was easy to do. I don't think I was really a "hard guy," or a guy who didn't care about other people's feelings; it wasn't that. But I really wanted to get a certain sound and sometimes I had to let a good guy go. Guys would come in to play and I would have to fire them. You read a lot of stories about that, Sonny Rollins anecdotes about me hiring and firing guys on the same night. But I had to do it.
>
> In retrospect, that was probably something I did not like doing, getting Elvin and Wilbur while these other guys were on the gig. But I had to do it, because I wanted to play with Elvin and Wilbur, and I wanted them on the record.

Sonny's ruthlessness is an indication of how fiercely he was committed to his musical vision, stubbornly doing whatever he had to do to achieve a certain sound. Sudden changes in personnel were an aspect of Sonny's career as a group leader for virtually its entire course. He had particular difficulty with drummers:

> Changing drummers so frequently is a challenge to me as a player because drummers are such a great influence in bringing out certain

areas of horn playing. Every time you have a new drummer it gives you a chance to get into something else. I do enjoy the challenge of a new drummer, the way he acts and speaks and his concept of rhythm and all of that. It proceeds into what I want to do and gives me new ideas.

A Night at the Village Vanguard ultimately included only one track with the Bailey-LaRoca trio, Dizzy Gillespie's "A Night in Tunisia." In the 1970s, Blue Note would release a twofer, *More from the Vanguard*, with another track by the Bailey-LaRoca group, Cole Porter's "I've Got You Under My Skin." (The entire session is now available on two CDs.) When one compares this and "Tunisia" with the music recorded with the Jones-Ware rhythm section, it is clear why Sonny preferred the latter. Elvin was not playing with the same power and polyrhythmic thunder that he would evince during his famous stint in the Coltrane quartet of the 1960s, but he was clearly working toward his mature style. He was now almost as ideal a drummer for Sonny as Max Roach had been.

Wilbur Ware had been playing in Thelonious Monk's quartet, which for several months of that year had included John Coltrane. He, too, was an suitable accompanist for Sonny. Ware's style, like that of LaRoca and Jones, prefigured the innovations for the bass that would occur in the 1960s. Ware's beautiful, deep tone made him a perfect accompanist but, like Charles Mingus, he was more than just a timekeeper. His melodic and harmonically inventive style was, like Sonny's own playing, a bridge between the jazz advances of of the 1940s. In the future, he would work with a number of key "New Thing" players such as Archie Shepp and Sun Ra.

Sonny was recently asked to choose the albums he believed to be his best out of the dozens he had recorded over a span of fifty years. He replied that he would have to choose *Saxophone Colossus* because so many fans and critics seem to think of it as special. But his own choice would be *A Night at the Village Vanguard*: "It came out pretty close to what I wanted to do." It should be no surprise, given Sonny's attitude toward playing at the recording studio, that a live album would be his favorite. He was to record live a number of times later in his career, and he still cites the Vanguard album as his personal favorite.

A sense of stubborn purpose is heard in the Vanguard recordings, as if Sonny is determined to shape his horn around his increasingly idiosyncratic musical vision. Perhaps that is why he names these recordings as his best: they are both a summing up of the gains he had made since his bop period, and the beginning of the musical journey he would take for the next forty years or so.

The repertoire heard on the Vanguard sessions includes a few of Sonny's own compositions, such as the up-tempo "Striver's Row"; classic jazz tunes—"A Night in Tunisia" and "Woody 'n' You"; pop songs, such as "Old Devil Moon" and "Softly As in a Morning Sunrise"; and the ballad "I Can't Get Started." This latter performance reinforced Sonny's reputation for being able to improvise at ballad tempo. This ballads were now even more effective because his tone had smoothed out and was now comparable to the tone of a great cellist like Pablo Casals. Despite the new smoothness of his tone, Sonny had not forfeited any of the power of his sound; if anything, it was more muscular than ever.

The most revealing track is the initial performance of one of Sonny's most popular tunes, the descending blues line "Sonnymoon for Two." Once again, he creates a complete and well-shaped musical statement through the continual use of a simple phrase abstracted from part of the melody itself. He begins by repeating this phrase several times with only slight alteration. As the solo proceeds, his playing gets more complex, but no matter how far he wanders from the phrase, he continually finds his way back to it. The solo is almost like an astronaut's space walk in which he floats farther and farther from the craft to which he is tethered. No matter how far he drifts, he always finds his way back. There is a very thin line between reiterating a phrase over and over with little embellishment, and using a single phrase to organize a complete and coherent musical statement. Once again, Sonny is the courageous tightrope walker, risking disaster once again and triumphing.

As good as the Vanguard album is, it is still not on the level of Sonny's best live performances. As Martin Williams pointed out in his essay on Rollins, "Even the 'live' Rollins can be a frustration. *A Night at the Village Vanguard* . . . is a fine example of generally high-level playing, but it does not have the brilliance of Rollins 'live' at his best."

Williams had been seeing Sonny perform quite often at the time of the Vanguard sessions, so he was aware of how good Sonny's playing then was. Here is further evidence that Sonny does not perform at his peak when he is being recorded, *even in a live situation.* He is not being perverse; of course he would love to play at his best no matter what the context. His belief in the transitory nature of jazz improvisation has been ingrained into his deepest musical instincts.

Jazz is essentially an existentialist art form, and that is one of the main reasons why it is so profoundly modern. A number of critics deride me for being pretentious and overstating my case, but I do not know any other way to describe Sonny Rollins's approach to his art and especially in the daring way he launched his career as a leader. His goal is to make music that reflects his identity as a person, and toward this end he has put himself on the line with the greatest risk a jazz musician can take: genuine improvisation, without nets. Accompanied only by bass and drums, Sonny puts himself squarely in the limelight with nobody to rescue him. It is the ultimate test for him, both as a musician and as a man.

Sonny did not choose this approach as a stunt. To him, it is a trade-off: by giving up the help of a chordal accompanist or another soloist, he gave himself the ultimate freedom. Sonny gladly made this trade-off because having the freedom to explore the "open sky" of music was the greatest joy of his life. Now that he had survived drug addiction through his own powerful will and had gained respect as a jazz player from both musicians and fans, it was time for him to fly.

Sonny was now "officially" a leader in his own right, but his next recording project was as a sideman. This was an opportunity he could not turn down, a group led by Dizzy Gillespie. In addition, on some of the tracks they would be joined by another great bopper, Sonny Stitt. Over a decade after being one of the chief architects of the bop revolution of the 1940s (along with Thelonious Monk and Charlie Parker, both of whom Sonny had recorded with), Dizzy was one of jazz's elder statesmen, but he had not given up his love of musical adventure. Although he coasted at times, performing the same tunes with similar solos and entertaining his audiences by singing bebop kitsch and comic routines, he still had the ability to blow virtually any other trumpeter off the stand when he was in the right mood. On this recording date, when Dizzy was challenged by both Stitt and Rollins, who came to play, his musicianship was among his best on record since the heyday of bebop.

For many listeners, the real fascination with this session was the contrast between the Sonnys. Stitt was a bop emissary whose style, on both alto and tenor, was similar to Charlie Parker (before he died, Bird told Stitt that he was giving him the "keys to the kingdom"). Dizzy used three configurations: he recorded separate sessions with both Rollins and Stitt and another session with both saxophonists. To listen to Rollins after a Stitt solo (or vice versa) makes plain how far Sonny had developed from orthodox bebop—in particular, rhythmically. Stitt is a classic bebopper, in a way even more than Dizzy, whose playing had evolved since the bop era. Stitt's rhythmic conception is a streamlined version of Charlie Parker's. We have already discussed Sonny's use of "sprung rhythm"; on this session, the unique nature of Sonny's rhythms is made crystal clear, since we can hear him right alongside two of the most important boppers. Rollins's elastic rhythmic conception, often implying polyrhythms, is a sharp contrast to the rhythms of Gillespie and especially Stitt.

The piece from these sessions that best illustrates the disparity between Sonny and the boppers is the Avery Parrish blues classic "After Hours." Played in a funky, slow, loping tempo, the tune tempts the soloists to let loose with every blues cliché ever known. But all of them (including the pianist, Ray Bryant, one of Sonny's favorites) play with imagination and emotional pungency, none more than Sonny Rollins. Actually, his playing is so emotionally powerful that a listener is almost embarrassed by his willingness to expose so much of his inner self. The raw emotions of Sonny's playing here, as well as his vocalized effects and speechlike phrasing, remind one of the great blues shouters, like Big Joe Turner and Bessie Smith. It is a remarkable and indelible performance.

Sonny was now in a position to just enjoy his status as a major jazz star; but, as we have seen, he had been brought up to believe that there is more to life than just professional success. He felt a need to do more than just reap the rewards due him.

Sonny was devoted to playing the best music that he could, but he had also begun thinking about using his talent for social change. His next major project reflected his thinking in this regard, but it would also make him an increasingly controversial figure in the jazz world.

8

The Freedom Suite

The recording session with Dizzy Gillespie was Sonny's last in the role of sideman, unless you count a brief appearance with the Modern Jazz Quartet at the Music Inn. He had become one of the most influential and respected of all modern jazz musicians, and his strong musical personality tended to overwhelm other players, although he never purposely tried to grab the spotlight. Sonny once jammed with Gerry Mulligan in a legendary concert that in earlier eras would have been called a "cutting contest," with each saxophonist trying to outdo the other in invention and swing. Mulligan tried his mightiest, but finally he shrugged and smiled—there was no way he could ever hope to top Sonny. Mulligan was one of the top names in jazz at the time, as well as an innovative and highly inventive player. His surrender was a special triumph for Sonny.

After his success at the Village Vanguard and the sessions he had recorded there, Sonny decided to keep leading a trio. He also decided that, now that he was on his own, he wanted to record an album that would make a social as well as musical statement. The need to do such a project had been on his mind for several years. Now, by recording *The Freedom Suite* for Orrin Keepnews's Riverside label, Sonny expressed an expanded commitment to social concerns.

In the 1960s albums with social overtones, particularly regarding the plight of African Americans, became almost commonplace. In 1960, Max Roach released the *Freedom Now Suite* (among the players on that album was Coleman Hawkins, who sounded as youthful and vital as ever). Archie Shepp would compose tunes about lynching and in other compositions alluded to Malcolm X; John Coltrane recorded "Alabama," dedicated to the memory of the four young girls killed in the 1963 Birmingham church bombing.

Sonny did not use his current trio for this project. Instead, he hired his compadre Max Roach and, on bass, Oscar Pettiford. These men were among the greatest players of their instruments; it is a mark of the high regard in which they held Sonny that these players were willing to be his sidemen. There was probably another reason why they were willing to play on this project—the boldness of the theme at the heart of *The Freedom Suite*. Sonny was insistent that the album's back cover include a message about the concerns central to the *Suite*. Sonny wrote the statement himself: "I remember that I worked so hard to make sure that my syntax was correct, and yet I wanted my feelings to be clear. I really sweated over writing it!" This is what it said:

> America is deeply rooted in Negro culture; its colloquialisms, its humor, its music. How ironic that the Negro, who more than any other people can claim America's culture as his own, is being persecuted and repressed, that the Negro, who has exemplified the humanities in his very existence, is being rewarded with inhumanity.

Today such a statement wouldn't raise an eyebrow unless it was made by Jesse Helms, Strom Thurmond, or David Duke. But in 1957, it was extraordinarily bold. Such talk seemed "uppity" to many white people, who ignored its truth and viewed it as a threat rather than what it really was, a plea. Sonny was well aware of the controversy the statement would produce. "I insisted that Orrin include those few sentences when the album was released. . . . After the album was put out, I received a lot of flack for it."

Probably no other label but Riverside would have touched a project like this, and Orrin Keepnews should be saluted for supporting it. In his liner notes, Keepnews pointed out that "freedom" in this context had more than one meaning:

In one sense . . . the reference [to freedom] is to the musical freedom of this unusual combination of composition and improvisation; in another it is to physical and moral freedom, to the presence or absence of it in Sonny's own life and the life of other Americans to whom he feels a relationship. This is not a piece *about* Emmett Till, or Little Rock, or Harlem or the peculiar election laws of Georgia or Louisiana, no more than it is *about* the artistic freedom of jazz. But it is about all these things, as they are observed by this musician and as they react—emotionally and intellectually—upon him.

Some accused Keepnews of watering down the album's message. But this was simply untrue; Keepnews fully backed Sonny's decision to include his statement on the back cover. As Sonny himself said, "I was just happy that he accepted *The Freedom Suite*."

The impact of Sonny's statement may be better understood if we remember the state of race relations in 1958. Earlier in the decade, Louis Armstrong had taken quite a bit of heat merely for saying that President Eisenhower should do more about integrating the schools in Little Rock, Arkansas. Lovable Louis was suddenly accused of being an angry black militant. In 1960, Miles Davis bluntly expressed his anger toward white racism in a *Playboy* interview (the very first *Playboy* interview), shocking some jazz fans who branded him an antiwhite racist. This was a ridiculous charge—Miles's first band, the *Birth of the Cool* nonet, was mostly white. Even in the early 1960s, the white British singer Petula Clark unleashed an outpouring of vitriol when she patted Harry Belafonte on the arm in a TV special.

Keepnews's notes may seem a watering down of Sonny's message at first glance, but to a degree that may be understandable. If you keep in mind incidents like the ones just described, the album note seems brave and even heroic. Sonny undoubtedly realized that he might anger some fans with his heartfelt sentiments, especially in a period when he was attempting to successfully launch his career as a leader. It is an indication of Sonny's strong feelings about social issues and his commitment to honesty regardless of the consequences. In the 1960s, many jazz musicians would be outspoken about America's racism; they expressed their anger in both their music and their public statements. The entire New Thing movement was assumed to be an expression of black power and militancy, which is one reason it scared off many white jazz fans. Long before that movement, jazz musicians were more knowledgeable and angry about racism than nonmusicians because they toured so much, visiting places that enforced legal segregation, and constantly experiencing the pain and sorrow caused by bigotry. They also knew that certain parts of the world were far more tolerant than America, even if racism was not entirely absent. The difference was that older musicians expressed these feelings only to each other and had not made clear to their audience their anger toward racism. Sonny was simply stating what many of his colleagues already believed.

Beyond its social import, *The Freedom Suite* is a significant musical accomplishment. It is a cohesive work, almost twenty minutes long, that ardently addresses the whole idea of freedom in musical terms. The three main sections are held together by a linking episode. The guiding structure of the piece—that is, the composition apart from the improvisation—is already familiar to us. As Orrin Keepnews explains in his notes:

> The *Suite* is built on a very simple musical basis: it consists, fundamentally, of a very simple melodic figure which is developed and improvised upon through several different phases. The difference between one of its separate sections and another may be a matter of tempo, or of rhythm or simply of mood. These differences are actually secondary to an overall feeling of unity of expression; the suite makes up a single complete whole.

Sonny uses thematic development once again, this time as a guiding logic for the parts of the *Suite*.

That *The Freedom Suite* is composed thematically is revealing, and paradoxical. Sonny used the same technique of thematic development to give cohesion to his improvised solos in such outstanding improvisations as those for "Wagon Wheels" on *Way Out West*, "Sonnymoon for Two" from the *Night at the Village Vanguard* sessions, and, most famously, "Blue Seven" from *Saxophone Colossus*.

There is a rather complicated process going on here. *Suite*—as a composition—uses a principle very similar to that of Sonny's improvised solo on "Blue Seven," and similar to his other solos that utilize thematic development. Sonny had to be consciously aware of the principles of thematic development in order to have written the *Suite*. He didn't compose this long, complex piece solely through intuition.

Ultimately the question concerning a programmatic piece with a theme like that of *The Freedom Suite* is whether it conveys the strong emotional jolt that Sonny intended, whether it makes us feel and comprehend what he is trying to tell us. I believe that it does. If one listens to the *Suite* without reading Sonny's note, it might be possible to hear the intense emotionality of the piece, but not to understand the source of those feelings. If one listens to the *Suite* after reading the note, its underlying intent becomes obvious. This is why Sonny insisted on including his note—*it is as much a part of this piece as the music itself*. The note does not stand alone and neither does the actual *Suite*.

Orrin Keepnews's note is something quite a bit more than just an attempt to smooth over Sonny's intent. *The Freedom Suite* displays the many layers of Sonny's genius, because it is a kind of musical pun. Programmatically, it is about African Americans' freedom, or rather lack of freedom. It is also very free musically. First of all, the trio format is inherently liberating, as Sonny has explained. Second, Max Roach's drumming, especially in the first section, is so free and abstract that he sounds more than a bit like one of the innovative drummers of the 1960s, such as Tony Williams or Andrew Cyrille.

This first section seesaws between two different meters, 4/4 and 3/4, and is almost as harmonically ambiguous as "Blue Seven." The section that links the three main parts of the piece (it is played, without improvisation, between the first and second piece and again between the second and third piece) includes an ominous, driving variation of the theme that gives the entire piece dark intensity. The second part is a ballad that begins mournfully and then seems to evolve into a somewhat brighter mood. The last piece is the freest of all the sections. A variation of the theme, played at a fast tempo, it develops as a series of "conversations" among the three players. Both Roach and Pettiford once again seem to prefigure the innovations of the advanced rhythm sections of the sixties, like Scott LaFaro and Paul Motian in the first Bill Evans trio, or Ron Carter and Tony Williams in the great Miles Davis quintet of that decade.

Sonny's solo in the third section is the most emotionally raw of his entire career up until this point. There is no doubt about the depth of his feelings regarding the theme of his *Suite*.

The Freedom Suite, besides its musical brilliance, was also innovative in treating modern jazz as program music. The real innovator of the jazz program suite was Duke Ellington, who wrote several suites, probably the most famous being *Black, Brown, and Beige Suite* in the early forties. He went on to write, along with Billy Strayhorn, a long series of suites, including the magnificent *Far Eastern Suite*. But *The Freedom Suite* was the first time a postbebop ("modern" would be the wrong word; Ellington was always "modern") jazz musician had attempted this kind of work. It would be followed by Max Roach's *Freedom Now Suite*, John Coltrane's *A Love Supreme*, Charles Mingus's *The Black Saint and the Sinner Lady*, and John Lewis's *The Comedy* (with the Modern Jazz Quartet). More recently, Wynton Marsalis created *Citi Movement* and *Blood on the Field* (which won the Pulitzer Prize), and George Russell composed his masterly *The African Game*.

The same group that recorded *The Freedom Suite* recorded other tunes for the second side of the original LP. Most of the cuts are short and the playing is not nearly as good as that on the *Suite*. The tunes largely seem to be throwaways, perfunctory at best. One has to wonder whether Sonny was deliberately pushing listeners to focus on the *Suite*. *The Freedom Suite* is certainly a highlight of Sonny's career, but the other pieces on the album made it increasingly clear to those following his career that, for Sonny, recording was a professional obligation; the studio was not a place of aesthetic epiphany.

Sonny discovered, not surprisingly, that his boldness had consequences.

After *The Freedom Suite* came out I got a lot of flack for it, especially when I went down South. I was traveling with a package group that included Maynard Ferguson's big band, the Dave Brubeck Quartet, the Four Freshmen, and my trio. We were traveling together in a bus and we played a number of places in the South. We didn't go into the deep South, like Mississippi or Georgia. We played Virginia and places in that area of the country. . . . Several fans, white fans, confronted me and wanted to know what I had meant in my comments that accompanied the album. Some of them were obviously upset. I felt pressure to rescind my statement, but of course I did not do that.

There was a fair amount of tension on that tour. A lot of things happened. All the other groups were led by white musicians, although there were a couple of black players in Maynard Ferguson's band, like trombonist Slide Hampton. And then there was the bassist with Brubeck's group, Gene Wright. I was friendly with a lot of the musicians on that tour, black and white. But a lot of the tension was caused by the fact that I was getting more praise than the other acts. What I was doing was revolutionary, playing in a bass, drums, and saxophone trio. We were playing things at breakneck tempos so that I was standing out, even [apart from] the fact that I was the only black leader. We were received in some places better than some of the other acts, and of course that added to the feeling of tension. It was that, added to *The Freedom Suite*. Someday I want to sit down and write about that tour because so many interesting things happened.

Despite the fallout from *The Freedom Suite*, Sonny would stubbornly continue to fuse his strong social concerns with his musical career. Within a few years, he once again sparked controversy, this time among African Americans as well as whites.

The next time Sonny recorded, he caused a very different kind of controversy. This recording was for yet another label: Verve. Verve pretty much reflected the taste of its founder, Norman Granz; it recorded little hard-bop-oriented jazz. Ella Fitzgerald, Ben Webster, and Stan Getz were among the staples of the label, and they made a number of classic albums for it.

The album Sonny recorded for Verve used three configurations. The first was the closest he had come, up until this point, to recording with a big band—he was backed by a brass ensemble arranged by Ernie Wilkins, one of Count Basie's favorite composers and arrangers. On the rest of the album he played with a trio, except for the solo version of "Body and Soul" that I have already mentioned. This last piece became the source of quite a bit of attention in the jazz world. Although Sonny had already recorded a solo piece ("It Could Happen to You" on *The Sound of Sonny*), either "Body and Soul" was far more successful or others simply slept on Sonny's first solo attempt, because the track gained a great deal of attention. As masterful as it was, it would be dwarfed by Sonny's later unaccompanied solos, many of them lengthy codas to pieces played by the full band. Some of these codas were far longer than the pieces they ended.

Sonny refers to this time as the golden age of jazz. It came to an end roughly around the time John Coltrane died, in 1967. It was an exciting time to be a jazz musician and there was great hope that the music would continue to evolve and win a larger audience. The success of the Newport Jazz Festival seemed to mark harvest time for jazz. One manifestation of this golden age was the establishment of the Music Inn in Concord, Massachusetts, a new kind of school for jazz, in which established musicians shared their wisdom with up-and-coming players.

For a while, Ornette Coleman and his colleague Don Cherry went to the Music Inn, supposedly as students. They wound up amazing some and unsettling others. Sonny was invited and he wound up sitting in with the Modern Jazz Quartet, with whom he had recorded a few years earlier. That session was not very notable, either for Sonny or the MJQ. The two sides he recorded at the Music Inn with the group were not much better, although they were live. No doubt part of the problem was that the MJQ's rhythm section—pianist John Lewis, bassist Percy Heath, and drummer Connie Kay (who had replaced Kenny Clarke in 1955)—while among the greats, was the wrong one for Sonny. He has always needed a strong drummer to complement his rhythmic conception; Connie Kay's subtlety made him an ideal drummer for a chamber jazz group such as the MJQ, but he was not the best drummer for Sonny.

Sonny's next recording project after *The Freedom Suite* was another album for Blue Note. This time, however, he used a traditional quartet rather than another trio. This was another sterling group: the bassist was Doug Watkins, who had been one of the original Jazz Messengers; Philly Joe Jones, who first recorded with Sonny on the 1955 Miles Davis session with Charlie Parker, was the drummer; and the pianist was Wynton Kelly, one of the few pianists whose accompaniment truly aided and inspired Sonny rather than distracting him.

Because of the superb rhythm section—an ideal one for Sonny (at least in the quartet format)—or simply because Sonny felt like playing, this is an especially brilliant and enjoyable album. The album's title, *Newk's Time*, refers to a nickname Miles Davis had given Sonny a couple of years earlier. Don Newcombe—"Newk"—was a pitcher for the Brooklyn Dodgers and one of the dominant hurlers of his time. Sonny bore a remarkable resemblance to Newcombe, and undoubtedly Miles considered Sonny as dominant in jazz as Newcombe was in baseball. In the tight little world of jazz, the nickname took hold, at least among those in the know.

Newk's Time is one of Sonny's best studio recordings of the 1950s. Although it is just a straight-ahead date, at times he is as inventive as on *Saxophone Colossus* and his playing shows how far he has advanced since that date, two years earlier. One of the cuts is Kenny Dorham's "Asiatic Rays," a lovely but tricky tune that Sonny handles with aplomb. As Joe Goldberg points out in his liner notes,

> [The] tune [has] a difficult structure and shifting rhythms which Sonny negotiates with ease. Most musicians use such rhythms only on the tune itself, going into a straight four for their improvisations. Sonny has the grace to improvise on the rhythms of the song.

He had already demonstrated his ease at playing with shifting rhythms, in the first section of *The Freedom Suite*. One of the pieces on *Newk's Time* joins the long list of unlikely tunes that Sonny turned into fine jazz vehicles: "Wonderful! Wonderful!," which had been a big hit for Johnny Mathis around the time this album was recorded. The song, previously associated mainly with swooning young women, works, surprisingly enough, as a valid jazz vehicle. Most jazzmen would not have touched it, but Sonny did not let snobbery get in the way of hearing the jazz potential of this melody regardless of the tune's pedigree.

The two most important cuts are, once again, demonstrations of Sonny's increasingly complex use of thematic development. The first of these is Rogers and Hammerstein's "The Surrey with the Fringe On Top" from *Oklahoma!*, first used as a jazz vehicle by Ahmad Jamal, then by Miles Davis's 1950s quintet. Sonny plays this tune for a duet with Philly Joe; Wynton Kelly and Doug Watkins lay out for the entire performance. As Sonny states and restates the tune, he pulls apart its melody, almost like a surgeon, almost reducing it to a series of sounds. But he never completely relinquishes the melody; it is a kaleidoscope of sound, turning crystals of notes that form a variety of new shapes. Without either chording by a pianist or the implication of chords by a bassist, Sonny is able to focus almost completely on the melodic, rather than harmonic, structure of this famous tune.

The second provocative piece is "Blues for Philly Joe." It belongs on the same list as "Blue Seven" and Sonny's performance of "Sonnymoon for Two" heard on the Vanguard sessions. That is, it is a blues line, which Sonny uses for thematic improvisation. These three blues are signposts indicating Sonny's increasingly complex and sophisticated conception and ability to create form as well as fresh melodic ideas.

In his essay on Sonny, Martin Williams brilliantly analyzes Sonny's solo. Williams states that in this piece "Rollins plays a kind of free, spontaneous blues rondo." Williams outlines the solo this way, using "A" to stand for the original melody and numerals to indicate variations on that theme:

A
A
AA-1
A-2
A-3
B
C
A-4
D
D-1
E(A-5?)
Wynton Kelly's piano solo
Exchange of four-bar phrases with drummer Philly Joe Jones
A(A-6?)
A

Williams points out several instances in the solo in which Sonny is able to give form and logic to this series of variations:

For example the new material Rollins introduces in A-1 appears again in variation A-2, thus tying these two choruses together.

Subsequently this double chorus idea is echoed in D and D-1 at approximately the middle of the piece and again at the end of the piece. A-3 is almost, but not quite, a nonthematic chorus; it is almost as if Rollins's strong departures from the theme were preparing our ears for B. . . . The two final saxophone choruses are thematic, but neither is an absolute restatement of the A theme, although the final chorus is closer.[1]

If reading Williams's analysis of this solo seems to indicate that Sonny's playing is more calculated than it might seem on the surface, it is important to note that Sonny's sense of structure is arrived at as intuitively as his sense of rhythm or melodic invention. There is no doubt that one of Sonny's missions was to bring to modern jazz a dedication to spontaneous improvisatory structure in addition to emotional pungency, speechlike phrasing, and sprung rhythm. Sonny has processed these concerns through his keen intuition, as he himself point out:

> You learn harmony and all that sort of stuff, and then push it to the back of your mind when you play because you have to be spontaneous. You just have to digest all that stuff so it will come up intuitively and spontaneously.

When Sonny recorded *The Freedom Suite* and "Blues for Philly Joe," other musicians were also working to expand the melodic freedom of jazz improvisation. In that same year, 1958, Miles Davis told Nat Hentoff:

> I think a movement in jazz is beginning away from the conventional string of chords, and an emphasis on melodic rather than harmonic variation. There will be fewer chords but infinite possibilities as to what to do with them. . . . The music has gotten thick. Guys give me tunes and they're full of chords. I can't play them.[2]

Despite their different approaches, both Miles and Sonny were dealing with the same problem in modern jazz. This should not be a surprise. As Sonny has already said, back then jazz musicians were a social and musical brotherhood, constantly sharing ideas and fresh discoveries.

That the move toward greater melodic, or horizontal, freedom came at the same time as the increasing insistence among African Americans on true freedom as American citizens is no coincidence. Freeing themselves from the dictates of harmonic structure had a special meaning beyond the purely musical: it pushed the music closer to its African and non-Western roots and further away from those elements which were essentially European. Part of this was a reaction to the cool jazz movement earlier in the decade, which consciously attempted to create jazz that was closer in some ways to European classical music. Many jazzmen wanted to explore more throughly the African roots of the music. And then there was simple restlessness among the more adventurous jazzmen to explore uncharted musical territory.

Miles's own solution was to use modes, or scales, rather than chords. He had first learned about the possibilities of modes from the brilliant composer and jazz theorist George Russell. Russell had used modes as far back as the 1940s, when he collaborated with Dizzy Gillespie on "Cubana Be, Cubana Bop." Russell spent years working out his theory, which he called the Lydian concept of tonal organization.

After learning the basic idea from Russell, Miles believed that he now had the answer to the problem of increasingly dense harmonic structure in modern jazz. In 1958 he recorded his first modal composition, "Milestones" (its title was eventually changed to "Miles," so as to prevent confusion with a different tune he had written in the 1940s with the same title). When Miles and Gil Evans collaborated on their version of *Porgy and Bess*, they used scales rather than chords on some of the tunes, most famously their version of "Summertime," a miracle of musical understatement. The following year, Miles recorded his modal masterpiece *Kind of Blue*. Jazz was going through another great period of change and Miles and Sonny were leading the way, taking separate, but parallel, paths.

Sonny returned to California in the fall of 1958, this time as a leader rather than as a sideman in Max Roach's group. He recorded for Lester Koenig's Contemporary label once again. Koenig assembled some of the best West Coast players to accompany him, hoping that he would produce another classic comparable to the magnificent *Way Out West*. It didn't turn out that way.

The group accompanying Sonny was fine enough: pianist Hampton Hawes, guitarist Barney Kessel, bassist Leroy Vinnegar, and, once again, Shelly Manne. Sonny's playing on the resulting disc, *Sonny Rollins and the Contemporary Leaders*, is probably as good as any other top tenorman's, but not on the high plane of *Way Out West*. However, there are a few notable things about this session. His tone is simply gorgeous, more cello-like than ever before. Earlier in his career, Sonny had been attacked for the coarseness of his tone, but at least with respect to this album, such criticism was not likely. Also, this was Sonny's last album before his second withdrawal from the scene, in 1959. Although *Contemporary Leaders* is an enjoyable enough album, for a perfectionist like Sonny, it was, perhaps, evidence that he needed to go back to the drawing board again.

The highlights of the set are its two versions of "I Want a New Baby," the original take and an alternate that was only released on the CD reissue. "I Want a New Baby" is a very old song, a favorite of Dixieland players. Modern jazzmen had rarely, if ever, covered it, but as usual Sonny turns it into a perfectly viable vehicle for modern jazz. On the master take, Sonny reduces his "thematic development" strategy to a single note. For almost an entire chorus, he just repeats a single note played in varying phrases and with varying rhythmic accentuation. At the end of the chorus, he dances away from the note only to return to it throughout the solo. He finishes the solo by using another single note in a manner not unlike the first section of the solo. This track is a wonderful example of Sonny's joy in musical play and of his sense of humor. His ability to use a single note as the essence of a convincing musical statement makes one believe that Mozart would have greatly appreciated Sonny Rollins's sheer joy in the act of creating music.

The alternate take of the song is completely different and it is useful just for illuminating what a pure improviser Sonny is. For many jazzmen, alternate takes usually involve a series of variations rather than completely different improvisation. In this alternate, Sonny does not use thematic development—indeed, he seems to be pushing hard at the harmonic perimeters of the tune. It is as close to "outside" improvising as anything Sonny would do on record in the 1950s and was a clear indication of the direction he would be going toward in the next decade. Since this was the last album he recorded before dropping out of the scene, this limited evidence of his direction is significant.

Sonny made his first tour of Europe in early 1959. It was an extensive one, including Denmark, Sweden, France, and England. He was the featured performer at Italy's San Remo Festival.

After this trip, Sonny regularly toured Europe. Unlike his old friends Kenny Drew and Act Taylor, as well as many other jazzmen, he never seriously entertained the idea of becoming an expatriate, despite his frequent disgust with many elements of American life.

> I have thought many times about leaving America. Almost every day! When I was in India I thought a lot about that, living someplace other than this country. I really like Denmark, and I have stayed for lengthy periods in London. I thought that I could be very compatible with the people there, but I never seriously thought about living there. I never really felt comfortable in other places that I have been to.

> Although I complain about this country, how would I go about moving somewhere else? Sure, if I lived in Africa I would be happy in that circumstance. But now I'm over here and I've gotten used to it, living in this technological society. It is hard to change back. I can't say it is something I couldn't do, but it is hard to rearrange all the mundane things that we deal with on a daily basis.

> So you get used to life here and you have so much in your life and you don't have the time needed to get the proper environment. You settle where you can.

Sonny recorded an entire set for a Danish radio broadcast—the only recording he sanctioned for 1959. His group was the trio with Pete LaRoca and Henry Grimes.

His choice of Grimes was significant. Henry Grimes was born in 1935 in Philadelphia. He studied bass at Juilliard and later played with a wide variety of jazz musicians, from Anita O'Day and Gerry Mulligan to Lennie Tristano. He first played with Sonny in 1957 and eventually became a member of Sonny's touring group along with Pete LaRoca. In the 1950s, Grimes became a favorite with the New Thing musicians of that decade; he would play with such revolutionaries as Cecil Taylor, Albert Ayler, Don Cherry, and Perry Robinson. He also recorded with his own trio on the ESP label. According to the *New Grove Dictionary of Jazz*: "His early bop style was powerful, raw and strongly percussive with a rocking rhythmic feeling." This made him a perfect bassist for Sonny.

A few years after the European tour with Sonny, Grimes became associated with the avant-garde. When Grimes began to regularly play with free-jazz musicians, his "conventional timekeeping usually gave way to drones, and unmetered countermelodies, played both pizzicato and arco," says the *New Grove*. Both Grimes and LaRoca were forward-looking jazzmen whose musical sensibilities would blossom in the radical jazz scene of the 1960s (LaRoca, though, never became as committed to the more extreme New Thing music as Grimes did).

The music he recorded during this period makes it obvious that the musical landscape Sonny had been exploring since the time of *Way Out West* and the Vanguard recordings was changing. Sonny was ready to move on. His break with bop was now almost complete—the bopper heard in, say, the Bud Powell recordings or his early recordings with J. J. Johnson and Miles Davis was now nearly gone. Sonny's melodic conception was becoming increasingly abstract, at times seemingly concerned with pure sound itself. As his playing became more fractured and unpredictable, he naturally gravitated toward other young musicians who were looking far into the horizon.

One of those musicians was his longtime friend John Coltrane. In 1959 Coltrane made two significant recordings that clearly showed he had become a master improviser. As a member of Miles Davis's sextet, he recorded the classic *Kind of Blue*; his solos throughout the album were so masterful that for many he seemed to dominate the session. He also recorded his own classic *Giant Steps*. It was obvious from these albums that Coltrane had finally arrived as a major jazz musician. One result, unfortunately, was the advent of a supposed rivalry between him and Sonny. Some fans and jazz critics insisted that Coltrane had taken over as jazz's most important tenor saxophonist. He soon started winning the polls and became one of the central jazzmen of the 1960s. The supposed rivalry was a hot topic in the jazz world, and for a short while it bothered Sonny; but, he says, it never interfered with their friendship:

> Coltrane and I never discussed it, never. We spent a lot of time together but we never discussed this. For a short time, these comparisons did bother me. Coltrane and I were friends for a long time and I think he had a lot of respect for me and vice versa. We *loved* each other. We used to hang out and practice together and we were very close. But I have to admit that for a while I was immature enough to let the press, the PR build-up of the so-called rivalry, affect me. They do not have polls in other art forms. There was no poll about whether Picasso was "greater" than Kandinsky. It is very hard to have that kind of sane observation in a very competitive business. In the jazz world, everybody is scrambling for crumbs, so to speak. A big write-up in *Down Beat* or *Metronome* or something could mean that you would be able to get a lot of work. Now, today, I am beyond this kind of stuff. But for a while, I have to admit, I bought into this idea that Coltrane and I were rivals. I did think that way for a short while. I emphasize "short" because I kind of realized that it was a big trick.
>
> It would have been a shame to have admitted that I was thinking that way to Coltrane. Because, really, I think we were so far beyond that as buddies and serious musicians. I hope I never betrayed those feelings to him. I don't think I did. . . . Some musicians would try and sustain these kinds of rivalries. This guy once came up to me and asked me, "Who is the greatest saxophonist around?" I said, "Coleman Hawkins." He said, "Oh, no. Lester Young." This is such a sophomoric, adolescent approach to art. So for a short period, yes, I was affected by this so-called rivalry. But then I realized, "Wait a second. What am I doing? This is Coltrane! We are too tight for this!" You know, whenever we were asked who our favorite tenorman was, Coltrane would say me and I would name him. That is how we felt about each other as musicians.
>
> This is one of the worst parts of the system, this artificial competition, which goes along with greed and consumerism. These things are rewarded in our society, so it should be no surprise to find it in jazz, this American art form.

Sonny continued to tour, going to California in the spring of 1959. Despite his growing popularity, he was growing increasingly restless, and he worried that he still was not playing on the high level he was trying to reach. He was about to make a drastic decision that would surprise, if not shock, most of those in the world-within-a-world of jazz.

9

The Bridge

In 1959, two musicians whom Sonny Rollins had met during his first visit to California, Ornette Coleman and Don Cherry, began a lengthy stand at the Five Spot club in New York's East Village. They caused a sensation. Ornette, the group's leader, played a plastic alto saxophone; his partner, Don Cherry, used a small "pocket" trumpet. But their instruments were not what caused the ruckus. Their music was "free" in that it mostly ignored harmonic structure and was, for the most part, totally "horizontal," or melodic. Coleman did not shy away from any effects he could produce with his horn, including vocalized effects not dissimilar to those used by Sonny. So here, at the inception of the 1960s, the gates of freedom seemed ready to open—at least for jazz. A number of musicians, including Charles Mingus, Miles Davis, George Russell, and, of course, Sonny Rollins, had been attempting to give jazz improvisation greater melodic freedom. They all had been uneasy with the strictures of European harmony that most musicians continued to adhere to in the late 1950s. Those doors were now being flung open by Coleman and Cherry. Jazz would never be the same.

Coleman was not the first jazz musician to attempt to break out of the harmonic box. In the late 1940s, Lennie Tristano recorded the first truly "free" jazz, having his band improvise with neither harmonic nor any other formal structure. Later in the 1950s, Charles Mingus, Jimmy Giuffre, and others attempted atonal jazz (Leonard Feather, for example, wrote "Twelve Tone Blues"). These experiments, while interesting, were nevertheless singular; they didn't open fresh new frontiers. Ornette's free jazz was different; it grew organically out of the jazz tradition. His playing was clearly imbued with the deep blues of his Texas background. Unlike the earlier experiments, his work never seemed self-conscious or anything other than sincere musical expression. In its own way, it swung hard. This music was too stunning and emotionally powerful to be ignored.

Not surprisingly, the Coleman-Cherry group was a pianoless quartet—two horns plus bass (Charlie Haden) and drums (Billy Higgins). The Gerry Mulligan pianoless quartet of the early 1950s was clearly an influence. At least as important were Sonny's trios. Sonny seemed to be on a parallel course with Ornette's developing ideas.

Musicians, fans, and critics flocked to the Five Spot, trying to decide whether this was the most revolutionary jazz since bebop or just a musical fraud. Forward-looking musicians such as John Coltrane and the reedman Eric Dolphy, who had also come East recently, were fascinated. Many wondered if Ornette's music was indicative, to use the title of one of his albums, of a "change of century," or just musical chaos. While many musicians and fans disdained Coleman's music, an increasingly large number believed it was a major new advance for jazz.

Coleman's stand at the Five Spot, for all intents and purposes, ushered in the free jazz era. This revolution in jazz reflected what was occurring in American society, especially for African Americans, just as bebop had. The cries of "Freedom now!" could have applied not only to the civil rights movement but also to this latest evolution in black American music. Jazz musicians were increasingly rejecting the most European element of jazz: "Let's just play the music," insisted Ornette Coleman, by which he meant playing melodically, without being tyrannized by harmonic structure. Already Sonny had made this connection between musical and social freedom in *The Freedom Suite*.

For Sonny, Ornette's stand at the Five Spot brought in a needed freshness to a jazz scene that was beginning to get stale:

> I remember one night going to see Ornette when he first came to New York and was playing at the Five Spot. After catching him and

his group, I went to the Jazz Gallery [a now defunct club] and the group over there sounded so hackneyed after hearing Ornette. The music had no real life. I guess that is what the people wanted and it was what musicians were supposed to do, ad infinitum.

In some ways Sonny viewed Ornette's music as a vindication of the musical direction he had been taking for a number of years. Coleman took devices Sonny used, such as speechlike effects, vocalized cries and wails, and tonal distortion, to far greater extremes; he often employed squeals and screams. This technique, called multiphonics, would become even more important to many of the post-Coleman saxophonists, such as Albert Ayler and Pharoah Sanders, as well as to the later playing of John Coltrane. In addition, Ornette's melodic invention was often at least as abstract as Sonny's; and, like Sonny, he had a sense of rhythm and time that was elastic and unpredictable. The most important component of Sonny's playing that influenced Coleman and his generation of free jazzmen was the unyielding, often coarse truth of his playing, and its raw, unsettling beauty. This is not to say that Sonny's music, or Ornette's, was simply "angry" or "filled with rage," although many critics and fans understood it that way (the reaction was even stronger to the 1960s music of Coltrane and most of the players of the New Thing movement). But, like the work of previous generations of jazzmen, Sonny and Ornette's music did reflect the worldview of a specific generation of African Americans.

The great splash made by Ornette, and his vindication of Sonny's ideas, were seemingly a good thing for Sonny and his career. Yet in 1959 he withdrew from the jazz scene. This time it was not because of personal problems; his private life had never been better. His new marriage, to Lucille, was a good one. But Sonny felt that he had work to do.

Basically what was happening back then was that I was getting a lot of good press, and the jazz press had finally accepted me, to a large degree. I had not been accepted by them for a long time. Then I began to make some records that they liked and they started to say, "Okay, Sonny Rollins is good after all." The problem was that I really wasn't good enough for myself. I was getting a lot of engagements where I was top-billed and people were beginning to expect a lot from me that I felt I couldn't deliver.

One particular job I remember was in Baltimore. Elvin Jones was with me and I picked up a bassist and piano player, or whatever we were using at the time. There were a lot of people there, a lot of jazz fans to whom the name "Sonny Rollins" evidently meant a lot. However, I didn't really play. The job wasn't very good. I just didn't feel confident in what I was doing. I felt that my name was bigger than my talent at that time. So the feeling of that, of being on a high pedestal, and not feeling you could do it, and disappointing the people, that was enough to make me realize, "Well, I'm going to get away and get myself straight." There were certain things that I wanted to work on, certain things I wanted to do that I wasn't able to concentrate on and nail down because I was working, trying to gig and all this stuff. So that is basically why I did it. I said, "Well, I'm going to do it," and I stopped playing for a while.

Sonny also wished to address certain aspects of his lifestyle:

After I got off drugs, I wanted to improve myself both physically and spiritually. I wanted to get away from all the detrimental things in the life of a jazz musician, such as cigarettes, drugs, and alcohol. I wanted to be healthy and play music and not be a guy who is playing music and all messed up. I took up bodybuilding and I tried to eradicate some of [my bad] habits. . . .

Like both Miles Davis and Coltrane, Sonny found smoking the most difficult habit to break free of. "That was a hard one. The tobacco hung on. I finally kicked it but it hung on for a while and it took me a while to do it. I did all these things to build up my health and just to try to be the perfect man." Sonny had expressed his desire to step away from the scene for these reasons as far back as 1956. He was even more specific in a 1958 interview:

Right now, I just want to get away for a while. I think I need a lot of things. One of them is time . . . time to study and finish some things I started a long time ago. . . . I never seem to have time to work, study, and write. Everything becomes secondary to going to work every night and wondering how the band sounds and whether our appearances are okay.

Many fans were startled by Sonny's withdrawal from the scene. He had reached the highest level of respect and recognition by this time; why was he not simply enjoying his success? Those who wondered did not know Sonny, did not understand his virtually religious devotion to playing music. Success was secondary.

Sonny and Lucille were living in a flat in lower Manhattan, not far from the river. Sonny's only income was "meager royalty checks that I got from time to time." Lucille was working to support the two of them, giving Sonny the freedom to do the hard musical work he felt was necessary. It was crucial for him to be able to practice any time of the day or night, not a considerate thing to do in an apartment building. Also, they were living next door to a pregnant woman; as sensitive as always, he especially did not want to bother her. He needed a place where he could practice regularly whenever he wanted to. He finally found the perfect rehearsal studio.

> I just happened to be on Delancey Street one day and I looked up and saw these steps going up to the Williamsburg Bridge [which connects Manhattan and Brooklyn]. So I walked up the steps and here was this big empty space and nobody there. So I walked across the bridge and I said to myself, "Wow! I can come up here and practice. There's nobody here!" Very few people were walking across the bridge, even when I began going out there regularly. A few people used to go across as if for exercise, but not many.
>
> It was a beautiful, perfect place. I had the view of the river and all the boats going back and forth and I was able to be on a part of the walkway where I wasn't visible to the subway trains and traffic which were crossing. I felt like it was God-sent. So I said, "Wow! This is it!" So I went. I could blow as loud as I wanted. It was exactly what I wanted.
>
> I brought a few musicians up there just to show them the spot. [Soprano saxophonist] Steve Lacy came up there. I think Jackie [McLean]. Nobody went up there a lot, but it became my studio.

Steve Lacy, like Sonny, had played with and learned from Thelonious Monk. He had long admired Sonny as a player; once he got to know him as a person, he became deeply respectful of him as a man, too. Joe Goldberg asked Lacy about practicing on the bridge:

We do practice on a bridge. It is not the Brooklyn Bridge, but I'd rather not say which one because it is such a wonderful rehearsal spot, everyone would like to go there. . . . There are two levels—a pedestrian level and an automobile level—and you can stand there late at night and look at the skyline and watch the tugboats going by, and no one bothers you. It is very hard to get a sound there, with the wind whipping by, so if you can play there, it would be the simplest thing in the world to play at a club. We don't have any particular material that we're rehearsing, just whatever comes to mind. We're just trying to find out about ourselves musically. We practice fingering, intonation, scales, intervals, everything. I've never seen anyone as in love with the tenor saxophone as Sonny is. He's the best player of that instrument I've ever seen.[1]

As usual, the jazz scene was soon rife with rumors about why Sonny had withdrawn from it. In 1962, when he had been away for two years, Blue Note's Alfred Lion said: "I think that Sonny's working on a new style. I think he was worried about some of the young tenor players coming up, but he better come back soon because people forget fast in this business." Was Sonny concerned specifically about John Coltrane's rapid ascent?

That sort of thing was not what was concerning me when I withdrew from the jazz scene back then. It certainly was not in front of my mind. I always have to rethink things, but no, that wasn't it. My battle has always been with myself, trying to get things better, trying to get myself better. It has always been me trying to improve myself for my own reasons.

Shortly after returning to the scene, Sonny told Whitney Balliett: "When I quit working, I tried to revise the way I played the horn. Completely. Then I amended that. Instead, I have made an exploration of the horn." Later, looking back on his "bridge period," Sonny said:

I did not go on the bridge to change my style. That's not why I went on the bridge. I went on the bridge to build up some of my rudimentary things. I realize that that is what many people expected: "Oh, well, he went away—he must be coming back with a new style." It had nothing to do with that. I went to practice the rudiments on my instruments—to get more proficient on my instrument, that sort of thing. I was also taking some composition lessons, and all of this stuff was why I went on the bridge. So when I came back, some people might have said, "Gee, he didn't change his style after all." They wouldn't see why I went on the bridge, which would be understandable, because there would be no reason for them to see it. But there *was* a reason for me. I had more confidence in what I was doing, and I felt better about my own rudimentary playing—technique and all of these things. That's why I went on the bridge.

Meanwhile, the jazz scene was changing rapidly. John Coltrane had left Miles Davis's group in 1960 and formed his own quartet, one of the great jazz groups of that era or any other. Coltrane had also begun experimenting with a second horn, the soprano saxophone. At one of the first recording sessions with his new group he had played on soprano a version of "My Favorite Things" that was a lot closer to the ragas of India than to the Trapp Family Singers. It caused a sensation and made Coltrane a jazz superstar. The comparisons between him and Rollins now became even more ubiquitous.

In late 1961, after two years of intense work, Sonny decided it was time to return to the scene. He felt that he was playing with more confidence. In addition, he felt more certain of his direction, with respect to both his technical mastery of his horn, and his musical direction as a player and composer.

Alfred Lion's fear that Sonny would be "forgotten" if he stayed away too long turned out to be unfounded. If anything, Sonny's withdrawal from the scene had added to his renown and increased the public's interest in him. There had been published a story about his practicing on the bridge, and by now it had become a jazz legend. His return excited people.

Sonny had had plenty of time to think about what kind of group he wanted. He put together a quartet, instead of the trios he had been playing with for most of the late 1950s. The bassist was Bob Cranshaw, who had played in one of Sonny's trios a few years earlier. Cranshaw would become a favorite Rollins sideman for decades, playing in various groups with him right up until the present.

Cranshaw, who was two years younger than Sonny, was born in Evanston, Illinois, and first gained notice playing in the Chicago jazz scene. He came to New York in 1960, where he joined a band called MJT+3 until he hooked up with Sonny and through him gained notice as one of the better young bassists on the scene.

The drummer for Sonny's new group was either H. T. Saunders or Ben Riley (as usual, Sonny had a hard time finding the right drummer).

As the fourth member of the quartet, Sonny decided to use a guitar player—a great one: Jim Hall.

Many in the jazz world were surprised that Sonny had chosen Hall; some even questioned his choice because Jim Hall was white. Sonny described his reasons:

> Number one, because I wanted a more airy sound. I wanted a little more freedom. A piano can be constricting. That's why I wanted a guitar, because I felt that a guitar was not as constricting as a piano.
>
> I had met Jim a couple of times before, when I was on the West Coast and he was with Chico Hamilton. Then I saw him in New York with Jimmy Giuffre. I admired him and he was no slouch musician, you know. I thought he was a good, good musician. I love Jim Hall.

Hall had been born in the same year as Sonny, 1930, in Buffalo, New York. He moved to Los Angeles early on and became associated with the West Coast jazz scene. He first gained fame for playing in Chico Hamilton's chamber jazz quintet and a little later joined another chamber jazz group, the wonderful Jimmy Giuffre Three (which for a while consisted of Giuffre's reeds, Bob Brookmeyer on trombone, and Hall—no rhythm section). His résumé made Hall a surprising choice for playing with Sonny, at least at first glance. But this view was merely an attempt by writers, and some fans, to put musicians and music into pat categories.

Sonny's choice of Hall made a lot of musical sense. Hall's trademark is his rounded, luminous tone, which makes his playing instantly recognizable. At its best, his playing is lean, subtle, sinuously lyrical, full of nuance and quiet charm, almost always inventive, and emotionally profound. If this sounds as if his playing was a great contrast to Sonny's bravura tenor, it was. Many jazz groups have included this kind of contrast; think of Miles Davis's reticent sparseness and angular lyricism, and John Coltrane's wailing outpour of notes. Miles understood the power of such a pairing, having offered a similar contrast to Bird when he was in Parker's quintet during the 1940s.

Hall had admired Sonny for a long time and jumped at the chance to play with the tenorman:

> I first met Sonny at a jam session with Clifford Brown and Richie Powell. They helped carry in my equipment from the taxicab. I loved the [Brown-Roach] group. I knew Sonny a bit. I didn't understand what a great player he was, although I remember liking his playing a lot. Actually, I always preferred his playing to that of John Coltrane. I thought it had more components to it. And as much as I admire John Coltrane, there was always something slightly one-dimensional about his playing. And I especially loved Sonny's sense of humor.

Hall was surprised to learn that Sonny wanted to hire him:

> I had been working with Jimmy Giuffre when John Lewis called me while I was in California and told me to come to New York, that there were a lot of things for me to do there. So I sublet [pianist] Dick Katz's apartment in the Village. One day I got a handwritten note in my mailbox saying, "Dear Jim, I want to talk to you about music," and it was signed by Sonny Rollins. That was typical Sonny Rollins.
>
> So eventually we made an appointment. When Sonny came over to my apartment, he was carrying a little plastic bag, which he put down on the table. So we sat down facing each other and he started talking to me. And he was offering me a job with his quartet. And then the bag started to kind of wiggle. So I said, "Sonny, what's in the bag?" He said, "We'll talk about that later."
>
> I thought about it later—this guy had offered me probably the most important job of my life, and he is so incredibly dignified and gifted, and his bag is wiggling away. After he offered me the job, he

opened the bag and smiled; there was a lizard or chameleon in it. "Look at this!" he said. "Isn't it great?"

After he had joined the group, Jim Hall's respect for Sonny as a musician grew even deeper. He found playing with Sonny a challenge:

> I was discovering every night just how great a player he is and then I had to play a solo after his. So it was kind of frightening. It really got my attention. I was practicing a lot back then. Boy, I was practicing a lot. I was also working on a John Coltrane type of thing, on the guitar, the kind of arpeggiated things that Coltrane would do.
>
> We did rehearse a lot, but as I recall, the rehearsal had more to do with getting sensitized to one another than anything else, because he's liable to do anything on the bandstand. It had nothing to do with what we rehearsed, although we did have a few things that we were supposed to do together.
>
> Boy, there was always lots of surprises on the bandstand, which was part of the charm of it. For example, we would be in the middle of a tune, romping along, and then suddenly he would be playing and somehow brought us to completely stop, just by the strength of his playing. He was such a strong player that he could stop us like stopping a freight train, just by playing something. Then he would play alone for a while and then he would bring us back in, maybe at a different tempo. So that was a big influence on me, all that stuff.
>
> I played at the Apollo with Sonny and it was great fun. We in the rhythm section would start off playing onstage and then Sonny would come stalking out from the wings and everybody would go crazy. We would milk that a little bit. And the audience would get on me, which was flattering, and Sonny would be standing in front of me sometimes, saying, "Don't let them get you." But that audience would get on everybody.

Sonny hired Jim Hall for reasons beyond his musical ability:

> I wanted to have an integrated band. I definitely wanted to make a statement by having an integrated band. I took a lot of flack for it, a lot of flack. There was one well-known black writer who gave me a

lot of grief for hiring Jim. For a long time I couldn't understand it. But then I looked back and said, "These guys feel that since I did *The Freedom Suite* I would feel the way that they did about this stuff. Before that I wrote "Airegin." And I played "The House I Live In" and the Negro National Anthem at the end of it. This was very race-conscious stuff! So I guess the militant end of the black community–jazz community felt betrayed by me. I couldn't understand this. You know, Miles's first band was made up almost completely with white guys! Miles was always hiring white guys—Bill Evans, Lee Konitz, Gil Evans. So at first I was really befuddled about why they would come down on me. I figured they thought I was even more of a black nationalist than these other guys, like Miles. But you cannot say that it is all right to be a racist as long as it's against white people.

Despite the flack that Sonny received, this quartet was a superb unit. The contrast between Hall's lyrical guitar and Sonny's speechlike phrasing gave the group a sound all of its own. Hall was able to keep pace with Sonny even at the fastest of tempos (although he does not like playing very fast), and he was sensitive enough to stay constantly tuned to Sonny's wavelength no matter what new corner Sonny turned. Sonny was experimenting with chugging tempos, or at times playing completely out of tempo as a group and then at the right moment once again playing with the original tempo. Doing this virtually required his sidemen to have ESP in order to anticipate his every spontaneous move. This type of playing indicates the direction of Sonny's music—toward a freer conception, in terms of both the group and his own playing.

Sonny's withdrawal from the scene and the mystique that had arisen concerning his lonely jaunts on the Williamsburg Bridge gave rise to a great deal of interest when he finally returned. Sonny now found himself in demand by several record labels. The best offer was from RCA Victor. For the first time, Sonny was signed to a major label rather than an independent. He was given an advance of approximately $90,000, which even today is extraordinary for a jazzman. It was not just the large advance that made the deal with RCA so attractive: a major company could both back more costly projects and market albums far more successfully than an independent jazz label such as

Blue Note or Riverside. But there were aspects of the deal that made Sonny uncomfortable:

> After they signed me, RCA didn't know what to do with me. Part of the reason they signed me was because of the bridge and the romantic legend, and that was about it. It was a tremendous thing for these guys in the business: "We can really use this and use this guy. Wow, he's going to make some money for us!"

Much to his credit, Sonny did not deviate from his musical agenda, despite RCA's commercial concerns; in fact, he now entered the most avant-garde period of his entire career. Much of the music Sonny recorded for RCA was hardly the stuff of radio play and mass consumption.

In January 1962, Sonny made his first album since *Sonny Rollins and the Contemporary Leaders* in 1958. Titled, naturally, *The Bridge*, it was the most traditional of all his RCA albums, a straight-ahead date with his new group. Although many consider it a great album, it does not compare to what he was playing in live performance with this group, according to those who heard him play then.

The Bridge clearly exhibits the fruits of Sonny's work during his years of withdrawal. He sounds far more confident and certain of his direction than on his previous album, *Contemporary Leaders*, and his tonal shadings are far more developed. As Loren Schoenberg wrote in the notes for *The Complete Sonny Rollins RCA Victor Recordings*: "With the slightest variance of pitch and timbre, he can make a 180° turn on a dime."[2]

Sonny's rhythmic conception had advanced, too, during his time "on the bridge." His new rhythmic mastery is most obvious on the album's two up-tempo pieces, both of which he composed: "The Bridge" and "John S." This last tune is not named after the *New York Times* jazz critic of that time, John S. Wilson, as many have thought. "I used that title because a guy came to me and wanted me to give him lessons. I told him that he should ask Coltrane instead because his approach to playing was much more conventional than mine. So I was thinking about him and me and this was my private code—'John S.,' John and Sonny."

In comparing these fast-tempo pieces with similar ones from the 1956 *Tour de Force*, such as "B. Quick" or "B. Swift," Sonny's rhythmic advances are quite apparent. On the earlier pieces, his ideas are fragmented and thin. Sonny was simply trying to play ridiculously fast, not even attempting the kind of cohesive musical statement he was able to create at medium or slow tempos. His mastery on *The Bridge* was due to the musical sprung rhythm that he had been working toward for a long time and apparently achieved during his absence from the scene. On *The Bridge*'s fast pieces, Sonny does not seem to be holding on for dear life; he is in full command, improvising with the same sense of logic, design, and melodic inventiveness as at less sizzling tempos. From here on, Sonny's playing at up-tempos brings to mind a man standing on a surfboard, riding a huge, fast-rushing wave. Despite the watery onslaught, he remains standing and triumphant, conquering the forces of nature.

The most emotionally profound piece on *The Bridge* is Sonny's version of the Billie Holiday classic "God Bless the Child." Sonny had known Holiday, who died in 1959, the same year as his withdrawal from the scene, and he never forgot her:

I was thinking about her the other night, 'cause I was in a cab with her one time, and when the cab stopped short, she almost fell out of her seat. This was not too long before she died. I tried to know her because I was really in love with her, just as a person. I was more of a fan than anything. She gave me her book [her autobiography, *Lady Sings the Blues*] and she autographed it. I befriended her and she let me accompany her home. It was wonderful to know that Billie Holiday could trust me.

Sonny is disgusted by the Diana Ross film about Holiday: "It was a travesty. Diana Ross didn't have the breadth to play her. That is why I have never seen any films made about people I have known, like the Clint Eastwood movie about Charlie Parker. I still have not seen it, and I never will."

Sonny takes "God Bless the Child" at a mournfully slow tempo; this is some of the most impassioned playing of his career. Perhaps he was recalling the ironic smile on Billie's face when she sang this particular song. Those who believe that Sonny's music is not as emotionally valid and heartfelt as that of anyone in jazz should listen to this track. It is, quite simply, a devastating performance.

The Bridge completely validates Sonny's choice of Jim Hall. Hall's solos seem to glow with warmth, and the pianist's sense of logic and melodic economy, his ability to select just the right note, made him a perfect complement to Sonny's more garrulous style. This was undoubtedly one of Sonny's greatest groups, comparable in its way to such great jazz combos of the 1960s as the Coltrane quartet and Miles Davis's Hancock-Williams-Carter-Shorter quintet.

Sonny took the group back to California, where they played on Ralph Gleason's *Just Jazz* PBS-TV show for its entire half-hour. This weekly show presented jazz with the appropriate respect for both music and musicians. Gleason mostly just let the groups play, sometimes doing a short interview. Sonny and Hall performed quite well, better than they ever had in the studio.

One of the tunes they played on *Just Jazz* was a bossa nova version of "If Ever I Would Leave You," a song from Lerner and Loewe's *Camelot*. The musical had recently opened on Broadway when Sonny recorded the song for his second RCA Victor album, *What's New*. According to Martin Williams, it did not compare to a version of the same tune he had heard Sonny play at a club around this time. In his book *The Jazz Tradition* he wrote: "Rollins's final piece was a kind of spontaneous orchestration on 'If Ever I Would Leave You' in which he became brass, reed, and rhythm section, tenor soloist and Latin percussionist, all at once and always with musical logic."[3] Sonny has the remarkable ability to look at things from a global perspective, to observe and create from a variety of angles all at once. This is how he tackles ideas and, by this period of his career, it had also become the way he approached music. Evidence of his sharp and wide-ranging mind, it is also what gives his music such substance and depth. Listening to a great Rollins solo over and over again inevitably brings forth fresh perspectives.

What's New was the closest Sonny ever came to recording a completely Latin album. Stan Getz and Charlie Byrd had recently ushered in the bossa nova craze with their 1962 *Jazz Samba* album and the hit from that record, "Desafinado." Virtually every jazz musician was jumping on the bandwagon and producing bossa nova albums hand over fist. The result was not just a fad; the Brazilian fusion of jazz and samba had produced some wonderful music, especially the songs of Antonio Carlos Jobim and Luiz Bonfá (of course, it also produced kitsch such as Eydie Gormé's "Blame It on the Bossa Nova"). The bossa nova rhythm was exhilarating for jazz musicians to improvise on, especially at a time when 4/4 straight-ahead swing seeming increasingly tired and used up—thus many musicians' experiments with different meters.

Jim Hall was among the first musicians to discover the new Brazilian music and bring the sound back to America. As he recalls:

> I was playing with Ella Fitzgerald and we went to Brazil, which was an amazing experience. I thought Brazil was all jungle; I didn't know anything about it. The bossa nova was just kind of taking over, it was the rage in Brazil. Roy Eldridge and I would go out at night to hear groups playing bossa nova. I came back with a stack of records, and one of them was a João Gilberto.

What's New was not just another product of the bossa nova fad. There are only two genuine bossa nova cuts on the album, "If Ever I Would Leave You" and "The Night Has a Thousand Eyes" (from the film of that name). Sonny seems completely at ease in the bossa mode, although he rarely played jazz samba later on.

The other tunes on *What's New* ranged from the calypsos "Brownskin Girl" and "Don't Stop the Carnival" (both with a chorus of singers) to a duet with the conga player Candido called "Jungoso," to "Blueso," a trio with Candido playing bongos and Cranshaw on bass. "Jungoso" is the most interesting cut on the album, and the one closest to indicating Sonny's direction at this time. Here his use of extramusical effects, especially tonal distortion, seems to presage Albert Ayler, Pharoah Sanders, and John Coltrane in his last period. Sonny, like those players, seems fascinated with pure sound rather than with a string of ideas. His tone at times becomes so gruff and woody that the listener can almost feel the splinters. What is also brought into focus is the percussive nature of Sonny's phrasing. At times he seems to be playing his horn in imitation of Candido's conga.

The controversy created by Sonny's hiring of Jim Hall continued despite the brilliance of the band's music. Sonny did not waver, although he recalls other problems caused by the hiring of Hall:

Well, all that flack didn't affect me. But as I look back, there was something that did really bother me. You see, whenever you have a white guy in your band and a black guy is the leader, you get treated funny. This was not the Jim Hall–Sonny Rollins band or the Sonny Rollins–Jim Hall band. It was the Sonny Rollins quartet. That is not how we were treated by club owners or technicians. It wasn't Jim's fault, it was none of his doing. But what happened a lot of times is that we would go to a certain venue and the technicians would all run over to Jim and ask him questions: "Well, what should we do about this?" or "Where do you want this set up?" They simply ignored me, treated me as if I was the sideman. Eventually that began to annoy me. I want to emphasize that none of this was Jim's fault. Jim had nothing to do with this. He didn't solicit this kind of thing. If he felt that this was a problem, he would have been the first one to do something about it. He is that kind of guy. This is where the dilemma comes in. He never acted as if he expected or required them to act this way. But that is what invariably happened. Maybe I felt more strongly about this because of the criticism I got from the black community. Invariably that sort of thing would happen at most of the venues we went to. This really bothered me. It was just time that I was ready to change bands anyway. That is nothing new with me, but that did have something to do with it.

Another reason why Sonny broke up the wonderful band with Jim Hall was because he wished to explore some of the more arcane areas hinted at in *What's New*'s "Jungoso." It was a time of tumult and revolution in jazz, and the Hall band may have seemed rather tepid compared to the work of colleagues such as Coleman, Coltrane, and Mingus.

Coltrane had Eric Dolphy in his group at the time and his music was causing great controversy. One critic called a performance by the group "anti-jazz" although it was not nearly as "outside" as Coltrane's music would become about three years later. There was a fresh wind blowing in the jazz world, and Sonny knew that he had been a key figure in ushering it in. He liked the "airiness" of the group with Jim Hall, but he needed even more harmonic freedom to play the kind of music that he now wanted to explore:

The *Bridge* group, which was called Sonny Rollins and Company, that was okay and it served my needs at the moment, but it wasn't enough for my mind after a point. So I changed the band. I've been changing bands all my life. I wanted to play with Don Cherry, who I had been practicing with ever since he came to New York. So that was the next thing I could do, at that moment. Some other people I could play with.

As much as he loved playing with Sonny, Hall too eventually realized that it was time to move on:

Sonny was kind of going in a different direction. He and Don Cherry had been practicing together and then Don joined the group for a while. It became a quintet and, although I could handle it now, back then I wasn't ready. It was a little freer than what I was used to. There was no room for a harmonic instrument to play chords and I began to feel uncomfortable. After we played the Village Gate with Don Cherry, I could kind of sense that I was on my way out of the group. Sonny had a long talk with my wife, Jane; I knew he felt bad about letting me go. But I could read the handwriting on the wall.

Much significance is given to the fact that Sonny seemingly hired half of Ornette's band, trumpeter Don Cherry and Billy Higgins. It was as if this was an attempt by Sonny to hop on the Ornette bandwagon. Sonny says is this just another pat explanation for a far more complicated process:

It was really just another step, not necessarily up or down, but just sideways, just another avenue, another change in the things I was trying to do in order to express myself. The [jazz] writers all tried to imply that when Ornette came to New York it was some kind of big revelation for me. It may have been a revelation to them, but it wasn't to me. I had practiced with Ornette years before. But they tried to sully my reputation by implying that I was just hopping on the bandwagon. I had been playing without a harmonic instrument for years by that point. The only thing that people can say was that I made a record with Don Cherry and [the drummer] Billy Higgins. What we were doing was more extended playing. We'd play for a long, long time, and we used less song forms that way.

To many ears, this group played free jazz, which is to say that the musicians ignored harmonic structure and simply improvised melodically. It was more complicated than that. Sonny did not throw away the entire concept of harmony:

> When we were playing in the free style, or whatever you want to call it, we didn't play, say, a chord progression like C, F, G, C. What we played was phrases. Within those phrases there was the essence of the chord. In other words, every phrases that you play, within itself, has some kind of a logical sequence of chords. But in the sense that you're playing, for example, "I've Got Rhythm" from one chord to the next chord, no, we didn't play that way. That's what Ornette and those guys were playing. So whatever phrase I would play had its own inner logic. It just wouldn't follow the straight C following G, and G following D, and D following A, or whatever it would be. You would play one phrase that might last for that duration of time, and in that phrase there would be a certain type of logic which would follow some kind of sequence. It wouldn't be a formalized sequence, or four bars; eight bars; eight bars; sixteen bars, like some of the other forms that people were playing. That's how I would explain it.

Sonny brought his new band to the Village Gate in New York's Greenwich Village for a lengthy stay. George Avakian, or somebody at RCA, figured out the perfect way to record Sonny: live, at a club. It had been done before, for Blue Note's *A Night at the Village Vanguard* sessions, but this time, as Sonny recalls, it was different:

> We were playing at the Village Gate and they wanted to do a record of that date. So I told the A&R guy, "Well, okay. We're gonna be there for ten nights so we will record every night." So they recorded every night. Now, for a while, I was kind of aware that they were recording me so it would kind of inhibit me and it might have inhibited some of the guys. After a while, after three or four nights, we sort of forgot about it, and played more naturally.

This is obviously the ideal way to record Sonny Rollins. As good as the 1957 Vanguard sessions are, who knows how good the resulting album would have been if Blue Note had recorded Sonny's entire two-week stand?

RCA issued the album with the title *Our Man in Jazz*. This album was part of a marketing ploy, in which several albums with RCA artists were released with titles that began *Our Man in.* . . . The album led by Al Hirt, the Dixieland trumpeter, was called *Our Man in New Orleans.* Rollins's contribution to the marketing strategy must have brought little joy to the RCA executives who had made the unprecedented investment in Sonny, as Loren Schoenberg points out in his notes. *Our Man in Jazz* is undoubtedly the most avant-garde album Sonny has ever released. It has only three tunes, including a twenty-five-minute version of "Oleo"; the two other pieces on the album are the old standard "Dearly Beloved" and a fifteen-minute-plus version of "Doxy." Sonny had first recorded "Oleo" and "Doxy" eight years earlier for a session led by Miles Davis, and he had first recorded "Dearly Beloved" for Riverside's *The Sound of Sonny* album during his "promiscuous" recording era, 1957. Sonny's versions of those tunes in *Our Man in Jazz* are so different that it is a little difficult to believe he is the same musician.

The *Our Man* "Oleo" is an extraordinary performance, unprecedented in any of Sonny's earlier recordings. It is *literally* free jazz; that is, there seems to be nothing taken for granted. Sonny plays both within and without the chord changes; tempos change; shifting and contrasting moods blend. What starts out as an abstracted, almost piecemeal performance turns into a medium-funky blues, all within this one piece. The most vivid moments of Sonny's solo are rhythmic. Sonny begins the piece at a very fast tempo. Midway through his solo comes that medium-funky blues, while the rhythm section continues at the same fast tempo. It is an amazing effect, another example of Sonny's aural legerdemain. It brings to mind an image of a man trying to walk up a down escalator, creates the illusion of sonic slow motion. When the rhythm section finally slows down and plays at the same tempo as Sonny, the listener feels an almost visceral lessening of tension.

There are many instances of such group inventiveness throughout *Our Man in Jazz*. Another example: in the middle of Don Cherry's "Oleo" solo, Higgins drops out and Cherry plays with only the bass for accompaniment for a long interval. A couple of years later, Miles Davis put together his 1960s quintet, which did this same sort of group improvisation, changing tempo, meter, texture, and mood as a group, often several times within a single tune. Many groups would try to play in this mode in years to come. Free jazz harked back to the group improvisation of early jazz while being at the same time genuinely avant-garde.

Also fascinating is Sonny's interplay with Cherry. In the early 1950s, Gerry Mulligan led a famous pianoless quartet with the trumpeter Chet Baker. They became famous for their counterpoint, which was a kind of substitute for a harmonic instrument. Sonny and Cherry took this practice even further, making it more abstract and often ignoring harmonic structure. Their interplay reaches its zenith on "Dearly Beloved." There seem to be absolutely no ground rules for this piece. The two horns constantly either duet or back the other up. That interplay (it is too abstract and unspecific to be labeled "counterpoint") dominates the piece.

Cherry shared Sonny's off-kilter musical sense of humor, and *Our Man* is the best expression of Sonny's sense of humor up to that time. There are some laugh-out-loud moments, as when Sonny suddenly breaks into a bugle call and Higgins breaks into a martial drill. Quotes from other tunes lurch out of the solos at unexpected moments and then disappear without a trace into the flow of notes. The interplay of Sonny and Cherry during "Dearly Beloved" is especially witty. Some of their quotations are out of left field—melodies ranging from "There's No Business Like Show Business" to "Reveille."

The most advanced element of Sonny's playing on *Our Man* is rhythmic. At times there seems to be only the thinnest and most tenuous connection between what he is playing and what the rhythm section is doing. Through the sheer domination of his instrument and by iron determination he creates a rhythmic propulsion that swings hard on its own terms, and delivers a powerful message to the listener.

Our Man in Jazz was not the only music Sonny recorded with this group. He also brought them into the studio to record three off-kilter (and relatively brief, at least compared with the music on *Our Man*) versions of some favorite standards, "There Will Never Be Another You," "I Could Write a Book," and "You Are My Lucky Star." Most of the solos virtually abandon the harmonic structure altogether. For "There Will Never Be Another You," Sonny reverts to thematic development, deconstructing and freely reassembling the tune in constantly inventive ways. In a couple of these pieces, Higgins takes a solo and proves that the great drummer Tony Williams, who rose to fame as a member of Miles Davis's 1960s quintet, must have listened very closely to both his accompaniment and his solo style while coming of age as a player.

Although *Our Man in Jazz* is truly free jazz and the playing is often extremely chromatic, it is not the sort of avant-garde statement that leaves the listener behind. This music is *fun*—the listener is constantly made to wonder what these fellows are going to do next. How far are they going to stretch this music? The ideal way to listen to the music is to come to it without any preconceptions about the limits of music, but just to give yourself up to it. *Our Man* may require novice listeners to adjust to music that is so spontaneous and totally unpredictable. Once that adjustment is made, the album is extraordinarily exhilarating for its celebration of true freedom. Not only are the musicians liberated, but by listening to this music, we are too.

In many ways, *Our Man in Jazz* was a culmination of many areas in his music that Sonny had been developing over the years. Its emphasis on horizontal rather than vertical structure was where Sonny had been heading since the mid-1950s. He could not have played so freely if he had not become far more confident both technically and musically during his two years or so away from the jazz scene. As he has commented, he did not withdraw from the scene in order to change his style; he did build on his ability to take his music in any direction his mind and heart pointed toward whenever he was on the bandstand. Now it was time to spread his wings and soar into the "open sky."

10

Now's the Time

Sonny Rollins is not usually thought of as one of the dominant musicians of the 1960s. John Coltrane, Ornette Coleman, Archie Shepp, Cecil Taylor, and Albert Ayler were considered the chief innovators of that era. This has more to do with trendiness than with musical accomplishment. The series of albums Sonny released during this decade, particularly for RCA Victor, are at least as strong and as innovative as any produced by many of the musicians who have been deemed central to the jazz of this era. Although he had clearly been one of the key prophets of the new jazz revolution, the fact that he still played standards and usually worked with musicians associated with straight-ahead postbop meant that in the 1960s a few jazz fans and writers saw him as something of a conservative.

Sonny has never had the slightest interest in being trendy. He has always had his own agenda, and has never attempted to be au courant for its own sake. His entire focus has been on playing music that was as close as it could be to who he was as a person. In the latter half of the 1950s, he was considered a hard bopper, but his music had always been far too idiosyncratic and profoundly personal to be part of any school. The only school he belonged to (at least after his earliest period, when he was a young bebopper) was the "Sonny Rollins School." Much of the music Sonny played during the early 1960s was just about as adventurous and free as the work of many New Thing players.

A case in point is *Sonny Meets Hawk*, the album he made after *Our Man in Jazz*, at the height of his free jazz period. For the first (and last) time, Sonny recorded with the man he had idolized since childhood, Coleman Hawkins.

Sonny had assembled a new band by this time, and had hired a pianist, Paul Bley. Bley was not an ordinary pianist by any stretch of the imagination. He had been associated with the avant-garde for years, having led a group between 1956 and 1958 that had included Ornette Coleman and Don Cherry. He was something of a prodigy. He had made his debut on records at the age of twenty-one, leading a trio that included Charles Mingus on bass and Art Blakey on drums. He had played in a wide variety of groups since then, working for Mingus and Jimmy Giuffre and with his own trios. The choice of Bley is another example of how big Sonny's ears are—while many musicians had trouble with the nuances of Bley's angular style, Sonny recognized Bley as the perfect accompanist for him during this period, one who would not have trouble supporting even his most eccentric ideas, who would even encourage him to be as adventurous as he wanted to be. Bley's accompaniment for Sonny was a model for any pianist who wishes to help an improviser explore rather than to impede him in flight. They were truly tuned in to each other on the bandstand, as Sonny recalls:

> I enjoyed playing with Paul. I will never forget one time when we were playing together at a club in Philadelphia. We were sort of playing free, free format and some very unusual patterns. We just played it together and we were trying to get on the same wavelength and we just came up with something at the same time. It was really remarkable. I really enjoyed playing with Paul and I like him as a player and as a person.

It may seem surprising that, given the difficulties Sonny had had after he hired Jim Hall, a little later he would hire Paul Bley, who is white. However, it turned out that clubowners and producers did not ignore Sonny and defer to Bley, as had happened with Hall. Sonny emphasizes, again, that this does not make the original problem Hall's "fault": "I didn't have any trouble with Paul. I think this is because Paul is more aloof than Jim is. I didn't blame Jim. Paul was the type of guy these people wouldn't approach. He had, I guess, a kind of abstract personality and a weird style. Jim seems like a more regular guy."

Despite the avant-garde nature of Sonny's music at this time, that he would record with Hawkins may have seemed inevitable. There was a fashion during this time for one major jazz musician "meeting" another in the recording studio (Gerry Mulligan made a long series of such albums). The idea was not Sonny's:

> The date with Hawkins came about through my producer at RCA, George Avakian. Of course, George knew my feelings about Hawkins, and Hawkins had expressed the fact that he had liked my playing. Coleman came up and we played some stuff together, which really attested to his sense of experimentation and his freshness and openness to play with us, especially since this was a very free band with Paul Bley on piano. A lot of guys of his stature and his reputation wouldn't do that.

It is even a greater testament to Coleman Hawkins that, after playing with Sonny at the 1963 Newport Jazz Festival and hearing how "outside" his music was, he was still agreeable to recording with Sonny's band. Hawkins had been already scheduled to play at Newport in a group of musicians assembled by the festival's director, George Wein. Since Sonny was scheduled to play at the festival with his group, it seemed like pure serendipity to have these two great, big-toned tenormen from different generations finally play together.

Hawkins would have had every right to balk at the idea of playing with Sonny's group. It seemed to be a conventional straight-ahead jazz quartet, but it was actually anything but that. Both Grimes and Bley were basically avant-gardists, although both were empathetic and knew how to give any player support. The amazing thing is how well Hawkins fit in.

Or perhaps it is not really so amazing. Hawkins had been an important player for close to forty years and he had always fit in to the music during every period. He was one of the first major jazz musicians who acted like a true artist onstage rather than an entertainer. That sense of dignity and artistic seriousness alone impressed the boppers of the 1940s. And Hawkins was the leader of what are now considered some of the very first "bebop" recordings. In the 1940s he hired Monk and Fats Navarro to play with him, and he sounded completely at home in a bop context. He never sacrificed his personal style or musical conception simply for the sake of being current or hip, but he had remained relevant in the jazz scene of the late 1950s and early 1960s. His influence on all saxophonists was undeniable. For example, Coltrane's "sheets of sound" period—with its reliance on arpeggiated chords rather than on melodic development—was continuously compared by critics to Hawkin's harmonically oriented style and his dramatically roiling arpeggios.

At the time of the 1963 Newport Jazz Festival, Hawkins was fifty-eight, a ripe age for a jazz musician (jazzmen often kidded Hawkins by referring to him as the Old Man). As his meeting with the genuinely avant-garde Sonny Rollins group proved, musically he remained as youthful as ever, if age is measured by openness to fresh new ideas and concepts.

The Jazz Festival meeting between Rollins and Hawkins did not work out as Sonny and Wein had hoped, although it seemed to have so much potential. As John Chilton states in his biography of Hawkins, *Song of the Hawk*:

> The Rollins-Hawkins set was a fascinating meeting of two big-toned tenor saxists who, despite being from different eras, were sometimes described (too conveniently) as having a similar approach to improvising. Both relied heavily on form and connecting musical ideas, but their ways of implementing their musical thoughts was usually quite dissimilar.[1]

The comparison is, as Chilton implies, based mainly on surface characteristics. Hawkins was mainly a harmonic or vertical player, while Sonny, at least during this period, was primarily a melodic improviser and, as we have seen, at times virtually aharmonic. The aspects of Hawkin's playing that deeply influenced Sonny were his dramatic bravura, his concern for improvising cohesively, his big sound, and his total dedication to his art. Lester Young, in his focus on melodically oriented improvising, was obviously as important an influence. But, as he himself points out, Sonny is certainly not the first musician to be deeply influenced by both "academies" of post-Armstrong improvisation:

That is what Charlie Parker was doing—he got his harmonic sophistication from Hawkins and the guys who played like Hawkins (like Don Byas and Chu Berry), and he also learned from Lester about melodic improvisation.

Sonny began his Newport set with Irving Berlin's old tune "Remember," played in such an abstract and fragmented way that few in the audience can have recognized it. His playing on this tune was a good example of his ability to tear apart the classic song form, twist it, and reassemble it into something altogether different. It was like the way Picasso could take a familiar shape, such as the human form, and recreate it on canvas as if it were being viewed from multiple points of view simultaneously.

Then Sonny announced, "And now, the great Coleman Hawkins!" Hawkins launched into a medium-fast "All the Things You Are," sounding full-blooded and feisty. But the solo seemed unfocused and discursive, to an extent, because of the rhythm section's effect on Hawkins. Like most players of his generation, Hawkins needed strong and empathetic accompaniment; this group, based around Sonny's fragmented and abstract style of this period, was far from ideal for the Old Man. Bley took a wonderful solo that displayed his rather odd, off-balance chromatic lyricism at its best; one has to wonder what Hawkins was thinking while hearing it (although at times Bley evoked Earl Hines, who was an avant-gardist back in the 1920s).

The next piece was a favorite of Sonny's, "The Way You Look Tonight." Those in the Newport audience expecting to hear the Sonny Rollins of a decade earlier, when he memorably recorded the tune with Thelonious Monk, were in for a shock. Yet those who had been closely following Sonny's development since that time should not have been so surprised. Sonny was simply taking some of the musical concepts that he had been exploring for years to their logical conclusion.

Shortly after Newport, Sonny and Hawkins went into the RCA studios for *Sonny Meets Hawk*. If RCA executives hoped that Sonny would be earthbound in his playing in deference to his idol, they couldn't have been more wrong. *Sonny Meets Hawk* is one of the most bizarre albums ever recorded. Talk about "the sound of surprise"! It is almost as if Whitney Balliett had been listening to this album when that phrase came into his mind (the theory falls apart because the book with that title appeared several years before the album). Instead of playing down to the Old Man, Sonny reaches a height of unpredictability and musical eccentricity not heard in any previous recording of his. There have been rumors that Sonny took drugs for this session or was having a brief psychotic episode. He says the wild adventurousness of his playing has a much more down-to-earth explanation:

> Everybody was trying to expand perimeters [then]. That is how we were playing and how I was playing with the group that I had. Also, I was just trying to hear as much as I could. When I played with Hawkins, I was trying to make a contrast between Hawkins and myself, really make a *sound*. I didn't want to try and sound like him, because I could not sound like him anyway. It's pretty hard to sound like Coleman. A lot of people played that style, but I wanted to make a contrast. I thought it would make a more striking record.

Sonny did not have to worry much about being mistaken for Coleman Hawkins on that album; not even a novice listener to jazz would have the slightest difficulty in differentiating between the two tenormen.

The most amazing thing about this album is how unruffled Hawkins is by the often strange sounds being created by both Sonny and Paul Bley (the band was the same as at Newport, although Bob Cranshaw substituted for Henry Grimes at the second session). The first tune, on the album, "Yesterdays," begins with Sonny's unaccompanied introduction, during which he briefly alludes to the famous Bird blues "Now's the Time." As the tune goes into tempo, Hawkins states the theme, or rather *implies* the melody. His statement is typically dramatic and moving, never for a moment sounding anything but utterly modern and never sacrificing his inimitable musical persona. Sonny begins by emulating Hawkins's brief trill at the end of his solo; Sonny makes it the core of his own improvised solo statement, using it as the basis of his solo just as he had in the past used melodic fragments for thematic development. The exploration of pure sound throughout this album prefigures the work of Albert Ayler, Pharoah Sanders and, in the last couple of years of his life, John Coltrane.

Perhaps the strangest and most interesting cut on this album is "Lover Man." One has to wonder if Sonny was recalling the first time Charlie

Parker recorded this tune. This was in Los Angeles, where, due to a drought of heroin, Parker had been going through drug withdrawal and had been drinking alcohol to minimize the agony. He was in terrible shape and his playing reflected it. His solo on "Lover Man" was erratic and fragmented, and that is just why the performance is so chilling. Technically, Parker could barely play, but his emotional intensity makes his performance galvanizing. Parker never wanted any of the music from this session released. Nevertheless it was; any music by Charlie Parker was valuable to the most fanatic of bop fans. Charles Mingus actually named "Lover Man" as his favorite Bird on record, hearing something in it of the sound of a man facing directly into the void. Parker later re-recorded "Lover Man," but that version, fine as it was, didn't have the emotional power of the first.

On *Sonny Meets Hawk*, Hawkins plays with the larger-than-life grandeur that is solely his. His playing throughout proves that even now he was still growing and developing as a player; his improvising on the album is equal to that during any period of his long career. Sonny's solo, even at ballad tempo, is as exploratory as any on the album. Every aspect of orthodox jazz improvisation is challenged in these improvisations. He seems to be drawn to the upper register of his horn, and he ends his solo by whistling through his horn, creating a rather unsettling sound, which he continues throughout Hawkins's final statement.

Yet once again, no matter how far into the cosmos Sonny takes the music, it is never inaccessible or off-putting, as some avant-garde music can be. Sonny's is a wild trip, but he never leaves us behind. This is not easily accomplished; this kind of playing demands courage and absolute mastery of both the instrument and every element of music-making if it is to work. There is a great deal of difference between chaos and free creativity. Some in the avant-garde believed that music must reflect the chaos of life in order to be relevant. But art is not just a reflection of nature. It is *artificial*. It is stylized creation, not a mirror of our world. Sonny's playing during this period is never chaotic; like the playing and compositions of Thelonious Monk, it has its own inner logic, albeit a logic unlike that of any other musician. This music, rather than reminding us of the ineluctable grind of a senseless universe, forces us to be braver, to find our own compass, and to unabashedly be who we truly are.

In its own off-kilter way, *Sonny Meets Hawk* is a great jazz album. There are some who criticized Sonny for his "outside" playing on it, assuming that his improvising must have confused and annoyed Hawkins. I believe that Sonny's adventurous playing was actually a tribute to Hawkins. Sonny challenged him into playing some of the most spontaneous and freshly inventive music of his later career. On the last cut, an original tune by Sonny called "At McKies," Hawkins at times seems to be parodying Sonny, playing with the same high-flying abandon as the younger man. This album is what jazz, at its best, is all about. The performances are not perfect. More than once, Sonny and Hawkins take a route that goes nowhere, or they play ideas that seem more eccentric than inventive. Miles Davis once said that when they release jazz albums on which all the mistakes are left in, then they will be releasing genuine jazz albums. True spontaneity has its cost, but carries with it its own quite profound rewards: emotional immediacy and the ecstatic joy of true freedom.

On *Sonny Meets Hawk* we can hear the entirety of jazz history captured in one session. It is all here: the early jazz roots of Hawkins, from his days with Fletcher Henderson through the lessons in swing he received from playing with Louis Armstrong. We can clearly hear elements from the bop era, in which Hawkins was involved in its earliest moments and which Sonny became involved in during his first years as a musician. Sonny's playing reflects the latest revolution, that of free jazz. This album is not just a signpost along the way of the jazz tradition. It *is* the jazz tradition.

During this "post-bridge" period, Sonny made other changes than the purely musical. Wanting a more striking visual image, he had his hair cut into a Mohawk, and then later shaved it off. He began doing things in live performance that caused many in the jazz scene to wonder if he had become a genuine eccentric. During a live performance, often right in the middle of a solo, he would walk off the bandstand and move around the club, at times playing directly to certain members of the audience. Occasionally he walked backstage where the audience could barely hear him and even, at times, headed into the street. Lucille Rollins, who has been observing Sonny's live performances since 1957, remembers the reaction to these post-bridge performances:

> A lot of people thought that Sonny was crazy because he would
> do some very unusual things, like walking into the street while play-

ing and things like that. I have a friend who has known Sonny for years and he thought Sonny was crazy when he was younger. . . . He had that reputation for years. Of course, Sonny referred to himself as an average Joe.

Sonny had his own reasons for his behavior. As usual, they were down-to-earth and had their own straightforward logic:

> Sometimes I would leave the bandstand just to separate myself from an inadequate band. Part of the reason I started to walk around the club was that I discovered that blowing your horn in one part of the club gets one sound, and then if you turn around and blow in some other part, it gets a completely different sound, perhaps a more conducive sound for what I was trying to do. Just being in a different area of the room produced different possibilities. I also wanted to get a closer proximity to the people, and it afforded me a chance to interact with their vibes. There is one more reason—it was a demonstration that the music I was playing was happening right here, even if I walked into the street. Even then, the music was going on.

The next two (and last) albums that Sonny recorded for RCA must have seemed a safe bet. The first one, recorded in 1964, was titled *Now's the Time*; the idea was for Sonny to play a number of famous modern jazz pieces, most of them associated with bop. The album turned out to be anything but nostalgic. Instead, it sounds almost like a manifesto, a declaration of the great distance Sonny had evolved *away* from bebop. I very much doubt that listening to this album brought tears of nostalgia to the eyes of jazz fans who fondly remembered bebop's glory days. Comparing Sonny's work on this album with that of his early bop period—such as the Bud Powell date or the J. J. Johnson Savoy sides—instantly makes clear just how much Sonny had changed. For this reason alone, the album is fascinating despite RCA's insistence on keeping the cuts short and "radio-friendly."

Most of the cuts on *Now's the Time* are between three and five minutes long; RCA did not seem to understand that jazz fans were fascinated by Sonny's ability to sustain lengthy solos and that such brevity would be a real turnoff. Sonny did record longer versions of a few of the tunes, but there were not released until a French division of RCA produced an album of rejected takes from the session, *The Alternative Sonny Rollins.*

As Orrin Keepnews explains in the notes to *The Complete Sonny Rollins RCA Victor Recordings*, many of these takes were not really "alternative." Sonny was recorded on some tunes at different sessions with different sidemen, but some of the takes were rejected only for being too long to fit into the format of the album. In virtually every case, the longer versions are far superior to those that were originally released. The exception is "Four," a tune usually attributed to Miles Davis (although it was actually written by the blues singer and alto saxophonist Eddie "Cleanhead" Vinson). The longer, and superior, version was chosen for the album.

The most spectacularly different takes are the two versions of the title tune, "Now's the Time," a famous blues composed and performed by Charlie Parker in 1945 for the first recoding session he ever led (the sidemen included a teenage Miles Davis, who soloes for the first time on record). One of Sonny's versions of this blues is clocked in at 4'01" and is relatively perfunctory; the other lasts almost sixteen minutes and is one of the most extraordinary solos Sonny ever recorded in the studio. For whatever reason, he broke free of RCA's manacles and simply stretched out.

The only possible comparison would be to Sonny's version of the title piece he wrote for the movie *Alfie* a few years later. This is one of the few recorded examples of Sonny playing on a level close to that of his live performances. His rhythm section for the session included two members of Miles Davis's quintet of the period: the pianist Herbie Hancock and the bassist Ron Carter. The drummer was Roy McCurdy, whom Sonny had been regularly using during this period. It is fascinating to hear Hancock attempting to keep up with Sonny, whose playing breaks through the envelope in so many unexpected ways that Hancock eventually gives up and lays out for a long period, letting Sonny wander in any direction. Nobody who is attentive will find this solo inaccessible or incomprehensible. There is something inherently gleeful about hearing someone dare to break free from the expected and mundane, to celebrate in music the awesome range of possibilities in life. No matter how experimental Sonny's playing is, his powerful control of all the elements of his music give us confidence in his ability to make great leaps of imagination without falling off the high wire.

There were some who wondered if Sonny's music being so outside and unpredictable during this period probably had something to do with the then-commonplace use of psychedelic drugs. A number of free jazz players admitted that their playing was influenced by LSD and other psychedelics. But Sonny does not believe that his use of these drugs affected his music nearly as much as national events of that time:

I have used LSD, but I was not an acidhead. I didn't take it that much. I was probably smoking some pot. The thing that most affected me was the social revolution taking place back then. I enjoyed taking LSD, although "enjoy" is not the proper word. It was more like a sacrament. I used pot the same way. I mean, it wasn't just to hang out with girls and get high. It was really to get inside of myself. A lot of people use it for that, and many of them become more aware as human beings.

Taking psychedelic drugs may have a peripheral effect of making somebody feel more free. But the main thing that affected me during this period was the change going on in this country with the civil rights movement and the Vietnam War. That is the main reason for what happened with music during this time: things just reached a point where people wanted to say something about it. This was reflected in the music we were making at that time.

People were trying to escape from the restriction of society, all this racism and these kinds of things, so that in doing that, they felt that they should break down these song forms. It was just a way to show something new, and to get away from some things that were obviously not positive for a lot of people. There were some attempts to break down a lot of these conventions.

Recently I was doing an interview and we were talking about standard songs, and I was telling him that although these so-called American standards are good, and that they are useful, and there's a close relationship between them and jazz, that maybe in the music of the future, at least my music—I may want to get away from that. I would like to play something more primitive. That is what people wanted in the 1960s: to get away from standards, and the whole society. They wanted to break down barriers because they were restrictive. Restrictive in the social sense and restrictive in the musical sense. People fused the two.

One has to wonder, given Sonny's strongly felt political and social views, whether working with a large corporation like RCA, especially in the context of the 1960s, gave him the aggressive edge so prevalent in his RCA recordings. Perhaps he was rebelling against the bland expectations RCA had for him. He simply refused to be RCA's "man in jazz" (at least in the recordings he made after the relatively sedate *The Bridge*). In the 1960s, many felt a keen anger toward large corporations like RCA, which they perceived as war-mongering and exploitive. Sonny definitely shared those feelings. Other things, too, disturbed him:

> As my contract ran out, the RCA executives insisted that I record shorter cuts. It was all in their hands, anyway. All I did was play the music. I had control of what I recorded because I've always been my own producer. George Avakian may have suggested I do a song, saying "Gee, Sonny, this is a good song. I wonder if you've ever played it." That would be about as far as anybody would go, in so far as trying to produce me. So I have always been my own producer. I had no control over how they put it out. They owned the "property" and they put it out in their own way. My concern was about making the music. They put it out their own way. Later they reissued this music in some pretty strange ways. But by that time it was long after I left RCA.

Perhaps when he made that statement, Sonny was thinking of the last album he recorded for RCA. It must have seemed a sure bet to the company executives: *The Standard Sonny Rollins* was exactly what the title implied, Sonny playing a collection of standard pop songs. Once again the idea was to create an album of short tracks that might be attractive for radio play. But Sonny took the classic songs and subversively twisted and turned them into virtually unrecognizable pure sound, pointillistic abstractions.

The personnel for the sessions are those of *Now's the Time*, with one surprise: Jim Hall plays the guitar on a few tracks. These two great musicians complement each other and together create a gorgeous sound. The contrast between Sonny's deep, dark tone and angular melodicism and Hall's incandescent sound and melancholy lyricism is one of the great delights in all of jazz.

A chief difference from *Now's the Time* is the method by which RCA insured that most tracks lasted no more than three or four minutes: they simply faded out the track in the middle of a Rollins solo. There is nothing more heartbreaking, or maddening for that matter, than hearing a jazz musician of Sonny's caliber being faded out in musical midflight. If the RCA honchos thought that by keeping the selections short they might make the album more attractive for radio play, they must have been dismayed at how jaggedly abstract Sonny's playing is on most of the tracks, even on some of the ballads.

The best example on record of the contrast between Jim Hall's style and Sonny's is the tune "Love Letters" from this album. It begins with a lovely introduction by Hall. When Sonny begins his solo, he totally destroys the distilled emotion of Hall's introduction by launching into a double-time solo that is reminiscent of a painting by Kandinsky, all jutting angles and unexpected contours. It constantly contradicts our expectations. Sonny enjoys throwing in offbeat quotes, although here they frequently have a surreal quality—for example, within the first few bars of his "Love Letters" solo, he plays a mercurial allusion to "Stranger in Paradise" from the musical *Kismet*.

After this off-kilter ballad, he surprises us again. "My One and Only Love" is rhapsodic and hauntingly romantic, one of his best ballad performances from this period (and at 5'59" it is also the longest cut on the original album). There is very little improvising by Sonny on this piece, but his phrasing, beautiful cellolike sound, and lovely ornamentation of the melody creates a lush and beautiful statement.

The most fascinating cut is Sonny's version of "Traveling Light," a tune associated with Billie Holiday, who always imbued it with poignancy and melancholy. In addition to Hall, the bassist David Izenzon, who plays arco throughout the track, creates a droning effect that perfectly complements Sonny's sound. French RCA included an alternate version of this piece for its double LP that is over twelve minutes long (the version included on the original album was 4' 06"). It is obvious why RCA would not have used this longer version. Sonny at times emulates Izenson's arco wail, playing high drones that don't sound like Western music. Although it never quite coalesces, the point of this piece seems to be to create music that has no center and that seems to drift into the air like smoke, dissolving into nothingness. It is a strange, ghostly performance, haunting and unsettling.

The Standard Sonny Rollins, Sonny's last album for RCA, is an indication of where he was heading musically. The playing is not as "ouside" as on the previous three albums. Rather, Sonny seems to be consolidating his explorations into his arsenal of techniques and musical possibilities; at times, his improvising moves "in" and "out" within the space of a few bars.

All in all, Sonny's RCA Victor recordings stand out as one of his greatest achievements, producing jazz that was a culmination of the advances he had been making ever since he recorded *Work Time* at the end of 1955. For various reasons, Sonny was able to overcome his usual problems with playing in recording studios; he improvised at a very high level of creativity, although the single greatest album from this period is undoubtedly *Our Man in Jazz*, recorded live during the two-week stint at the Village Gate.

Part of the reason for the high quality of his Victor recordings was work he did during the two-year break that preceded them. Part of it also was his rebelliousness against the idea of working for the kind of large corporation that he has always distrusted. For whatever reason, he played the most adventurous music of his career and greatly expanded the possibilities of jazz improvisation. I place great emphasis on the word "recording" in this last sentence; as we have previously noted, Sonny's studio sessions, for the most part, have borne little resemblance to what he was playing at clubs or concerts at the same time. The RCA sessions are an exception. He took the kind of chances that he rarely does in studio albums. Moreover, *Our Man in Jazz* better represents the way Sonny was playing at the time than any of his other live albums do, including the Vanguard sessions.

As popular as he had ever been, Sonny was once more ensconced in the jazz life. He has always been one to look deep inside himself and make decisions that might surprise and confuse others. Once again he was questioning his role as a musician and a man. Was he going down the right course? With his continuing concerns about social and political matters, the 1960s made him look even deeper within and question who he was and what he was doing with his life. Once again, despite great success, he would exit from the scene.

11

Playin' in the Yard

While Sonny was recording his final albums for RCA Victor in the mid-1960s, the free jazz revolution was in full swing. In 1965, John Coltrane recorded "Ascension," a manifesto declaring his allegiance to the New Thing movement. The large group he assembled for this lengthy piece included many of the Young Turks of this new jazz revolution: Archie Shepp, Marion Brown, Pharoah Sanders, and John Tchicai, most of whom had previously recorded only for small independent labels such as ESP, or hadn't been recorded at all. "Ascension" was viewed by many as an attempt to bring these New Thing musicians into the mainstream of jazz and out of the lofts and small, out-of-the-way clubs that had been the only places where they could play.

As Coltrane was getting further and further involved in the free jazz revolution, Sonny seemed to be, at least on the surface, retrenching. A famous jazz writer who had a weekend jazz radio show introduced a selection from the first studio album Sonny recorded after leaving RCA by saying, "It seems that Sonny has finally come down from outer space." Indeed, his playing on that album, *Sonny Rollins on Impulse!*, seemed on first hearing far more conservative than that on *Our Man in Jazz* or *Sonny Meets Hawk*. But Sonny was concerned with exploring whatever avenues led to the music of his soul. He had not rejected his "outside" explorations. Instead, he had incorporated these techniques into his style, giving himself an additional range of possibilities that enabled him to push his agenda forward. This was simply a continuation of how he had continued to develop as a musician:

I use a variety of systems. . . . What I'm trying to do is to get to the point where I can have a really complete expression of what I'm thinking about. . . . That is what I am looking for, that's what I'm trying to get to. I don't completely accept anything as final. If I did, I would be playing the way I did in 1951 or something—which, regardless of its merits or demerits, is fine, but I can't do that. I'm not that age, I am not in that time, and I simply can't play like I did in 1951. If I did that, I would turn into a guy who copied, and I can't copy. It's not my style of playing; it's not my nature. I'm trying to play jazz, creative jazz, where you play things in the moment, at the moment that I get it—it comes into your mind and you're able to play it. So I can't go back, I can't play like that.

As far as harmonic style goes, I'm trying to be able to play whatever comes into my mind. So . . . I'm trying to be conversant with any musical skill which will help me to do that. That would mean being at least relatively familiar with different ways of playing. Not that I could play like Coleman Hawkins completely, or Ben Webster, or John Coltrane, or anybody you could name. But I have been trying to appreciate what they are doing, to the extent that I am conversant with it, so that can help lead into playing Sonny Rollins and being able to do whatever it takes to have that kind of knowledge about what I am doing. I have to have knowledge of the music, so I am able to play some Fletcher Henderson, or know something about what Louis Armstrong plays, in order to really play free, expressive, in-the-moment jazz. . . . I'd do anything. I might use any kind of technique or harmonic system. . . . everything is going in the service of trying to reach Sonny Rollins and play myself.

Sonny Rollins on Impulse! is evidence of the truth of this latter statement. Although the group was a standard jazz quartet (Walter Booker on bass, Mickey Roker on drums, and the pianist from *Work Time*, Ray Bryant),

Sonny's playing is plainly different from his late 1950s style. He has incorporated some of his explorations into a style that was now even more idiosyncratic and that owed very little to current trends.

John Coltrane had now become a dominating force in jazz, and virtually all modern musicians were affected by his style and musical conception, especially saxophonists. Stan Getz, who was usually classified as a leader of the cool jazz movement, became more rhythmically aggressive and pungently emotional. Even Coleman Hawkins's playing seemed to nod toward Coltrane occasionally.

Sonny was one of the very few exceptions. This is borne out simply by listening to a Coltrane album from 1965, such as *John Coltrane Quartet Plays*, and comparing it with *Sonny Rollins on Impulse!* Turn back the clock nine years and listen to the title tune from Sonny's *Tenor Madness* (1956), when, for the only time on record, the two tenormen play together. Even those unfamiliar with their styles would have no trouble hearing the difference between them on the 1965 albums. Novices would probably find it was harder to distinguish between the two on the '56 album. For those obsessed with the cutting edge, Sonny might have seemed irrelevant to the jazz scene of the mid-sixties. He was simply doing what he had always done, seeking his own muse and finding his own way. This is exactly what John Coltrane was doing, too, but his often cacophonous excursions seemed to be more timely during this tumultuous decade. Both men were seeking and creating music that reflected their innermost soul.

The two men shared something else: a record company, Impulse, a division of ABC. Impulse had aggressively sought out many of the most important modern jazz names of the time, but its biggest coup was signing John Coltrane in 1961, just when his career as a leader was really taking off. Impulse put considerable creativity, freshness, and skill into packaging its albums. The label's producer, Bob Thiele, had been making great jazz records for decades and was well known for being sympathetic to musicians. Coltrane was given a great deal of freedom to record whatever he wanted and as frequently as he had something to say musically.

The success of Sonny's friend was one factor that encouraged him to sign with Impulse:

> Everybody sort of knew each other in those days, so I knew they
> were interested in signing major jazz musicians. Coltrane never tried

to convince me to sign with Impulse. I think I just realized that they were doing a good job with him, and so I thought that maybe it would be good for me too.

Sonny "had high hopes about working for Impulse," but his attitude changed:

> It turned out that they were a rough group of people, and they really screwed me out of stuff. Not only that, the way they did it—these guys were really just thugs. Their lawyers were really tough. I never had any problems with Bob Thiele. Bob was a very accommodating fellow. . . . I did have problems with the ABC lawyers and business people who twisted my arm while I was doing business with them. I was kind of naive and I didn't have anybody representing me at the time when I was doing contracts and working out a royalty agreement and all that kind of thing. I really got used.

An example of the label's strange practices is the very first album Sonny recorded for it, about a month before *Sonny Rollins on Impulse!* Impulse had recorded a Rollins concert at Manhattan's Museum of Modern Art. (MOMA had regular jazz concerts during the summer in its sculpture garden then.) The problem was that nobody told Sonny he was being recorded. His playing is magnificent, but he is off-mike much of the time. Listening to this album is painful, since Sonny was playing so much better than he does on his first Impulse studio session. Two of the tunes he played at the museum concert, "On Green Dolphin Street" and "Three Little Words," are far superior, at least as far as anyone can actually hear on the album, to the studio session.

This performance had some other bizarre features. It was raining, and there was no shelter for either the musicians or the audience. The group Sonny used included the pianist Tommy Flanagan, who had played with him on *Saxophone Colossus* almost a decade earlier; Bob Cranshaw, who had become one of his favorite bassists; and *two* drummers, Mickey Roker and Billy Higgins, who did not alternate. They played simultaneously. Why? "At the time, I liked both of them as drummers and I did not want to let either of them go. And I had heard that Duke Ellington had been using two drummers and I thought it might work out." Apparently it was not all that successful; Sonny never tried it again.

It is amazing how well Sonny plays despite the rain and the two drummers. The key is that he did not know he was being recorded. We shall never know if he would have played just as well if he *had* known, but I doubt it. Just having to play into the mike rather than strolling around the stage would probably have been enough to make him too self-conscious to play at his best. Sonny was rightfully angry when this album was released in 1978 (with the title *There Will Never Be Another You*), several years after his contract with Impulse had ended. "For one thing," he explains, "I was not paid to do that record. And also it should never have been released, just because I am off-mike so much. It was just another example of their gouging more money out of the public by selling them an inferior product."

Sonny was given a great opportunity in 1965. During a successful engagement at Ronnie Scott's club in London, he was approached by a director to create the music for the movie *Alfie*, about the dalliances of an amoral, cocky Cockney cad played by Michael Caine. Sonny wrote and performed a lively and attractive score for the film—part composed, part improvised—but it was only sparingly used in the film itself. He then re-recorded the tunes with a ten-piece band, arranged and orchestrated by Oliver Nelson.

The title piece is a funky blues reminiscent of "Sonnymoon for Two." Sonny takes a lengthy solo that invites comparison with the alternative version of "Now's the Time" a couple of years earlier. At a bouncy medium tempo, Sonny plays a long, discursive solo that shows him once again incorporating his entire musical history; his occasional wanderings "outside" are only part of his musical arsenal. There is also a lovely ballad, which Sonny plays with great tenderness and deep sincerity. Nelson's arrangements are spare, but they do set off the solos and establish moods. Along with the Verve session with brass, and one of his later Milestone albums (in which he is backed by a brass choir not too dissimilar to that of the Verve *Brass & Trio*), this is the closest we come to hearing the way Sonny would have sounded with a big band. His big, domineering sound might have worked beautifully with Duke Ellington's band.

The film *Alfie* was a major hit, and it launched Michael Caine's career. Sonny's music was little noticed because it was so sparingly used in the film. The song "Alfie," written for the movie by Burt Bacharach and Hal David, became a huge hit and became the tune associated with the film; it over-shadowed Sonny's excellent score. However, he feels that doing the score was a good experience: "I enjoyed writing and playing the score for *Alfie* very much. However, if I were offered another opportunity such as this, I would only do it if the film highlighted the music rather than the story itself."

In May 1966, Sonny recorded his last Impulse album, *East Broadway Rundown*. On paper it had the makings of a Rollins classic. The rhythm section was that of Coltrane's quartet: drummer Elvin Jones (who had played on Sonny's Vanguard sessions) and the bassist Jimmy Garrison. Trumpeter Freddie Hubbard was on one track. The album has only three tunes, so one would expect Sonny to have more than enough room to stretch out. Yet *East Broadway Rundown* is not a great Sonny Rollins album—although it *is* a fascinating and revealing recording.

Listening to the title cut, one has to wonder if Sonny had been listening to Albert Ayler. At the time of this album, Ayler was becoming an increasingly dominant, and controversial, figure in the "New Thing" movement of the 1960s. He had played with John Coltrane, who had expressed great respect for his fellow saxophonist. Ayler justaposed simple melodies, tunes that sounded like old spirituals or ballads, with caterwaul-ing multiphonics, ripping the head off his listeners. Ayler had declared that "it's not about notes anymore," and it seems as if Sonny had been listening to that message. After all, Sonny says, "I have always thought of myself as an avant-garde player."

The most gripping aspect of the title cut, and the entire album, is Sonny's tone, noticeably stronger and more powerful than ever. It is still cello-like, but it is far too muscular to be mistaken for a cello. Undoubtedly this was at least partly due to the engineering of Rudy Van Gelder, who understood better than anyone else how to capture the sound of jazz in the studio. Sonny's first solo on the tune almost sounds like a parody of impro-visation, it seems so deliberately constructed. Just as he seems to be gath-ering heat, the solo comes to a stop and the listener is made to feel that he has crashed headfirst into a stone wall. After a fine Hubbard solo, Sonny plays through his horn with the mouthpiece removed, creating an eerie squeak that seems to fascinate him—it seems to go on for way too long a time. Any hope that Sonny will put the mouthpiece back in his horn and play another solo is dashed when he and Hubbard play the theme and take it out. It is a frustrating example of musical *coitus interruptus*.

As for the other two tunes on the album, "Blessing in Disguise," with just the trio of Sonny and the rhythm section, never seems to go anyplace, but the ballad "We Kiss in the Shadows" is lovely, the finest moment on the album.

East Broadway Rundown was not only Sonny's final album for Impulse but also his last for six years. This was his longest withdrawal from recording up to that point. His reasons were somewhat different than on the two earlier occasions.

The problems Sonny had with the ABC honchos and their lawyers left him greatly disillusioned with the business aspects of his career. He felt as if his gifts were being used simply as a commodity and that the record company's only concern was the bottom line. This was the 1960s, after all, when idealism was at its height and there was a growing movement to reject the materialism of American society. Sonny had been concerned with social issues for his entire life; now, during the social tumult caused by a seemingly endless, immoral war and the continuing struggle of the civil rights movement, he once again reconsidered his own life and career. He had been asking himself the same questions ever since he had kicked his drug habit. Now his cynicism about the music business extended to the whole of American society: what was he doing in this life, and what was his place in a society that had so disillusioned him?

In 1968, Sonny went on his second tour of Japan. This time he had other reasons for going in addition to playing; seeking spiritual rejuvenation, he was increasingly drawn to Eastern religion: "I visited some Buddhist temples while I was there. They were Zen temples. All this was building in my mind during this time. I wanted to get a more spiritual base to my life; that was all I was trying to do."

But Sonny did not find the answer to his spiritual questions in Japan. When he returned to America, he decided that he had to step away from the jazz scene once again. He felt desperate for the rejuvenation of his soul. When he was playing at his peak, he experienced spiritual transcendence, but increasingly that was not enough:

I guess I had a general disillusionment with American society. This included the jazz business, which was pretty mercenary. There was nothing happening there for me. I remember one guy at Impulse said about *East Broadway Rundown*, "Well, gee, we can't sell this record." I still don't get any royalties from that record. So I was disillusioned with the record business and I was very disturbed by all the social turmoil of that time. The injustice of it all bothered me then, and still bothers me now. Everything is still the same—really, we haven't gone anywhere. We have the same type of people leading the country, and the same type of shit that was going on then is going on now. As a musician and an artist it bothered me. Every time someone looked at me like I was an animal instead of a human because I was black. It could be then, it could be now. The same thing happens. That was the climate of this country, and it still is.

I was also getting deeper and deeper into spiritual pursuits as a way of getting away from all of that, and finding some sort of answer. I had begun to realize that it was impossible to get, on a day-to-day level, any kind of satisfaction out of this world. So I was getting more and more into the spiritual things. I decided to go to India because I believed that it was the place where I would be able to get deeper into the spiritual element of life and be able to find a way to deal with that kind of reality.

At this time, Lucille and I were separated. I went there by myself. . . . I just took my horn and a bag and got on the plane to India. There was one fellow on the plane who knew of several swamis and who knew of ashrams that would be hospitable to international students. I chose one of the places, an ashram called Sanddpany Sadhanalayna, that he mentioned because it was on Powaii Lake, close to Bombay, which is where I was going. The swami was Chinmayamananda. I had not heard of him before I got there. It was a nice environment and I began to study meditation and Vedanta and some of the Eastern sacred texts, such as the Upanishads and the Bhagavad Gita and several other holy texts. Women monks and young monks were studying [there]. I went strictly as a neophyte. I was just trying to find some real, deeper understanding of life. Nobody knew who I was, and I was unknown to them as far as who I was in the jazz world. There were a few Americans at the ashram, and one guy knew who I was. The focus was never on me. I only rarely practiced because I was in an ashram and I did not want any undue focus directed on me. The only time I ever played publicly at the ashram is when I did a solo concert for the people at the ashram. There was another musician there; he was an Indian guy who played an instrument that sounded like a big oboe. He played some and then I played. I also went to a kind of Indian dance where some musicians were playing Western instruments. I went there with some people from the ashram. I brought my horn and I sat in with them for a while.

I didn't play a lot of music while I was there, but I did hear a lot of music. There was a song I wrote called "Powaii." I used to hear the people at night from a far-off village chanting this song. It is on my album *Sonny Rollins in Japan*. I also went to an Indian music concert in Bombay. I know that there is an element of improvisation in Indian music and people sometimes compare it to jazz. It's hard to know because they have these Eastern harmonies and scales that make it hard for the Western ear to determine if they are really improvising or not. From what I know of it, improvisation is very limited in Indian music; the musician does not have nearly the amount of freedom that a jazz musician has.

I would say that I did learn a lot over there. I learned a lot about what I had to do with my life, which was that I really had to get into my music and play. That was what they call karma yoga, which means a life of work. This is how you find your salvation. And was no problem for me, because I am a person who was doing something he liked to do anyway, playing music. I just kind of rededicated myself through that and I was able to deal with other things that were bugging the shit out of me. I think I learned a lot over there.

After several months in India, Sonny decided to return home. It was now time to deal with "karmic yoga" and go back to work.

When I came back from India, where I was living in a place of great spirituality, both in its culture and its religion, I felt as if I was actually elevated. I felt like I was walking three feet over the ground. This lasted for maybe three or four weeks. Gradually I felt I was dragged back down to the reality of this way of life here, . . . dragged back down to earth, so to speak. But the experience over there was one that stayed with me, and I'm glad I went. I got a lot out of it. I met some good teachers. . . .

Going to India still affects my life. I do not practice meditation, at least not what people think of as meditation. I find it very hard to just sit down and make myself still. But I do practice my hatha yoga every day, and in that way I meditate. I find it very hard to practice meditation in this climate over here. This is such a different type of existence. . . . But I believe that playing my horn is a form of meditation. There are different types of meditation other than sitting down and trying to still your mind.

After returning to the United States, Sonny gave an unusual concert at Manhattan's Town Hall. The bassist Bill Lee (the father of the filmmaker Spike Lee) organized a group of seven bassists, a pianist, and a drummer, which he called the New York Bass Violin Choir.

Sonny had a new look. As Ira Gitler described it in *Down Beat*: "His powerful torso [was] encased in a dashiki, his head shaven and his formidable face adorned by a pair of fierce Oriental mustaches."[1] As six of the seven bassists played arco arrangements (with one bass being plucked in the usual style for jazz), Sonny walked among them soloing. A couple of times he wandered clear off the stage, into the backstage area where the audience could only faintly hear him.

Unfortunately, the group had less than half an hour's worth of arrangements. When the short set ended and the musicians left the stage, the crowd went wild, demanding that Sonny play more. He had been doing very few live engagements around this time and had not released a new album since *East Broadway Rundown* three years earlier. He finally came out and tried to reason with the crowd, then gave up, put his horn to his mouth, and played solo for a few minutes. The crowd demanded more. Sonny tried to explain, talking to the audience and finishing his sentences by playing a few bars on his horn. One had the feeling that he felt more comfortable explaining the situation through his saxophone than attempting to quiet the audience with actual words. It was an extraordinarily revealing spectacle.

Ira Gitler reported: [Sonny] made an effort, but a lot of disgruntled people left Town Hall that night. . . . Sonny admitted he should have played another set with just a rhythm section. "I could have played longer, I tried to show them that I was thinking of them. . . . I didn't intend it to be that way. . . . I didn't intend to be that way. . . . I usually don't play for that short a time. I worked very hard. I wear out suits playing. I hope that they forgive me."[2]

Sonny also told Gitler that he listened to soul as his "light" music, and he named Miles Davis, who at the time was beginning his exploration of jazz-rock fusion, as the jazzman he most enjoyed hearing at this time, "Miles and Coleman Hawkins," he said, "those people *are* jazz." Gitler asked Sonny what he was working on. "Right now," Sonny told him, "I want to do more writing and orchestrating my own material. I'm studying several ways of setting down my own music most efficiently. There are so many possibilities in music. It's an open sky."[3]

Following the Town Hall disaster, Sonny played a week-long stint at the Village Vanguard. After that he left the scene again. After his time in India, he found it virtually impossible to deal with the business aspects of his art form and the damage they had done to his soul.

During these years of Sonny's spiritual searching, the jazz scene had been going through some drastic changes. In 1967, John Coltrane died from cancer of the liver. Most people had been unaware of how sick he was and were shocked by the news. His death was also a blow to Sonny, who had known him for almost twenty years and had loved him like a brother.

Coltrane had become such a central figure in the jazz of his time that his death caused a crisis. He had brought the avant-garde into the main-stream, but now that he was dead those players found few allies in the jazz establishment. According to some, the free jazz movement had almost destroyed the idea of jazz as a "people's music" and had made it the province of a small band of elitists.

To make things even worse, the Beatles and other rock bands were hav-ing such enormous popular success that record companies increasingly marginalized jazz. Rock was also gaining interest and respect from the postadolescent audiences that had previously been so supportive of jazz. Such vastly popular rock bands as Cream, the Grateful Dead, and the Jimi

Hendrix Experience featured lengthy improvisations and were experimenting with electronic effects and the use of volume to create the sonic weight of a large orchestra. The growing counterculture used rock as a force for community, just as the Beats had used jazz. Record companies quickly realized that a rock group of even moderate popularity could easily outsell some of the greatest of jazz musicians. One of Sonny's favorite epigrams is Calvin Coolidge's remark that "the business of America is business"; from this point of view, jazz was a loser.

In 1969, there began a movement that gave new hope to many in the jazz scene. The group Blood, Sweat and Tears pioneered a kind of merger between jazz and rock that won it a great deal of popularity. Miles Davis, coming from another angle, used elements of rock and funk melded with jazz to create the album *Bitches Brew*, which gave rise to a new form of jazz that was dubbed fusion.

Miles had not been the first jazz musician to use elements of rock; a number of other musicians had been making this kind of experiment. Miles himself had been working on this development for a few years before recording *Brew*. The difference between *Bitches Brew* and the previous attempts to meld jazz and rock was that Miles had not just cobbled the two forms of music together but had found a way to join certain elements of jazz and rock so that the music seemed to be organic, to have its own inner logic. Despite those who insisted that Miles was playing rock and roll, *Bitches Brew*, like much of the other fusion music he created at this time, was certainly closer to jazz than to rock, but it reached a wider audience. *Bitches Brew* became the biggest-selling jazz album up until that time. Fusion looked like a way out of the box jazz seemed to be in; once again, here was a music that connected with the popular culture.

But many people believed that fusion was a debasement of the jazz tradition, a way of selling out. This was not true for Miles, who during this period produced some of the most innovative and complex music of his career. However, much of the fusion created in his wake was of dubious aesthetic value. That many jazzmen turned to fusion gave rise to cynicism. A few of these groups, such as Weather Report at its best, played innovative, personal music. However, most of the other jazz-rock groups played loud, bombastic, heavy-handed music, obviously meant to appeal to the huge, undiscriminating rock audience. If kids admired fast guitarists, the jazz-fusioneers could play three times as fast as any of the rock guitarists.

All the musicians had to do was to play music that was loud, fast, and banal and they could find an audience. What had happened to the subtle, nuanced, lyrical, and deeply personal music that jazz had once been?

Many in the jazz world of the early 1970s began to pin their hopes on Sonny as a possible savior of jazz—if only he would return to the scene. In a 1971 piece for *Down Beat*, "Needed Now: Sonny Rollins," Gordon Kopulos expressed the feelings of many:

> Once again Sonny Rollins has dropped out of the jazz world. . . . He just disappeared without any fanfare. . . . Silently, he just dropped out.
>
> Jazz, whether or not we like to admit it, is in a serious crisis. Though there are a few groups around who play in the bop or hard bop tradition, they are the vestiges of the past. They are not in the mainstream of jazz. In fact, there is no mainstream in the sense that was used in the fifties or sixties. The two forces vying to become that mainstream are the avant-garde and rock-jazz. . . . Logically, the solution to the avant-garde/rock-jazz seems to be a circumvention of the death-delivering aspects of both choices: the creation of a music which at once is capable of attracting a large part of the present rock audience, and also is true to the jazz tradition which the avant-garde loyally embraces.
>
> Dilemma solvers are always rare yet always needed. Jazz has never needed one more than now. Sonny Rollins is eminently qualified . . . the return of Sonny Rollins would be a glorious event—even if he didn't want to solve any problems.[4]

Kopulos was right: Sonny could never take upon himself the role of a savior. That would have been far too pretentious for Sonny, particularly after his sojourn in India. He had always viewed his playing of music as simply a form of work. After studying the concept of karmic yoga, he realized that his work was his spiritual salvation. Sonny certainly believed that jazz was important. But had he felt it was his burden to "save jazz," he would have been at least as self-conscious as he was after the Gunther Schuller "thematic improvisation" piece. That would undoubtedly have corroded the ability to play supremely well that was the joy of his life.

Moreover, Sonny was reluctant to get involved in the business side of music, which had been such a drag on his spirit. For a while, that prevented him from returning to the scene. Dealing with ABC/Impulse had demoralized and depressed him, but there was no way to avoid those aspects of the jazz life. He finally discovered a solution to this problem, one surprisingly close at hand:

> This was when Lucille came into it, in a big way. When I came back from India, [and] went back to playing, around 'seventy-one or early 'seventy-two, I realized that if I was going to survive in this business, I couldn't do it myself. I couldn't deal with the business part of my career by myself, so I got Lucille into doing it, because she is suited for it. She's worked within the system, and she is of the system; she can deal with the system, which is something I cannot do. I began taking Lucille to the studio when I was mixing records and let her sit in on the sessions. I encouraged her to learn about all of that sort of thing. I was handling a lot of jobs myself at the time. Guys would just call me up for a job. I began to get her into it, and she liked it. Now she handles all my business. If I had to deal with the people in the music business, I don't think I could survive out there. It was a lucky thing that I had someone I could trust to handle those kinds of things in-house, because there are a lot of people out there who are willing to work with you, but they steal your money.

Lucille discovered, to both her surprise and Sonny's, that she not only was very good at handling his business affairs, she actually enjoyed it:

> It started out that in 'seventy-one or 'seventy-two. I handled a couple of business matters for Sonny, things which I thought were mistakes and it turned out that I was right. It just evolved from there. Now I love it! I love the business. It's a challenge, and I feel that I am good at it. There was a period there when there was nobody around. We didn't have a booking agent and I was doing that, too, and I didn't like that. Now we have had the same booking agent for fifteen years and they understand what we want. Obviously I want what is best for Sonny, and I want to make him happy. Most agents and managers get a commission, so they always think about the money. Which I do, up to a point, but I think of

other things, too. I just love the business. Every time you think you have seen everything, somebody will do something else that will make you think, "I don't believe it."

Sonny's first foray back into the jazz world was an unusual one: a solo concert at New York's Whitney Museum. A number of jazz musicians had been given grants to create extended pieces, which were then played at the museum. Ornette Coleman wrote a piece for string quartet, and Jimmy Guiffre also wrote a piece for string quartet with the addition of his clarinet. Sonny was planning to write a similar extended piece, but it did not work out:

> I had been working on a piece for strings for the Whitney concert. I tried to find someone to work on it with me, to help with the orchestration and so on. I did not have the time or the skill to do it myself. Originally I was supposed to do something with a classical bent, but I just did not have my string quartet chops up, so I did the next best thing—a solo improvisation. It was not the first time I did it. Just before I went on the bridge, I performed at a jazz festival in Berkeley, California, where I performed solo. And of course, I had recorded a couple of solo pieces in the 1950s.

Sonny called his Whitney solo piece "Tone Poem for Saxophone." It was easily the hit of the concert. Nobody could ever accuse Sonny of lack of daring! To swing back to the jazz scene with such a risky undertaking was an example of the kind of challenge that exhilarated Sonny. Playing in such an exposed context meant putting his soul on the line, with no turning back. Sonny had been playing lengthy unaccompanied codas for years, but now, in this setting, he had no band to turn to if his inspiration ran out. For almost an hour, Sonny played solo with incredible invention, creating not only huge slabs of melodic invention, but also maintaining a strong rhythmic impetus that was felt as strongly as that of any rhythm section. Sonny himself seemed to be enjoying his own invention—his eyes often lit up with astonishment at his most piquant turns of phrase and unexpected quotes. This solo concert was unfortunately not recorded.

In the Whitney audience was Orrin Keepnews, of the now defunct

Riverside Records. He did not have a ticket; Sonny let him play roadie, carrying his horn into the museum so that he could hear the show. Keepnews had been the producer of Sonny's classic *The Freedom Suite*, but Riverside had gone into bankruptcy many years earlier. He was now the chief producer for the Milestone label, a division of Fantasy Records located in Berkeley (Fantasy had also bought the Riverside catalog and was reissuing most of the Riverside albums). Sonny had gotten along well with Keepnews before and he trusted him, so it was natural that he would record his first album in six years for Milestone.

After such a long layoff, many wondered whether Sonny was going to put forth something new and different. To a degree, he did. Sonny, too, had been listening to, or at least was aware of, the ubiquitous pop music of the day; he well knew that some musicians were experimenting with elements of rock and jazz. He had always been open to a wide variety of pop music and he was anxious to merge his jazz sensibility with funk and rock, at least to some extent.

Sonny recorded his first studio album since *East Broadway Rundown* in July 1972. The band he used was pianist George Cables, Bob Cranshaw (who now played electric bass in addition to "acoustic" bass) and either Jack DeJohnette or David Lee on drums. The album, cleverly titled *Sonny Rollins' Next Album* (an allusion, of course, to all those who had been waiting for it), set the pattern for most of the records Sonny would make for Milestone over the next twenty-five years or so.

He made no attempt at playing the long, soaring solos he was famous for in live performance. He had come to the realization that he had to go into the studio with a different agenda than he had in a club or a concert. He had gained enough experience by this time to make a solid if not outstanding record, and that is the best way to describe *Next Album*.

Sonny's playing on this album is noticeably more conservative than his work of the 1960s. He sounds more at peace and less iconoclastic than he had sounded even on the Impulse albums of the previous decade. His creativity is still molten, but he does not seem to be struggling as much with the very idea of music and his role as a musician.

For those who hoped that Sonny would be able to steer jazz away from the unorthodoxies of jazz-rock fusion, *Next Album* was a big letdown. The first tune, a composition by Sonny called "Playin' in the Yard," is a joyful bit of jazz-funk; it brings out the rhythm-and-blues influence that had always been an element of his playing, albeit one well camouflaged. The first saxophonist Sonny ever heard, after all, was Louis Jordan, who played an early version of R&B on his alto saxophone. On this piece, for the first time, Sonny used both electric piano and Bob Cranshaw's electric bass (Cranshaw would eventually devote himself to playing the electric instrument exclusively). It is an irresistible performance; it may not be Sonny's most profound improvising, but it is so ripely enjoyable that such criticism seems beside the point.

The album includes more than a few moments of transcendent beauty. The highlight is clearly the Hoagy Charmichael tune "Skylark," a classic Rollins ballad. There is also a calypso performance, "The Everywhere Calypso," in which Sonny is boisterous and extroverted; it's a perfect example of his mastery of polyrhythm. For the first time since he played an alto sax during his boyhood, Sonny uses a horn other than a tenor: a soprano saxophone. He had a very special, and poignant, reason:

> I played the soprano as a tribute to John Coltrane. I never pursued it very much after that period, due in part to my recurring dental problems. I did want to return to the alto saxophone, but once again dental problems prevented me from doing that.

Sonny achieves a nasal sound and style reminiscent of his old friend. The straight-ahead "Keep Hold of Yourself," with its streamlined harmony, also sounds like a tribute to Coltrane. Sonny makes a disappointingly abbreviated statement, but one can imagine how exciting a tune like this would have sounded during one of Sonny's live performances of this time.

Sonny Rollins's Next Album did get some good reviews. Two were of particular importance because they were written by perhaps the two best critics of American "vernacular" music: Robert Palmer and Gary Giddins. Writing for *Down Beat*, Giddins said: "It is as inconsistent as many of his albums but boasts two masterpieces ('Skylark' and 'The Everywhere Calypso'). . . . There is enough here to confirm that Sonny Rollins is the best saxophonist alive."[5] Palmer's review appeared in *Rolling Stone*, which rarely ran reviews of jazz albums; it was a tribute to the importance of Sonny's return to music that the magazine published Palmer's review. Palmer called Rollins "such a clear, conscious player that one can follow his lines of thought as they interact with recurring cycles of chords and phrases."[6]

Many in the jazz world derided Sonny for experimenting with jazz-funk fusion (although *Next Album* was for the most part straight-ahead). He found himself facing the same attacks that met such peers as Miles Davis and Donald Byrd. Some of those who attacked Sonny were old comrades, such as Max Roach. Like Davis and Byrd, Sonny was labeled a sellout who was cravenly attempting to win over the huge, youthful rock audience. To a degree the critics were right; Davis, Byrd, and Sonny, like a number of other jazz musicians, wanted to make jazz a "people's music" again, music relevant to the lives of their audience. The free jazz of the 1960s had confused many and turned them off. But, Sonny says,

I have never seriously entertained the idea of trying to reach a broader audience. I do things for my own edification. If, in the course of doing that, I get a wider audience, fine. I do things if I think there is something in it for me that is worth doing. At that time, there seemed to be a loss of vitality in jazz.

Jazz began to sound predictable and tired. Naturally I hated that. So the beat, the backbeat, put a little life in the music at that time. To me there was nothing wrong with it. I didn't see it as some kind of a betrayal of jazz. I mean, I just saw it as another way to play jazz.

I didn't start playing that music because Donald Byrd or Miles [was] doing it. It was because I wanted to play music that had more energy. I am an energy player. I have got to play with energy. There was no infusion of energy in jazz at that time (if you will excuse the pun). Even the guys I was auditioning at that time—the ones who were playing jazz-funk were the ones who had the energy I need to play and who made me feel energized. So the fact that Donald Byrd or Miles or Herbie Hancock were doing it—well, to me they were just trying to play where the energy at that time was. That was what I was into. It would have been ridiculous for me to play [like] the straight-ahead guys. They had reached a dead end. Everything they played was very predictable.

The thing that makes jazz so unique is improvisation. I don't care what kind of beat is going on in the background as long as you are able to do something creative with improvisation. I really do enjoy playing funk; I like the freedom. You see, it's an easier beat to play with. If you give a guy a backbeat, this beat is so strong and so dominant that anybody, any mediocre musician, should be able to play with it. Which is why guys in rock use it. I don't mean to put them down, but you can come out of high school and play because of that backbeat beating you over the head. So it's an easy beat to play with. It's easier to play with than a straight-ahead 4/4 beat. So the challenge is to really elevate it to something else.

Sonny and the other musicians exploring fusion were also pilloried for playing electric instruments, which supposedly were not part of the hallowed "jazz tradition." As Sonny puts it,

> For me it's the man in front of the instrument, not the instrument. If you want to use an electric instrument, fine, but you better be able to do something with it. That is what I believe. I have been vilified and crucified for that, but so what?

A case in point is Bob Cranshaw, Sonny's longtime bassist. His hands were damaged in a car accident; his fingers were no longer strong enough to play the string bass, so he decided to focus exclusively on the electric bass. Cranshaw concluded that the difference between the two was virtually nonexistent:

> Nobody can tell the difference between my playing and that of an acoustic bassist except they can hear me better. Most bass players use a pickup make these days anyway, so what is the difference? To me all of this stuff about the superiority of acoustic instruments is bullshit. I can play anything on the electric that I play on the acoustic. I love the acoustic tradition and all that, but I need more energy than that, and the electric has it.

Sonny has actually come to prefer the electric bass; it better complements his rhythmic conception than the acoustic bass:

> I having been using the electric bass for my group for a while. I have gotten used to the delay time that the electric bass gives you. It gives you a faster beat. When I tried playing with an acoustic bass again, it bothered me because the beat wasn't as quick. I have reached the point where I actually prefer the quick beat of the electric bass.

I have received a lot of flak from people for that. I know the arguments. But for me, I like that quick attack sound; it gives me more time to cement some of the ideas that go through my mind. I guess if I were on a desert island with only an acoustic bass, I would get used to it again. But I prefer the electric bass.

Sonny used to be bothered by bad reviews from critics. But in the last several years he has learned how to take them in stride:

Fortunately, the role of the jazz critic is not as crucial as it used to be. When I started out, the critics for *Down Beat* or *Metronome* had a disproportionate effect on your ability to get work. They could kill you. But now it doesn't really make any difference. There's a lot of people writing. I tell them all to go to hell, in my way, because I don't care. I'm trying to get my own music together and I don't care what some writer has to say about it. I don't have to care, because many of them dislike me and I still make my living. I've reached the point where I can live and pursue my career and that's it. I'm never going to have everybody liking me. So the hell with them.

Sonny brought to jazz-funk the same high standards and stubborn commitment to inventive improvisation that have always been hallmarks of his music. No critic, none or even a fellow musician, could impede Sonny's continuing search for new challenges and new opportunities in his lifelong musical mission.

With Lucille handling his business affairs, Sonny no longer had to concern himself with the aspects of his career that had sapped his spirit and interfered with his ability to focus completely on music itself, his karmic yoga, the work he had dedicated his life to. Sonny was finally free of the encumbrances that had held him down; his sky was now wide open for even further flights.

12

Silver City

Except for the time Sonny spent on the road or in Chicago in the early 1950s, and then in Lexington for his "cure," New York had been his home almost all his life. In the early 1970s he decided he needed a change:

> After I came back from India, Lucille and I got back together. We were living in Brooklyn, right across the street from the Pratt Institute. There was a nice, integrated middle-class development there. A lot of people who worked at the Brooklyn Navy Yard lived there. Then the neighborhood began to change, to go down. Lucille was working and I had to go and meet her at the subway when she came back from work every day. We began to feel that we had to leave, which we hated to do because we had a nice big apartment. We got a much smaller place in Tribeca in Manhattan, but we also started driving upstate looking for a home there. We used to do that every day, and finally we found a house. It was not perfect and it was a kind of compromise, but you have to compromise when you buy your first house. We began to spend every weekend up there. We have ten acres of wooded land and I have my own studio to practice in.

Sonny and Lucille began to spend most of their time there, in Germantown, although Sonny used the Tribeca apartment when he had business in New York, such as rehearsals and recording sessions.

In the country, Sonny is able to focus on practicing and playing music without the distractions of city life. He plays only about fifty dates a year, but he has reached such a plateau that his fees are more than adequate to keep him and Lucille comfortable. According to Sonny, that is all he needs: "I am not interested in being rich or more famous."

Sonny went on tour in 1976 with an all-star group made up of leaders who recorded for the Milestone label: pianist McCoy Tyner, bassist Ron Carter, and drummer Al Foster (who was not a leader, just a great drummer). Tyner had become famous as a member of John Coltrane's quartet of the 1960s, and both Carter and Foster had played with Miles Davis (at different periods of the trumpeter's career). This might have seemed an ideal situation for Sonny, but the album the group recorded turned out to be a disappointment. Tyner was anything but the right pianist for Sonny. His thick, thunderous chords were too domineering for a musician like him; he played at his best with minimal harmonic support. It was impossible for Sonny just to ignore Tyner's accompaniment; and his playing sounds distracted and earthbound. It is often the case that all-star groups seem like an exciting idea; but the musicians may not have all that much in common except for being well known.

At this point in his career, Sonny had ascended to the ranks of the greatest legends in American music. He was still surprised in 1980, when the Rolling Stones requested that he play on their upcoming album, *Tattoo You*. Sonny recorded two tunes with the group, "Slave" and "Waiting on a Friend." As Sonny recalls:

> That came about after Mick Jagger . . . [and] a British filmmaker who had made a documentary about me in the 1950s came to see me play. I didn't know it happened, but one day a little later I got a call from the Rolling Stones asking me to be on their album. Charlie Watts, the drummer, is a big jazz fan and I think it was probably him

who was behind this. They were going to cut the basic tracks in England and then I could overdub my parts in New York. I was supposed to get together with Mick Jagger in the studio, but that day I had a hard time finding the studio. I hate being late to anything, and usually I am not. But this time I was late, although not purposely. Mick seemed to feel that I was dissing him . . . but it was completely inadvertent. . . . I just could not find the studio.

. . . I thought that it came out very well. I was into what they were doing and it was a very successful record for them, but I would never want to play regularly with the Rolling Stones. They wanted me to be part of this big HBO concert they are doing. But I did not want to be a part of that. That is not who I am.

I realize that if I did stuff like that I could make a lot of money, and I could get a lot of visibility and that sort of thing, but I don't want to do that. All I want to do is to protect what I have now. I'm not trying to make more money. I am not trying to be more visible. I'm not trying to get on TV, which makes me a strange person among everybody else in the business.

Sonny's playing on the two Stones tunes is surprisingly spirited. He obviously completely understood what the Stones required of him and his improvising fit in perfectly. The blues are at the roots of the Stones' music, and Sonny has always exhibited a deep understanding of the blues sensibility. Some of his greatest and most important improvisations on record were blues performances, such as "Blue Seven" and "Blues for Philly Joe."

On July 8, 1985, almost fifteen years after the Whitney Museum concert, Sonny played another solo concert at a New York museum, Manhattan's Museum of Modern Art. This was the same place where, years before, he had played a bizarre, rain-soaked date that, without his knowledge, had been recorded and later released by Impulse. The solo concert at MOMA was not nearly the equal of the Whitney performance. Much of it seemed like technical exercises. Sonny seemed to be trying far too hard to get his inventiveness into gear, but he often seemed frustrated. What was the trouble?

Sonny's playing has never been consistent from performance to performance, but on this occasion there were other difficulties. For one, the concert was recorded, and Sonny was aware of the fact. As usual, being recorded made him self-conscious. As Sonny recalls, there were also other reasons why this solo concert did not turn out so well.

> For one thing, I had had dental work and I couldn't get my bite to where it should have been. I was playing under a certain kind of pressure, in a way. I needed to bite in a certain way, but I couldn't bite that way. . . . Also, I had smoked some pot just before playing, which was something I really shouldn't have done because I really didn't need it at that time. It was around that time when I was wrestling with smoking pot before I played. It was kind of weird because I had to smoke in the museum and there were a lot of people, of course, around guarding the works of art. It put me in a very defensive mood. That, along with the dental problem, [prevented] that second solo concert from coming off the way it should have been.

Nevertheless, the resulting recording (*The Solo Album*) proves that Sonny had many moments of extraordinary invention. The music lacks the cohesiveness of Sonny's best work; at times he sounds as if he is lost in a forest of sound trying desperately to find his way home. The album is proof of the dangers of improvising without a net. But it must be listened to, if only for insight into the nature of Sonny's musical imagination and thought processes.

After reaching an age when many jazz musicians have lost their earlier stamina, Sonny continued to play long, electrifying solos at least as brilliant as at any time in his career. However, he decided that he had to cut back on playing as often as he had in the past:

> I had to stop playing clubs for the most part, because it just became too difficult for someone who plays as hard as I do not to have a dressing room and that kind of thing. You have to be able to relax for a minute after playing. That's why I hate clubs. Other than that, clubs are fine because you are near the people and that is wonderful, but the physical part is too draining. . . . I have to really *concentrate*, play hard. That's how I get my stuff out. Playing

like that in a club just does not work out because I was never able to relax.

This happened to me recently when I was playing at Tramps [a club in Manhattan]. I was able to play a first set, which was reasonably okay. I did have a dressing room there, but after the first set they allowed a whole bunch of people back there. There were people talking to me from right after the first set until the time the clubowner said, "Okay, Sonny, we're ready for the next set." I can't go back and play at the level that I can reach without concentrating and being able to really play. I just do not have that much in me anymore to do that. I have to be able to rest between sets.

Sonny has continued to grow as a musician. Even now that he is in his late sixties, he is aware of changes in the jazz scene, such as the repertory movement. He has also been giving deep thought to where he is taking his own music. To use an apt phrase, Sonny is still listening to his own drummer:

My whole thing now, my new realization, is trying to go in a different direction, in a way of speaking. I wouldn't be so presumptuous to say that I am "taking jazz in a new direction"; I mean my own playing. I am trying to make my playing more primitive and even more intuitive than what classically oriented musicians might consider to be a higher form of music. I used to be intimidated by the difference between my music and classical music. I used to think, "Well, gee, this doesn't sound enough like how a Western classical player would play it." This is completely meaningless to me now.

Jazz is a *living art*. I mean, it is one thing to play music that was written a long time ago. Some of it is great music. I do think that there is a place for repertory or even for jazz musicians copying other jazz musicians. I wouldn't want to be the one to deny them or to say that what they are doing is wrong. But in the long run, jazz is a living art, it is something which is being created in the moment. We must be concerned with what we are doing now, not what was happening in 1929, as great as it might have been in 1929.

There is too much media and technology now. Jazz is meeting the media of sound bites now. Jazz can do all that because it's quick. So I don't put down Wynton [Marsalis] and those guys that are doing repertory. They are doing an especially important job by educating young people about this music. Maybe they can show stupid America that jazz is something other than, say, murdering your wife. I understand what they are doing and I appreciate it. I also appreciate Lunceford's music or whoever. That is not all there is to jazz. That is just a part of it.

Despite these feelings, in 1985 Sonny ventured into a whole new area of music-making: he was given a Japanese commission to compose a large-scale piece for saxophone and orchestra. It was a great leap for a musician who was primarily an improviser and a composer of short pieces intended for jazz combos. Sonny was intrigued by the challenge. He also realized that he could not write the piece without some help:

> I contacted a Finnish composer named Heikki Sarmanto to help me with the arrangements and the orchestration. I met him years ago, the first time I went to Finland. He is sort of a jazz player, he has his own groups, but he also works in bigger mediums. He works with orchestras, and he has written music for ballet and a number of other orchestral pieces. I contacted him and he agreed to work on it with me. I had certain themes and certain concepts that I wanted to work with. We worked very closely together and he wrote all the orchestrations.
>
> Just that made it different, that I was collaborating with someone else. There were certain things that might have worked for a small group but not with a large orchestra, and he helped me with that. There are certain imperatives when working with a full orchestra. It was my first attempt at something like this and it was a total learning experience.
>
> We performed it twice—once in Japan [in 1986] and then again in Italy the following year. The first performance of the piece (titled *Concerto for Tenor Saxophone and Orchestra*) in Japan wasn't as good as I thought it could be. When we did it in Italy it was a lot better. We also changed it to a degree; after its first performance, we realized that certain sections did not work. So it was really a work in progress and that is how it should be referred to. It was a fine experience and I am happy I did it. I am trying to be able to do it again. I have learned

so much about it since I began working on that piece and I think that if I did it again, I could get closer to what I originally intended to do.

The premiere of this "work in progress" has never been released on an American CD. It was filmed by Robert Mugge for a documentary about Sonny called *Saxophone Colossus*. Watching the movie is the only way to hear this ambitious work.

The concerto is surprisingly romantic; parts of it could pass as Rachmaninoff. Needless to say, Sonny's playing dominates the piece and probably the ear of most listeners. While it is not wholly successful, it is surprisingly accomplished despite Sonny's lifelong commitment to quite a different tradition. For anyone who has been following Sonny's development as musical thinker, hearing the concerto is a fascinating experience.

Mugge also filmed another Rollins concert, one held in 1986 in Saugerties, New York, not far from Sonny's upstate home. It was outdoors, on a stage several feet high. Sonny was playing superbly despite the fact that he was not only being recorded for an album but also being filmed by Mugge. Perhaps Sonny has simply learned to take things in his stride. For whatever reason, his fifteen-minute-plus improvisation on a composition of his called "G-Man" is probably the closest that Sonny has come since *Our Man in Jazz* to recording a solo that genuinely resembles the long, cosmically expansive solos he performs in person on a good night.

In the "G-Man" solo, it is clear that one of the most fascinating aspects of Sonny's style, at least in such a long, discursive solo, is the element of suspense. Just when you are certain that you know the direction Sonny is taking, he turns a corner and goes to a very different place. At times he is so "outside" that he could pass for Albert Ayler or any of the most iconoclastic of the 1960s New Thing jazzmen. No matter how exotic the music becomes, he finds his way back to the main theme again and again, using it as a taking-off point for further excursions into the ether. It is a riveting and often unsettling performance.

Something very strange happened at the Saugerties concert that, fortunately, Mugge also filmed. During a long unaccompanied solo, Sonny had a bizarre, painful accident.

It still hurts for me to think about this one! As you know, I used to walk around the clubs in order to find a better sound. So this was kind of a throwback to when I used to leave the stage and walk through the audience. I wanted to change the setting, to get closer to the people, and to explore other parts of this outdoor area to see how it affected my sound. So I jumped off the stage to get closer to the people but it was a little farther down than I thought. I landed on my heel and as soon as I hit the ground I thought, "Uh-oh!" I tried to stand up, but I couldn't. I didn't realize that I had broken my heel. And then the pain started. I continued playing my solo, not just because the show must go on but because I still was able to blow. I couldn't stand, but I could blow my solo.

It is no small miracle that Mugge was there to film Sonny's painful fall; the sight of him lying on the ground but continuing to play—and play brilliantly—is an indelible image of Sonny's stubborn commitment to music. If ever one needed proof of Art Blakey's statement that Sonny was the most determined man he had ever known, here it is.

Sonny has continued to record for Milestone up until the present (1999), cutting a new album every year or two. Most of his records have been quite similar to *Next Album* in the kinds of tunes they include (among them jazz-funk pieces) and in their inconsistency. Many critics and fans have expressed disappointment that Sonny has not recorded another *Way Out West* or *Saxophone Colossus*. Sonny believes it is hard to reach such peaks in a vacuum:

It is difficult for an artist who has been around as long as I have to make some kind of a product that's going to be universally accepted. The music changes and the audience changes. We were in the middle of the golden age of jazz when I made those albums. This is just *not* the golden age. The 1970s were not the golden age, and neither were the 1980s. So I as a musician can't expect to make what somebody might consider a "1960s classic Sonny Rollins record." It's impossible to do that in the 1980s or the 1990s.

There are some good players, but the golden-age people are not there. I can't use people like Oscar Pettiford, there's no Monk there, there's no Coltrane there, there's no Miles there. There is nobody playing like they played in the middle of the century there—the 1930s, the 1940s, the 1950s, or the 1960s. Times change, people die off, and new elements are produced, like the new electric instruments, or what they refer to as crossover, the backbeat playing a more prominent role as opposed to the classic form. All the things which happen in time. It's just like growing old. I can't stop getting gray hair.

The jazz critics, at least a lot of them, are judging me against a period when it was a golden age of playing and recording. In some areas I might agree with them. I may not be able to make the same kind of record as I used to. I am not one to argue with record reviewers over that. I just don't think that my energies are well spent over that. My energies are better spent trying to keep my own self vital.

A lot of critics have their own agenda. That's why I stopped reading them. My thing is to try to really make sure that my own standards are high and to try and get closer to my goal, my ideas, and hopefully progress to the point of reaching my ideals.

What many critics missed was that although none of Sonny's later records is consistently great, they offer quite a few notable performances. Some of these releases were better than others, but there were very few complete duds. One example of the latter is *The Way I Feel*. Sonny's playing sounds lethargic and unengaged. The problem is the album's slick but uninspired horn arrangements. Most of the Milestone albums have been far superior.

In 1978, Sonny recorded a two-LP set called *Don't Stop the Carnival*, partly recorded live at San Francisco's Treat American Music Hall and partly recorded in the studio. (It is now available on a single CD.) Among the musicians were the drummer Tony Williams, who had been part of Miles Davis's seminal 1960s quintet, and the trumpeter Donald Byrd, who had played on Sonny's first album for Blue Note over twenty years earlier.

Byrd, however, had not been playing much, and although he managed to hold his own, his soloing on this album is not the equal of his best work, particularly in comparison to the soloing of Sonny. The highlights of the album are the tracks without Byrd: "Silver City," "Autumn Nocturne" (a tune Sonny had originally recorded on his final RCA album, *The Standard Sonny Rollins*), and a typically rollicking version of the title calypso, which Sonny plays with a particularly gruff and gritty tone.

"Autumn Nocturne" is the centerpiece of the album. It consists largely of an unaccompanied solo that eventually goes into a brief playing of the melody in tempo with the rhythm section. This long introductory section is a superb example of Sonny's mastery of unaccompanied improvisation, maybe his single best such solo on record. It is a dazzling and breathtaking performance. "Silver City," "Autumn Nocturne," and, to a lesser extent, "Don't Stop the Carnival" are proof of Sonny's continuing ability in the mid-1970s to create expansive and exhilarating music.

In 1980, Orrin Keepnews left Milestone. From this point on, Sonny and Lucille produced their own albums. Keepnews remembers jokingly making a comment that since Sonny and Lucille would be producing Sonny's albums, he was losing out on the producing fees. Sonny offered to pay Keepnews's fees anyway even though he would not be the producer any longer. Of course, Keepnews explained that he was just kidding. This was another reminder to Keepnews of Sonny's genuine devotion to true friendship. Sonny had come to understand the best way for him to record in the studio and how to deal with his deeply felt aversion to it. Lucille, who was now coproducing Sonny's albums, knew how to help him feel more comfortable and to be productive despite his misgivings about the entire idea of recording jazz. She thinks that this new setup did make a difference:

> There is nobody extraneous in the recording studio now. I don't mean to say that Orrin [Keepnews] was extraneous—I am referring to the others. Now there is nobody but us. He can do exactly what he wants to do. He always did, to a certain extent. Nobody ever said, "Do this" or "Do that," but now there is less pressure on him. It is easier for him to relax in the studio, as much as he can *ever* relax in the studio, and just do everything his own way.

Indeed, the first session the two produced together, *Sunny Days, Starry Nights*, has an unusually relaxed, tropical ambiance, at least for a studio date.

Most of the 1980s Milestone albums received negative reviews from some critics, such as Peter Watrous of *The New York Times*. Some of the more perceptive writers realized that throughout Sonny's Milestone albums there were several brilliant performances, more than a few of which were equal to anything he had previously recorded. Gary Giddins was one of those critics, and in 1995 he wrote a piece for the *Village Voice* in which he enumerated enough superb selections for a set of at least two CDs.

When Sonny and Lucille saw the piece, they realized it was a wonderful idea. They added a few other selections of equal value and assembled a two-CD set, *Silver City*, named for one of the best cuts on *Don't Stop the Carnival*. Taken as a whole, *Silver City* is simply one of the few classic albums of the past twenty-five years; it proves beyond any doubt that Sonny has continued to grow as a musician since his supposed heyday of the 1950s and 1960s. The high level of artistry is heard not only in the ballads and straight-ahead tunes, but also in the fusion pieces, which are marvelous. For example, "Harlem Boys" is a hugely enjoyable jazz-funk tune, as emotionally vital as anything he has recorded. Sonny plays with the freshness and vitality that many, quite wrongly, associate only with youthful players. On tunes like this, he proves that a great artist does not have to be young in order to celebrate life.

There is one track (culled from the album titled *Falling in Love with Jazz*) that must have really disturbed those who insisted that Sonny's veering from the straight-ahead jazz tradition made him a traitor: the old Patti Page hit "Tennessee Waltz." On this track he is not fusing jazz and rock or jazz and funk, but rather jazz and country-and-western music! Sonny plays the familiar melody with great tenderness; perhaps he was thinking of Patti Page's voice when he recorded the tune. The guitarist, Jerome Harris, even recreates the poignant sound of a pedal steel guitar; it is a lovely, enraptured performance.

Sonny continued to change his groups, particularly the rhythm sections. He has very strong ideas about the kind of rhythm section he needs to give him empathetic support:

> First, the bass players. When I look for a bassist, I want a guy that's secure enough in his own musical ability that he doesn't get distracted by what I do. I want to be able to feel free to do whatever

I feel like doing. But of course I am doing it within certain rules. I'm not going up in the air with one wing. The bass player has to able to deal with that. This is hard to find. That is why I've worked with Cranshaw for so long. I want the rhythm section to stay basic and be solid. Lucille told me one time, "Oh, gee, you know how hard it is for somebody to play with you." I play stuff that would throw most people off. I thought that was a funny way to put it.

A drummer has to have good rhythm and he, too, should not get distracted by whatever I do. I've been lucky to play with a lot of great drummers—Blakey, Max Roach; these guys really have to know what they are doing. Then we can take the music to the next level. There are so many different senses of rhythm that the search goes on and on. For me, they simply have to be world-class players.

Another problem I have with rhythm sections is that I have a more varied repertoire than a lot of other musicians. I have to find a guy who will give me the freedom that I need, but he also must be able to adapt to my repertoire.

In the last few years, Sonny has recorded and played with a number of the supposed "young lions" of the last few years:

With a lot of these younger guys I have to bring in the [sheet music of the] tunes and show it to them. If I want to play, say, "Dancing in the Dark," a lot of these kids have not even heard that song. Sometimes that is hard, because just seeing the chord changes may not be enough for them to feel comfortable playing a certain tune.

I had a funny experience with this young trumpet player, Roy Hargrove. Now Roy is a guy who has done his homework, he knows his tradition. So I did a concert with him one time and the guys in my band were all about ten years older than Roy. I said "Let's play this tune," an old standard called "I Wish I Knew." And Roy knew it. The other guys in my band didn't! So I shouldn't say that the young guys don't know these tunes, this tradition, because some of them do. The better young guys know the jazz repertoire.

Sonny does not make much of an attempt to listen to the latest records or any other music:

The main reason why I do not do much listening is because music is so much in the forefront of my mind. I want to *get away* from music. It is just difficult for me to really be able to relax and listen to music. Another reason, although it is no longer as important as it may have been at one time, is that I do not want to be influenced by anybody else. That may be true to a lesser extent.

Unlike many musicians, Sonny has interests that range widely beyond music. Although he lacks formal education, Sonny has become knowledgeable in many areas. He is a voracious reader, and he takes the books that he reads very seriously, highlighting sections of importance and making voluminous notes in the margins.

Sonny still takes a dark view of the kind of country America has become. In many ways, he considers himself a pessimist, a melancholy prophet of where we are going as a nation:

> I keep saying this about all of life: it is not about black or white, it is about grays. And this is a metaphor for America. America likes to say that everything is black or white because it relates to its racist philosophy. Either you are black or you are white. But it is not that simple. There are things that meld, areas that are not that absolute. If you want to build a better society, a better world, a better music, you have got to understand these things. You just cannot put everything into black or white.

Sonny has become a stubborn Luddite, distrustful of the effects of modern technology. And in the last several years, the environment has become his chief concern. For Sonny, it is the ultimate problem facing the human race:

> The environment is going to straighten everybody out. With global warming, they will have to wake up. Nature is going to win out, it always does, over these arrogant people. This year [1998] is the warmest on record. And next year will be warmer than this one.
>
> The whole arrogant idea of this age we're living in is that we can dominate Nature. You have got to have a spiritual center to your life.

If you go inside yourself, you can't help but realize that spirituality and the mindless commercialism of this country don't work together.

Even world politics is unimportant next to issues concerning the environment. Once the environment kicks in and starts going down the tubes, everybody's going. Saddam Hussein is going, the Russians are going, America is going.

The problem is that we are being lied to by our leaders twenty-four hours a day. We are bombarded by these spin doctors who fill our heads with bullshit.

Despite my pessimism, I still hold out the hope that people will wake up to what is happening and save our planet before it is too late. We can still do it if we want to. If we can just connect to the Higher Power, we can save ourselves.

Once again, Sonny has fused his social concerns with his music, recording in 1999 what he calls his "environmental album," *Global Warming*. Just as he did with *The Freedom Suite*, Sonny wrote a statement, in this case a rap stating the album's theme:

We got to stop assumin'
We can just go on consumin'
Clean up the air, clean up the food
Forget that arrogant attitude
Live light on the planet, sister and brother
Cause if we kill it, there ain't no other
Not that much time left either

Sonny was recording *Global Warming* during part of the time we were doing our interviews for this book. As usual, he was very unhappy with how the sessions were going, or at least with his own playing. He was plagued by dental problems and because of them he had not been playing. He insisted that he was unable to play anything worthwhile.

The album belies that pessimism. It has some very strong work, particularly on the title track and the old standard "Change Partners." One track in particular is worth the price of the album: not surprisingly, it is a blues, "Mother Nature's Blues." Here Sonny takes a lengthy solo that flirts with polytonality, and that at times has a strange, Mideastern mood;

at one point he creates an eerie droning sound, almost as if he were playing the oud or some other non-Western instrument. This solo alone is certain proof that Sonny's imaginative world continues to expand.

The band on the album resembles the groups he has been leading in the last several years. There are two alternating drummers, Idris Muhammad and Perry Wilson. Sonny's nephew, Clifton Anderson, has been playing trombone with him for a while. Anderson is a fine soloist and with him Sonny is able to re-create the sonically pleasing sound of the dates that he did with J. J. Johnson and Jimmy Cleveland. The pianist is Stephen Scott and the bassist is that constant colleague of Sonny's, Bob Cranshaw. Sonny has been touring with this group, or variations of it, for the last few years.

Sonny remains as committed as ever to "pure" improvisation; although many jazzmen of his age simply reiterate old solos or licks and clichés, Sonny cannot even consider following that path:

> It is just my own creative process to play fresh improvised music when I perform. That does not necessarily mean that what I do is superior to musicians who know how to re-create moods and play the same thing over and over again. That is a skill, too. I know better by now not to denigrate that type of musician. It is hard to play. It's hard to do all those things. I am just a different kind of musician. I couldn't play the same thing, at least not to that degree. Everybody plays the same licks in order to get started, but being able to re-create moods and all that, I would say it's *impossible* for me to do that.

Sonny is continually asked to play the kind of music he did in the 1950s, or to play with comrades from that era:

> A lot of guys play like they did back in 1962 or whenever. Which is fine, because in 1962 it was great and it still is great. I am not trying to knock them. That is not where I am coming from. When people say, "Why don't you play with so and so from back then?" they don't understand that I have a different philosophy; I am trying to change all the time, and that must be taken into consideration.

There are other reasons why Sonny cannot turn back the clock:

Somebody asked [Miles Davis] why he wasn't playing like he did at an earlier period. Miles told him, "Well, really, man, I can't physically play like that anymore." That might be another reason not to go back to playing the way you did a long time ago. It may be physically impossible because of age, which I am beginning to see in my own case. I can no longer practice fifteen hours a day like I once did. You have to think about today. Even if you tried to re-create what you once did, you might be confronted with the fact of time. Instead, I try and get the most I can into two hours of practice and not dwell on the fact that there are now some things I just cannot do.

Despite these problems, Sonny does not believe that jazz is only a young man's art:

As I become older, I am able to get deeper into myself and I am able to play more of myself. The more you live, hopefully the more you learn about life. The more experience, the more you should be able to do. It's like when I heard Coleman Hawkins one night when he was sick and he really couldn't play all the notes that he usually plays. He only played certain notes, but the notes he played were great. He was playing less notes, but each note had such depth and power to it that it was a revelation.

Some guy was talking to me one time about Art Tatum. He was talking about the fact that he heard Tatum playing not long before his death and that he didn't have the technique he used to have and he was making a lot of mistakes. I resented what this guy was saying, because an older musician should be judged on what he is saying rather than on his ability to say it.

I am aware that I have to prove every time that I play before an audience that I can still do it. I have to demonstrate this to my audience now—that despite my age, I am still capable of playing and maybe even playing better.

If you think that Sonny means his own playing is weaker, you probably have not heard him recently. The best judge is Lucille, since nobody but

Sonny himself has been listening to him as long as she has: "I have heard Sonny play since 1957. He is playing better than he has ever has, no doubt about it." Sonny is unlike Hawkins in that, except for the fact that he no longer feels comfortable at very fast tempos, he has not noticeably lost any of his technical facility. (He may feel that he has lost some, but most listeners would never know it.) He is like Hawkins in that his music now is a summary of all he has learned, and explored, during the fifty years of his professional career. Getting older has not made it harder for Sonny to play with a sense of openness and freedom. Instead, endless avenues are open to him every time he plays. He is still discovering new areas, fresh musical concepts, and deeper aspects of himself as grist for his art.

When I first started talking to Sonny in 1997, he told me that he was working toward a new innovation. But a year later he was not as certain:

> There is something I am trying to get to, and it is clear at some times and not as clear at others. It is very difficult to embrace the whole thing. Then after I told you about this it pulled back a little. The vision, the concept is still there, it's just that right now, it is a little hard to grasp it. This will pass. Back then it was a little more clear, and I thought I could get to it a little bit quicker and I haven't gotten to it yet. You just have to live with these things, because you just can't create the kind of music I am trying to create all at once. Basically, what I am trying to do is to play a more primitive kind of music.
>
> By primitive, I mean less industrialized, more basic. Maybe one note instead of ten. There are more basic tones that convey a deep meaning which was just as important as far back as man can recall. Perhaps more potent, getting away from this technological society. So when I say "primitive," I mean sounds closer to nature.

Although he still hopes to achieve this more "primitive" style of playing, Sonny has also given some thought to what he will do if he does eventually lose the physical ability to play:

> If I had to give up the saxophone for some reason, I would compose. I think it would be difficult to do, because I love to play. So much of my creative juices flow from playing that I have to only

compose. I guess I could hone my skills a little bit and come up with some stuff if I ever had to stop playing.

Sonny has curtailed his performing schedule in the last few years, but music is still his greatest joy: "Being able to play improvised jazz in front of an audience is the greatest thing in the world, the best experience of my life." He hopes that his music provides enlightenment to those who open themselves to it.

Listening to him play those long solos that can veer in any and every direction, solos that he has created on the spot, and that will never be heard again, is a deeply spiritual experience. It reminds us that we are living in the here and now, in this very moment, even as I write these words or you read them. How many of us remain trapped by our past and spend so much time worried about the future, while life is flowing right through us?

During one of our interviews, we were discussing Thoreau's remark that most people live lives of "quiet desperation." "But," exclaimed Sonny, "why should people live in 'quiet desperation'? Look at how beautiful the day is, what an incredible world we live in! All the possibilities open to us!" That, perhaps, is the greatest lesson we can learn from Sonny Rollins's music: that life has infinite choices, that we are free to go forward and become the kind of people we want to be and create the kind of world that we want to live in. And ultimately, Sonny's beautiful improvisations tell us that life is like music: it, too, is an "open sky."

Notes

Chapter 2: School Days

1. Mailer, Norman. *Advertisements for Myself* (Cambridge, Mass.: Harvard University Press, 1991), p. 338.

Chapter 3: Blue Room

1. Williams, Martin. *The Jazz Tradition*, Second Revised Edition (New York: Oxford University Press, 1993), p. 181.
2. Nisenson, Eric. *'Round About Midnight: A Portrait of Miles Davis*, updated version (New York: Da Capo Press, 1996), p. 76.
3. Blumenthal, Bob. Liner notes for *Sonny Rollins: The Complete Prestige Recordings* (Berkeley, Calif.: Fantasy Records, 1992).
4. Ibid.

Chapter 4: "Oleo"

1. Nisenson. Op. cit., p. 87.
2. Khan, Hazrat Inayat. *The Mysticism of Sound and Music* (Boston: Shambala Publications Inc., 1991), p. 2.
3. Goldberg, Joe. *Jazz Masters of the 50s* (New York: Da Capo Press, 1965), p. 26.
4. Blumenthal. Op. cit.
5. Khan. Op. cit., p. 154.

Chapter 6: Saxophone Colossus

1. Williams, Martin, ed. *Jazz Panorama* (New York: The Coward-Collier Press, 1962), p. 239.
2. Ibid, p. 241.
3. Ibid, p. 248.
4. Hentoff, Nat. "Sonny Rollins," in *Down Beat: Sixty Years of Jazz* (Milwaukee: Hal Leonard Corporation, 1995), p. 94.
5. Ibid, p. 95.
6. Ibid.
7. Ibid.

Chapter 7: A Night at the Village Vanguard

1. Williams, *The Jazz Tradition*. Op. cit., p. 180.

Chapter 8: The Freedom Suite

1. Williams, *The Jazz Tradition*. Op. cit., pp. 185–6.
2. Nisenson, '*Round About Midnight: A Portrait of Miles Davis*. Op. cit., p. 142.

Chapter 9: The Bridge

1. Goldberg. Op. cit., p. 106.
2. Schoenberg, Loren. Liner notes for *The Complete Sonny Rollins RCA Recordings* (New York, 1997).
3. Williams, *The Jazz Tradition*. Op. cit., p. 187.

Chapter 10: Now's the Time

1. Chilton, John. *The Song of the Hawk* (Ann Arbor: The University of Michigan Press, 1990), p. 349.

Chapter 11: Playin' in the Yard

1. Gitler, Ira. "Music Is an Open Sky," *Down Beat* (May 29, 1969), p. 24.
2. Ibid.
3. Ibid.
4. Kopulos, Gordon. "Needed Now: Sonny Rollins," *Down Beat* (June 24, 1971), pp. 12–13.
5. Giddins, Gary. "Sonny Rollins' Next Album" (review), *Down Beat* (November 9, 1972), p. 19.
6. Palmer, Robert. "Sonny Rollins' Next Album" (review), *Rolling Stone* (December 7, 1972), p. 66.